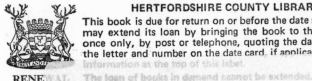

THE AUTOBIOGRAPHY OF
LIEUTENANT-GENERAL
SIR HARRY SMITH
BART., G.C.B.

Walker & Cockerell, ph. sc.

Lieut. General Sir Harry Smith, Bart.

THE AUTOBIOGRAPHY OF

LIEUTENANT-GENERAL

SIR HARRY SMITH

BARONET OF ALIWAL ON THE SUTLEJ
G.C.B.

EDITED

WITH THE ADDITION OF SOME SUPPLEMENTARY CHAPTERS

BY G. C. MOORE SMITH, M.A.

IN TWO VOLUMES

VOL. I.

WITH PORTRAITS AND ILLUSTRATIONS

LONDON
JOHN MURRAY, ALBEMARLE STREET
1901

PRINTED BY
WILLIAM CLOWES AND SONS, LIMITED,
LONDON AND BECCLES.

PREFACE.

THE Life of Sir Harry Smith here offered to the public consists of an Autobiography covering the period 1787 to 1846 (illustrated by notes and appendices), and some supplementary chapters contributed by myself on the last period of Sir Harry's life (1846–1860). The first volume carries the reader to the year 1829. This, it is interesting to remark, is a true turning point in the life of the great soldier. Till then he had seen warfare only on two continents, Europe and America (the Peninsula, France, the Netherlands, Monte Video, Buenos Ayres, Washington, New Orleans); from that date onwards the scene of his active service was Africa and Asia. Till 1829 his responsibility was small; after 1829 he had a large or paramount share in directing the operations in which he was engaged. This difference naturally affects the tone of his narrative in the two periods.

The Autobiography (called by its author "Various Anecdotes and Events of my Life") was begun by Sir Harry Smith, then Lieutenant-Colonel Smith, at Glasgow in 1824. At that time it was only continued as far as page 15 of the present volume. On 11th August, 1844, when he had won his K.C.B., and was Adjutant-General of Her Majesty's Forces in India, he resumed his task at Simla. He then wrote with such speed that on 15th October he was able to tell his sister that he had carried his narrative to the end of the campaign of Gwalior, that is, to 1844 (vol. ii. p. 132). Finally, on 7th September, 1846, when at Cawnpore in command of a Division, he began to add to what he had previously written an account of the campaign of the Sutlej, which had brought him fresh honours. This narrative was broken off abruptly in the middle of the Battle of Sobraon (vol. ii. p. 192), and was never completed. Accordingly, of Sir Harry Smith's life from February, 1846, to his death on 12th October, 1860, we have no record by his own hand.

The Autobiography had been carefully preserved by Sir Harry's former aide-de-camp and friend, General Sir Edward Alan Holdich, K.C.B., but, as it happened, I was not myself aware of its existence until, owing to the fresh interest awakened in Sir Harry Smith and his wife by the siege of Ladysmith early in 1900, I inquired from members of my family what memorials of my great-uncle were preserved. Sir Edward then put this manuscript and a number of letters and documents at my disposal. It appeared to me and to friends whom I consulted that the Autobiography was so full of romantic adventure and at the same time of such solid historical value that it ought no longer to remain unpublished, and Mr. John Murray, to whom I submitted a transcription of it, came at once to the same conclusion.

My task as Editor has not been a light one. In Sir Harry's letter to Mrs. Sargant of 15th October, 1844,* he says of his manuscript, "I have never read a page of it since my scrawling it over at full gallop;" and in a letter of 14th January, 1845, "Harry Lorrequer would make a good story of it. You may ask him if you like, and let me know what he says of it." It is clear from these passages that Sir Harry did not contemplate the publication of his story in the rough form in which he had written it, but imagined that some literary man, such as Charles Lever, might take it in hand, rewrite it with fictitious names, and so fashion out of it a military romance. The chapters † on Afghanistan and Gwalior, already written, were, however, of a serious character which would make them unsuitable for such treatment ; and the same was the case with the chapters on the Sikh War, afterwards added. Whether Lever ever saw the manuscript I do not know ; at any rate, the author's idea was never carried out.

---

* See vol. ii. Appendix iv.
† Sir Harry's original narrative is not broken into chapters.

It is obvious that now that fifty years have passed, some of the reasons which made Sir Harry suggest such a transformation of his story are no longer in force. The actors in the events which he describes having almost all passed away, to suppress names would be meaningless and would deprive the book of the greater part of its interest. And for the sake of literary effect to rewrite Sir Harry's story would be to destroy its great charm, the intimate relation in which it sets us with his fiery and romantic character.

The book here given to the public is not indeed word for word as Sir Harry wrote it. It has often been necessary to break up a long sentence, to invert a construction—sometimes to transpose a paragraph in order to bring it into closer connexion with the events to which it refers. But such changes have only been made when they seemed necessary to bring out more clearly the writer's intention; the *words* are the author's own, even where a specially awkward construction has been smoothed; and it may be broadly said that *nothing* has been added to Sir Harry's narrative or omitted from it. Such slight additions to the text as seemed desirable, for example, names and dates of battles,* have been included in square brackets. In some cases, to avoid awkward parentheses, sentences of

* The Peninsular dates are generally borrowed from *A British Rifleman* (Major Simmons' diary).

Sir Harry's own have been relegated from the text to footnotes. Such notes are indicated by the addition of his initials ("H.G.S.").

Sir Harry's handwriting was not of the most legible order, as he admits, and I have had considerable difficulty in identifying some of the persons and places he mentions. Sometimes I have come to the conclusion that his own recollection was at fault, and in this case I have laid my difficulty before the reader.

I have not thought it my duty to normalize the spelling of proper names, such as those of towns in the Peninsula and in India, and the names of Kafir chiefs. Sir Harry himself spells such names in a variety of ways, and I have not thought absolute consistency a matter of importance, while to have re-written Indian names according to the modern official spelling would have been, as it seems to me, to perpetrate an anachronism.

I have, indeed, generally printed "Sutlej," though Sir Harry frequently or generally wrote "Sutledge;" but I have kept in his own narrative his spelling "Ferozeshuhur" (which is, I believe, more correct) for the battle generally called "Ferozeshah." Even Sir Harry's native place (and my own) has two spellings, "Whittlesey" and "Whittlesea." In his narrative I have preserved his usual spelling "Whittlesea," but I have myself used the other, as I have been taught to do from a boy.

Perhaps it is worth while to mention here that Sir Harry's name was strictly "Henry George Wakelyn Smith," and it appears in this form in official documents. But having been always known in the army as "Harry Smith," after attaining his knighthood he stoutly refused to become "Sir Henry," and insisted on retaining the more familiar name.* As the year of his birth is constantly given as 1788, it is worth while to state that the Baptismal Register of St. Mary's, Whittlesey, proves him to have been born on 28th June, 1787.

While the documents put into my hands by Sir Edward Holdich enabled me to throw a good deal of additional light on the events recorded in the Autobiography, I thought it a prime duty not to interrupt Sir Harry's own narrative by interpolations. Accordingly I have thrown this illustrative matter into Appendices. In some of these, especially in his letters to his wife of 1835 (vol. ii., Appendix ii.), one sees the writer, perhaps, in still more familiar guise than in the Autobiography.

But I had not merely to illustrate the period of Sir Harry's life covered by his Autobiography; I

* Sir Harry's ordinary signature was "H. G. Smith." His letters to his wife were commonly signed "Enrique"; to members of his family, "Harry Smith"; to his friend and interpreter for the Kafir language, Mr. Theophilus Shepstone, "Inkosi" ("Chief"). He addressed Mr. Shepstone as "My dear Sumtseu" ("Hunter").

had a further task before me, viz. to construct a narrative of the rest of his life (1846–1860), including his Governorship of the Cape (1847–1852). For the manner in which I have done this, I must crave indulgence. At the best it would have been no easy matter to continue in the third person a story begun by the main actor in the first, and in this case the letters and personal memoranda, which were tolerably abundant for Sir Harry's earlier years, suddenly became very scanty when they were most required. Accordingly, for much of Sir Harry's life I had no more sources to draw on than are accessible to anybody—histories, blue-books, and newspapers. I can only say that in this situation I have done the best I could. My chief difficulty was, of course, in dealing with the time of Sir Harry's command at the Cape. It would have been inconsistent with the scope of the whole book to have attempted a systematic history of the colony or of the operations of the Kafir War. At the same time I could not enable my readers to form an estimate of Sir Harry's conduct at this time without giving them some indication of the circumstances which surrounded him. If I am found by some critics to have subordinated biography too much to history, I can only hope that other critics will console me by finding that I have subordinated history too much to biography.

Amid a certain dearth of materials of a private

kind, I do congratulate myself on having been able
to use the packet of letters docketed by Sir Harry,
"John Bell's and Charlie Beckwith's Letters."
General Beckwith was an earlier General Gordon,
and his letters are so interesting in matter and so
brilliant in expression that one is tempted to wish
to see them printed in full. Perhaps some readers
of this book may be able to tell me of other letters
by the same remarkable man which have been
preserved.

The latter part of this book would have been
balder than it is, if it had not been for the help I
have received from various friends, known and
unknown. I must express my thanks in particular
to the Misses Payne of Chester, who lent me letters
addressed to their father, Major C. W. Meadows
Payne; to Mrs. Thorne of Chippenham, who lent
me letters addressed to her father, Major George
Simmons; to Mrs. Fasson, daughter of Mr. Justice
Menzies of the Cape, and Mr. W. F. Collier of
Horrabridge, who gave me their reminiscences; to
Colonel L. G. Fawkes, R.A., Stephen A. Aveling,
Esq., of Rochester, Major J. F. Anderson of Faring-
don, R. Morton Middleton, Esq., of Ealing, Captain
C. V. Ibbetson of Preston, Mrs. Henry Fawcett,
my aunt Mrs. John A. Smith, Mrs. Farebrother of
Oxford, Mr. B. Genn of Ely, Mr. Charles Sayle
of Cambridge, Mr. G. J. Turner of Lincoln's Inn,
Mr. A. E. Barnes of the Local Government Board,

the Military Secretary of the War Office, and others, for kind assistance of various kinds. I am indebted to my cousins, Mrs. Lambert of 1, Sloane Gardens, S.W., and C. W. Ford, Esq., for permission to reproduce pictures in their possession, and to General Sir Edward Holdich for much aid and interest in my work in addition to the permission to use his diary of the Boomplaats expedition. Lastly, my thanks are due to my brothers and sisters who assisted in transcribing the Autobiography, and in particular to my sister, Miss M. A. Smith, who did most of the work of preparing the Index.

I shall feel that any labour which I have bestowed on the preparation of this book will be richly repaid if through it Harry and Juana Smith cease to be mere names and become living figures, held in honour and affection by the sons and daughters of the Empire which they served.

G. C. MOORE SMITH.

Sheffield,
September, 1901.

DATES OF LIEUT.-GENERAL SIR HARRY SMITH'S COMMISSIONS AND APPOINTMENTS.

———◆———

REGIMENTAL RANK.

Second Lieutenant, 1st Battalion 95th Regiment ...	8 May, 1805
Lieutenant	15 Aug. 1805
Captain	28 Feb. 1812
Major, unattached	29 Dec. 1826
Lieut.-Colonel, unattached	22 July, 1830
Lieut.-Colonel, 3rd Foot	13 May, 1842
Lieut.-Colonel, unattached	25 Aug. 1843
Colonel, 47th Foot	18 Jan. 1847
Colonel, 2nd Battalion Rifle Brigade	16 April, 1847
Colonel, 1st Battalion Rifle Brigade	18 Jan. 1855

ARMY RANK.

Major	29 Sept. 1814
Lieut.-Colonel	18 June, 1815
Colonel	10 Jan. 1837
Local rank of Major-General in the East Indies ...	21 Aug. 1840
Major-General	9 Nov. 1846
Local rank of Lieut.-General in South Africa ...	1847–1852
Lieut.-General	20 June, 1854

STAFF APPOINTMENTS.

PENINSULAR WAR.

A.D.C. to Colonel T. S. Beckwith	Oct. 1810
Brigade Major, 2nd Brigade, Light Division under Major-General Drummond, Major-General Vandeleur, Major-General Skerrett, and Colonel Colborne successively	Mar. 1811 to the end of the war, Mar. 1814

WASHINGTON EXPEDITION.

D.A.G. to Major-General R. Ross	1814

New Orleans Expedition.

A.A.G. to Major-General Sir E. Pakenham ...	1814
Military Secretary to Major-General Sir J. Lambert	1815

Waterloo Campaign.

Brigade-Major, afterwards A.Q.M.G. to 6th Division
    (Major-General Sir J. Lambert and Major-General
    Sir Lowry Cole successively)   1815
[Returns to his regiment.]

Occupation of France.

Major de Place of Cambray   1815–1818
[Returns to his regiment.]

Glasgow.

Major of Brigade to Major-General Sir T. Reynell
    (commanding Western District) and Lieut-
    General Sir T. Bradford (Commander-in-Chief in
    Scotland) successively   1819–1825
[Returns to his regiment.]

Nova Scotia.

A.D.C. to Lieut.-General Sir James Kempt, Governor   1826

Jamaica.

D.Q.M.G. under Lieut.-General Sir John Keane,
    Governor   1827

Cape of Good Hope.

D.Q.M.G. under Lieut.-General Sir Lowry Cole, Lieut.-
    General Sir B. D'Urban, Major-General Sir G.
    T. Napier, Governors, successively   1828
Chief of the Staff under Sir Benjamin D'Urban in
    the Kafir War   1835

India.

A.G. to Her Majesty's Forces, under Lieut.-General
    Sir Jasper Nicolls and Lieut.-General Sir Hugh
    Gough, Commanders-in-Chief, successively   ...   1840–1845

Sikh War.

In Command of the 1st Division Infantry   1845–1846

CAPE OF GOOD HOPE.

Governor and Commander-in-Chief   1847–1852

HOME STAFF.

In Command of the Western Military District   ...   1853–1854
In Command of the Northern and Midland Military
    Districts   1854–1859

STEPS IN THE ORDER OF THE BATH.

C.B. for Waterloo   1815
K.C.B. for Maharajpore   1844
G.C.B. for Aliwal and Sobraon   1846

BOOKS USEFUL FOR REFERENCE IN CONNEXION WITH SIR HARRY SMITH'S LIFE.

SIR WILLIAM F. P. NAPIER: *History of the War in the Peninsula.*

SIR H. E. MAXWELL: *Life of Wellington.*

SIR WILLIAM H. COPE: *History of the Rifle Brigade* (1877).

EDWARD COSTELLO: *Adventures of a Soldier.*

A British Rifleman (Major George Simmons' Diary), edited by COLONEL WILLOUGHBY VERNER.

SIR JOHN KINCAID: *Random Shots by a Rifleman.*

SIR JOHN KINCAID: *Adventures in the Rifle Brigade.*

Recollections of Rifleman Harris (1848).

SURTEES: *Twenty-five Years in the Rifle Brigade* (1833).

COLONEL JONATHAN LEACH: *Rough Sketches in the Life of an Old Soldier* (1831).

CHARLES DALTON: *The Waterloo Roll Call* (1890).

GEORGE McC. THEAL: *History of South Africa,* vol. iv. (1893).

SIR J. E. ALEXANDER: *Narrative of a Voyage, etc.* (1837). This work contains in vol. ii. a history of the Kafir War of 1835, with illustrations.

H. CLOETE: *The Great Boer Trek.*

The War in India. Despatches of Viscount Hardinge, Lord Gough, Major-General Sir Harry Smith, Bart., etc. (1846).

GENERAL SIR CHAS. GOUGH and A. D. INNES: *The Sikhs and the Sikh Wars* (1897).

J. W. CLARK and T. McK. HUGHES: *Life of Adam Sedgwick.*

HARRIET WARD: *Five Years in Kaffirland.*

J. NOBLE: *South Africa* (1877).

A. WILMOT and J. C. CHASE: *Annals of the Colony of the Cape of Good Hope* (1869).

ALFRED W. COLE: *The Cape and the Kaffirs* (1852).

W. R. KING: *Campaigning in Kaffirland* (with illustrations), (1853).

W. A. NEWMAN: *Memoir of John Montagu* (1855).

Correspondence of General Sir G. Cathcart (1856).

EARL GREY: *The Colonial Policy of Lord John Russell's Administration* (1853).

BLUE-BOOKS: *Cape of Good Hope* (1830-1852).

M. MEILLE: *Memoir of General Beckwith, C.B.* (1873).

CONTENTS OF VOL. I.

—◦—

LIST OF ILLUSTRATIONS.

VOL. I.

———◆———

On the Cover.

ARMS GRANTED TO SIR HARRY SMITH IN 1846.

They are thus described by Sir Bernard Burke :—

Arms—Argent, on a chevron between two martlets in chief gules, and upon a mount vert in base, an elephant proper, a fleur-de-lis between two lions rampant, of the first: from the centre-chief, pendant by a riband, gules, fimbriated azure, a representation of the Waterloo medal.

Crest—Upon an Eastern crown or, a lion rampant argent, supporting a lance proper ; therefrom flowing to the sinister, a pennon gules, charged with two palm-branches, in saltier, or.

The supporters are a soldier of the Rifle Brigade and a soldier of the 52nd Regiment.

THE AUTOBIOGRAPHY OF
Lt.-Gen. Sir Harry Smith,

BARONET OF ALIWAL, G.C.B.

———

CHAPTER I.

MONTE VIDEO AND BUENOS AYRES.
1806–7.

Written in Glasgow in 1824.—H. G. Smith.

I was born in the parish of Whittlesea and county of Cambridgeshire in the year [1787]. I am one of eleven children, six sons and five daughters. Every pains was taken with my education which my father could afford, and I was taught natural philosophy, classics, algebra, and music.*

* The birthplace of Sir Harry Smith in St. Mary's Street, Whittlesey, is now called "Aliwal House." In his MS. he left the year of his birth vacant, and it would appear that he was uncertain of his own age (cp. p. 73). This may account for the date of his birth having been often given wrongly as 1788. The east end of the south aisle of St. Mary's church was at this time partitioned off and used as a schoolroom, the vicar or curate teaching. It was here that Harry Smith received his education from the Rev. George Burgess, then curate, who survived to welcome him in Whittlesey in 1847 on his return after the battle of Aliwal. This part of the church, having been restored in 1862 as a memorial to him, is now known as "Sir Harry's Chapel."

Harry Smith's father, John Smith (son of Wakelyn Smith),

In 1804 the whole country was *en masse* collected in arms as volunteers from the expected invasion of the French, and being now sixteen years of age, I was received into the Whittlesea troop of

surgeon, born 1756, died 2 Sept. 1843, married in 1781 Eleanor (born 1760, died 12 Dec. 1813), daughter of the Rev. George Moore, M.A. (Queens' College, Cambridge), vicar of St. Mary and St. Andrew, Whittlesey, and minor canon of Peterborough Cathedral. They had in all fourteen children, but only eleven survived infancy, viz. 1, Mary Anne; 2, John Stona; 3, Eleanor Moore; 4, Elizabeth; 5, Henry George Wakelyn (b. 28 June, 1787); 6, Jane Alice (Mrs. Sargant), b. 1789; 7, William; 8, Thomas Lawrence (b. 25 Feb. 1792); 9, Anna Maria; 10, Charles (b. 10 Aug. 1795); 11, Samuel.

Mrs. Sargant, Harry Smith's favourite sister, resided for many years in Clapton Square, and died in 1869. She was the author of *Joan of Arc, a Play*, *Charlie Burton* (a tale, translated into French and German), and many other works.

Thomas Lawrence (frequently mentioned in this book) received his commission in the 95th (Rifle Brigade) on 3 March, 1808, and took part in the actions of Sir John Moore's expedition to the battle of Corunna. Like his brother Harry, he served with the Light Division throughout the Peninsular War to the battle of Toulouse, being dangerously wounded at the Coa. He was recommended for promotion for his conduct at Waterloo. He proceeded with his regiment to Paris, and riding as Adjutant at the head of the 2nd Battalion, was the first British officer who entered the city on 7 July, 1815. He went on half-pay in 1817. In 1824 he was appointed Barrack-master, in which capacity he served in Ireland till 1838, when he was transferred to Chatham. On the formation of Aldershot Camp in 1855, he was appointed Principal Barrack-master there, and held his appointment till 1868. On retirement he was made a C.B. and granted a special pension. He died in London on 6 April, 1877, and was buried in the cemetery, Aldershot.

Charles was present as a "Volunteer" with the 1st Battalion 95th at Quatrebras and Waterloo, after which he received a commission as Second Lieutenant. Two or three years later he retired from the army and settled at Whittlesey. He became J.P. and D.L. for Cambridgeshire, and Lieut.-Colonel of the Yeomanry Cavalry of the county, and died at Whittlesey on 24 Dec. 1854.

Further information about Sir Harry Smith's family was given to Mr. Arthur M. Smith, at his request, for his book *The Smiths of Exeter*, and will there be found, although, in the opinion of the present editor, no connexion between the two families can be established.

Yeomanry Cavalry, commanded by Captain Johnson.
During this year the Yeomanry in the neighbourhood patrolled through Norman Cross Barracks,
where 15,000 French prisoners were kept, when
the Frenchmen laughed exceedingly at the young
dragoon, saying, " I say, leetel fellow, go home with
your mamma; you most eat more pudding." In the
spring of 1805 the Whittlesea Yeomanry kept the
ground at a review made by Brigadier-General
Stewart (now Sir W. Stewart), when I was orderly
to the General, who said, " Young gentleman, would
you like to be an officer ?" "Of all things," was
my answer. "Well, I will make you a Rifleman, a
green jacket," says the General, "and very smart."
I assure you the General kept his word, and upon
the 15th [8th ?] May, 1805, I was gazetted second
lieutenant in the 95th Regiment Riflemen,* and
joined at Brabourne Lees upon the 18th of August.
A vacancy of lieutenant occurring for purchase,
my father kindly advanced the money, and I was
gazetted lieutenant the 15th September [August ?],
1805. This fortunate purchase occurred when the
2nd Battalion of the corps was raising and the

* In consequence of a representation made to the Government by
Colonel Coote Manningham and Lieut.-Colonel the Hon. William
Stewart, an "experimental Corps of Riflemen" was formed early in
1800, with Manningham as colonel and Stewart one of the lieut.-
colonels. It was actually organized by Stewart. On the 25th of
December, 1802, the corps was ordered to be numbered as the 95th
Regiment. In 1803 they were brigaded with the 43rd and 52nd as
part of Sir John Moore's Camp of Instruction at Shorncliffe. The
2nd Battalion was formed on the 6th of May, 1805, according to
Cope, and joined the 1st Battalion at Brabourn Lees, near Ashford,
in June (see Cope's *History of the Rifle Brigade*, p. 1, etc.).

officers had not been appointed, by which good luck twenty-seven steps were obtained by £100.

In the summer of 1806 a detachment of three Companies was directed to proceed from the 2nd Battalion of the corps from Faversham to Portsmouth, there to embark and form part of an army about to proceed to South America under the command of Sir Samuel Auchmuty. This detachment was under the command of Major Gardner, and I was appointed Adjutant, a great honour for so young an officer.* The army sailed for America, touching at Plymouth, Falmouth, Peak of Teneriffe, and Rio Janeiro, at which place it stayed one week to take in water, stores, etc., and, covered by the detachment of Riflemen, landed within a few miles of Monte Video upon the 16th of January, 1807. Some skirmishing took place the whole day with the light troops of the enemy. Upon the 17th and 18th the army halted for the artillery, stores, etc., to be landed. The outposts (Riflemen) were employed both of these days.

Upon the 19th the army moved forward, and a general action took place, the result of which was most favourable to the British, and a position was taken up in the suburbs of Monte Video. Upon the 20th the garrison made a most vigorous sortie in three columns, and drove in our outposts, and a heavy and general attack lasted for near two hours, when the enemy were driven to the very walls of the place. The

* For his diary of the voyage, etc., see Appendix I.

Riflemen were particularly distinguished on this occasion.

The siege of Monte Video was immediately commenced, and upon the morning of the 3rd of February, the breach being considered practicable, a general assault was ordered in two columns, the one upon the breach, the other an escalade. Both ultimately succeeded. Not a defence was destroyed nor a gun dismounted upon the works. The breach was only wide enough for three men to enter abreast, and when upon the top of the breach there was a descent into the city of twelve feet. Most of the men fell, and many were wounded by each other's bayonets. When the head of the column entered the breach, the main body lost its communications or was checked by the tremendous fire. Perceiving the delay, I went back and conducted the column to the breach, when the place was immediately taken. The slaughter in the breach was enormous owing to the defence being perfect, and its not being really practicable. The surrender of this fortress put the English in the possession of this part of the country.

I was now afflicted with a most severe fever and dysentery, and owe my life to the kind attentions of a Spanish family in whose house I was billeted. My own relations could not have treated me with greater kindness. My gratitude to them can never be expressed or sufficiently appreciated. *

* The following extracts from Hughes and Clark's *Life of Adam Sedgwick* (i. p. 76, etc.) refer to this time—

"Sedgwick went on December 17, 1804, to spend Christmas with

In the autumn * an outpost was established on the same side of the river as Monte Video, but nearly opposite to Buenos Ayres, at Colonia del Sacramento. This had formerly belonged to the Portuguese. It was situated on a neck of land, and a mud wall was carried from water to water. There were no guns up, and in one place a considerable breach. One particular night a column of Spaniards which had crossed the river from Buenos Ayres stormed this post, and were near carrying it by surprise had it not been for the valour of Scott and his guard of Riflemen, who most bravely defended the breach until the troops got under arms. The enemy were not pursued, as their numbers were not known and the night was dark. Why this breach was not repaired one cannot say,

Ainger at his father's house at Whittlesea. . . . He never forgot the simple pleasures which he there enjoyed. . . . It was on this occasion that he made the acquaintance of Henry Smith, son to the surgeon of Whittlesea, then a boy of sixteen. Sedgwick watched his career with affectionate interest.

"In 1807 he wrote to Ainger—

"'Pray has Henry Smith escaped the fate which many of our brave countrymen have met in Egypt? I believe his Regiment was in the expedition.'

"W. Ainger replies—

"'Whittlesea, August 3, 1807.

"'Henry Smith, after whom you inquired, did not go into Egypt, but to Buenos Ayres. His father had a letter from him after the engagement. His Captain was killed by his side in the outset; the command of the Company then of course devolved to Henry, who, I believe, acquitted himself very creditably, and did not, to use his own expression, get a single scratch. Last week brought his friends another letter from Monte Video, which acquainted them that he was then (in April) just recovering from the attack of a fever, which appears, Sedgwick, to have been not less formidable than yours was. He says he has lost all his flesh; but I find he retains all his spirit.'"

* *I.e.* the English spring.

except that in those days our commanders understood little of the art of war, and sat themselves
down anywhere in a state of blind security without
using every means to strengthen their posts.
Experience taught us better.

The enemy did not re-cross the river, but took
up a position about fourteen miles from Colonia,
in which Colonel Pack (afterwards Sir Denis
Pack), who commanded the British force, resolved
to attack them. The column consisted of three
companies of Riflemen, the 40th Regiment, two
6-pounders, and three light companies. It marched
upon the night of [6–7 June], and arrived in sight
of the enemy at daylight in the morning. They
were drawn up on an elevated piece of ground,
with a narrow but deep, muddy, and miry river in
their front. Their cavalry formed a right angle upon
the right of their infantry and they had seven guns
upon the left. The Rifle Brigade covered the
troops whilst crossing the rivulet, and in about
twenty minutes by a rapid advance the position was
carried, the enemy leaving behind him his guns,
tents, stores, etc., with a great quantity of ammunition. In the destroying of the latter poor Major
Gardner and fourteen soldiers suffered most dreadfully from an explosion. Some flints had been
scattered upon the field ; the soldiers took the shot
to break the cartridges, and thus the whole blew
up. About two hundred shells also exploded.
The army at a short distance lay down, and not
an individual was touched. Colonel Pack, with his

army, the captured guns, etc., returned to Colonia in the evening.*

A considerable force having arrived under General Whitelock, who took the command, the army was remodelled and embarked in August [really on the 17th of June], 1807, to attack Buenos Ayres. The post of Colonia was abandoned, and the three companies of the 2nd Battalion Rifle Brigade were embodied with five of the 1st just arrived from England, and I was appointed adjutant of the whole under the command of Major McLeod. The army landed upon [28 June], and was divided into two columns, the one consisting of the light troops under General Craufurd, and the other of a heavy brigade, the whole under Major - General Leveson - Gower. [Some epithets are here omitted.] His column was one day in advance of the main body commanded by General Whitelock in person. His orders were to march up to the enemy's outposts and take up a position. In place of obeying his orders, General Leveson-Gower immediately attacked the enemy in the suburbs of Buenos Ayres, and drove them in with great loss, leaving their cannon behind them. Having thus committed himself, in lieu of

* Cope says he could find no particulars of this affair of the 7th of June beyond the mention of it and the casualties. Pack's own report of the affair, however (with Whitelock's covering despatch), is given under his name in Philippart's *Royal Military Calendar* (1820). It is interesting to compare that account with the one in the text, as each has some details not in the other. It seems that the Spaniards, two thousand in number, were under Major-General Elio (see p. 79, below), and the name of their position was San Pedro.

following up the advantage he had gained and pushing forward into Buenos Ayres, which would have immediately surrendered, he halted his column and took up a position. The enemy recovered from his panic, and with the utmost vigour turned to and fortified the entrances of all the streets. (Buenos Ayres is perfectly open on the land side, but has a citadel of some strength within the town and upon the river. The houses are all flat-roofed, with a parapet of about three feet high.) The day after the affair alluded to, General Whitelock with his column arrived. The next day he reconnoitred the enemy, drove in their outposts, and partially invested the city. Some very heavy skirmishing took place in the enclosures, the fences consisting of aloe hedges, very difficult to get through, but making excellent breastworks. The Rifle Corps particularly distinguished themselves.

Upon the [5 July] the whole army attacked in four columns. The men were ordered to advance without flints in their musquets, and crowbars, axes, etc., were provided at the head of the column to break open the doors, which were most strongly barricaded. It must be stated that the streets of Buenos Ayres run at right angles from each other. Each street was cut off by a ditch and a battery behind it. Thus the troops were exposed to a cross fire. The tops of the houses were occupied by troops, and such a tremendous fire was produced of grape, canister, and musquetry, that in a short time two columns were nearly annihilated without effecting any impression. The column I belonged to, under Brigadier-General Craufurd, after severe loss, took refuge in a church, and about dusk in the evening surrendered to the enemy. Thus terminated one of the most sanguinary conflicts Britons were ever engaged in, and all owing to the stupidity of the General-in-chief and General Leveson-Gower. Liniers, a Frenchman by birth, who commanded, treated us prisoners tolerably well, but he had little to give us to eat, his citadel not being provisioned for a siege. We were three or four days in his hands, when, in consequence of the disgraceful convention entered into by General Whitelock, who agreed within two months to evacuate the territory altogether and to give up the fortress of Monte Video, we were released. The army re-embarked with all dispatch and sailed to Monte Video. Our wounded suffered dreadfully, many dying from slight wounds in the extremity of lockjaw.

The division of troops I belonged to sailed upon [12 July], under the command of Brigadier-General Lumley. I confess I parted from the kind Spanish family, who during my illness had treated me with such paternal kindness, with feelings of the deepest sorrow and most lively gratitude. The old lady offered me her daughter in marriage and $20,000, with as many thousand oxen as I wished, and she would build me a house in the country upon any plan I chose to devise.

Now that I am brought to leave the fertile

plains of the Plate, let me make some little
mention of its climate, soil, and productions. Its
summer is, of course, in January; during this time
it is very hot. Still you have a sea breeze and a
land breeze, which is very refreshing. During the
rainy seasons the weather is very tempestuous.
The climate altogether is, however, most mild and
salubrious. Corn of all descriptions grows with the
least possible care. The fertile grass plains are
immense. The country is not a dead flat, but un-
dulated like the great Atlantic a few days after a
gale of wind. Upon these plains thousands of oxen
and horses are grazing; they are so thick that were
an individual ever entangled amongst them he
would be lost as in a wood. These animals are,
however, all the property of individuals, and not wild
as supposed, and each horse and ox is branded.
You could buy a most excellent horse for two dollars
(I gave ten for one, he being very handsome, which
was a price unheard of before), a cow and calf one
dollar, a pair of draft oxen five (they are thus dear
in consequence of being trained). The country
abounds in all sorts of wild fowl and innumerable
wild dogs, which nature must have provided to eat
the carcases of the slaughtered cattle, many of which
are killed merely for their hides, a few of the prime
pieces alone being made use of for food. The
marrow is usually also taken and rendered into
bladders, with which they cook everything, using it,
in short, as we use butter, which makes their dishes
very palatable. The native inhabitants, called

"peons," or labourers, are a very superior race of men, almost Patagonians, are beautiful horsemen, and have a peculiar art of catching horses and oxen by what is termed the "lasso." This is a leathern thong of about thirty feet resembling the lash of a hunting-whip. An iron ring is at one end, through which the other end is passed, by which means a noose is formed ; the end is then fastened to the girths of the horse. The lasso is collected in the man's hand, he swings it circularly round his head, and when the opportunity offers, he throws it over the head of the animal he wishes to catch. He is sure of his aim ; the noose draws tight round the animal's throat, and he is of course choked, and down he drops.

In killing bullocks they are very dexterous. The moment the bullock finds himself caught he begins to gallop round ; the end being fast to the saddle, the horse turns gradually round so that he is not entangled. A second peon with his lasso gallops after the bullock, and throws his lasso round the hind leg above the hough and rides in a contrary direction to the other horseman, consequently the bullock is stretched between the two horses. The riders jump off and plunge their knives into the bullock, and other persons are employed to dress it, etc.

The fleet separated in a gale of wind off the Azores. During this gale the transport I was in carried away its rudder. Our captain had kept so bad a reckoning we ran four hundred miles after he expected to make the Lizard. In the chops of the Channel we fell in with the *Swallow*, sloop of war, to whom we made a signal of distress, and she towed us into Falmouth Harbour [5 Nov.]. It blew the most tremendous gale of wind that night. A transport with the 9th Dragoons aboard was wrecked near the Lizard, and this would inevitably have been our fate had we not been towed in by the sloop of war. The rudder was repaired, we were driven into Plymouth, and in the middle of December anchored at Spithead, where we delighted to have arrived. However, to our great mortification, we were ordered to the Downs, there to disembark.

I obtained leave of absence, and was soon in the arms of a most affectionate family, who dearly loved me. My mother's delight I shall never forget. There are feelings we possess in our youth which cannot be described. I was then only nineteen. My brothers and sisters were all well, and every moment called to my recollection some incident of juvenile delight and affection.

CHAPTER II.

WITH SIR JOHN MOORE—BATTLE OF CORUÑA. 1808-9.

I STAYED in this happy land of my sires for two months, when I was ordered to join. The Regiment was then quartered at Colchester. Although there were many subalterns present who were senior to me, I had given to me, for my exertions abroad as Adjutant, the command of a Company. This was the act of my kind and valued friend Colonel Beckwith, whom I shall have occasion frequently to mention in these memoirs, but never without feelings of affection and gratitude. The Company was in very bad order when I received it, which Colonel Beckwith told me was the reason he gave it me. I now procured a commission for my brother Tom, who was gazetted over the heads of several other candidates.

In the summer [spring] of 1808 10,000 men were ordered to Sweden under the command of Sir J. Moore. Three Companies of the Rifle Brigade under Major Gilmour were to form part of the expedition. By dint of great exertion I was appointed Adjutant to this detachment. We marched to Harwich to embark. When the fleet was collected, we anchored a few days in Yarmouth roads. The fleet arrived at Gottenburgh [on 7 May], blowing a heavy gale of wind. The harbour of this place is most beautiful. The army never landed, but the men were drilled, embarking and disembarking in flat-bottomed boats. I jumped against three regiments, 95th, 43rd, and 52nd, and beat them by four inches, having leaped 19 feet and 4 inches.

Commenced at Simla, Himalayas, 11th Aug. 1844.—H.G.S.

At this period Napoleon announced his unjust invasion of Spain, and Sir John Moore's army was ordered to sail and unite with the forces collecting on the coast of Portugal for the purpose of expelling Junot's army from Lisbon. On approaching the mouth of the Mondego, a frigate met us to say Sir Arthur Wellesley's army had landed in Mondego and pushed forward, and that Sir John Moore was to sail for Peniche, and there land on arrival. The battle of Vimiera had been fought [21 Aug. 1808], and the Convention was in progress. Sir John Moore's army landed one or two days after the battle and took the outposts. The three Companies to which I was Adjutant joined Colonel Beckwith and the headquarters of the Regiment, and I was appointed to Captain O'Hare's Company (sub-alterns Smith, W. Eeles, Eaton).

After the embarcation of the French army, an army was formed under Sir John Moore for the aid of the Spaniards, and it moved on the frontier of Alemtejo.

The 95th were quartered in Villa Viciosa, in an elegant palace. I occupied a beautiful little room with a private staircase, called the Hall of Justice. I was sent by Sir Edward Paget to examine the fort Xuramenha and report upon it, the fords of the Guadiana, etc., near the important fortress of Badajos.

In the autumn of this year (1808), Sir John Moore's army moved on Salamanca. As I could speak Spanish, I was employed by Colonel Beckwith to precede the Regiment daily to aid the Quarter-master in procuring billets and rations in the different towns, and various were the adventures I met with. The army was assembled at Salamanca, and never did England assemble such a body of organized and elegant troops as that army of Sir John Moore, destined to cover itself with glory, disgrace, victory, and misfortune. The whole of this campaign is too ably recorded by Napier for me to dwell on. I shall only say that never did corps so distinguish itself during the whole of this retreat as my dear old Rifles. From the severe attack on our rear-guard at Calca-vellos [3 Jan. 1809], where I was particularly distinguished, until the battle of Coruña, we were daily engaged with a most vigorous and pushing enemy, making most terrific long marches (one day 37 miles). The fire of the Riflemen ever prevented the column being molested by the enemy ; but the scenes of drunkenness, riot, and disorder we Reserve Division witnessed on the part of the rest of the army are not to be described ; it was truly awful and heartrending to see that army which had been so brilliant at Sala-manca so totally disorganized, with the exception of the reserve under the revered Paget and the Brigade of Guards. The cavalry were nearly all dismounted, the whole a mass of fugitives and insubordinates; yet these very fellows licked the French at Coruña like men [16 Jan.]. The army embarked the following day. I shall never forget the explosion of a fortress blown up by us—the report cannot be imagined. Oh, the filthy state we were all in! We lost our baggage at Calcavellos; for three weeks we had no clothes but those on our backs; we were literally covered and almost eaten up with vermin, most of us suffering from ague and dysentery, every man a living still active skeleton. On embarcation many fell asleep in their ships and never awoke for three days and nights, until in a gale we reached Portsmouth [21 Jan.]. I was so reduced that Colonel Beckwith, with a warmth of heart equalling the thunder of his voice, on meeting me in the George Inn, roared out, "Who the devil's ghost are you? Pack up your kit—which is soon done, the devil a thing have you got—take   ce in the coach, and set off home to your father's. I shall soon want again such fellows as you, and I will arrange your leave of absence!" I soon took the hint, and naked and slothful and covered with vermin I reached my dear native home, where the kindest of fathers and most affectionate of mothers soon restored me to health.*

* See his reference to this time, p. 159.

CHAPTER III.

BACK TO THE PENINSULA UNDER SIR ARTHUR WELLESLEY.

1809.

In two months I rejoined the Regiment at Hythe. From Hythe we marched for Dover, where we embarked for Lisbon [25 May] to join the Duke's * army. Having landed at Lisbon, we commenced our march for Talavera. On this march—a very long one—General Craufurd compiled his orders for the march of his Brigade, consisting of the 43rd, 52nd, and 95th, each upwards of 1000 strong. These orders he enforced with rigour (as it seemed at the moment), but he was in this way the means of establishing the organization and discipline of that corps which acquired for it its after-celebrity as the " Light Division."

We had some long, harassing, and excessively hot marches. In the last twenty-eight hours we

---

* The author, writing many years after the events described, does not discriminate the titles borne at different dates by his revered commander, but speaks of him as " the Duke," even from the time he was Sir Arthur Wellesley. At the risk of offending the historical sense of some readers, I have made no attempt to remove such a harmless anachronism.

marched from Oropesa to Talavera, a distance of
fourteen Spanish leagues (56 miles), our soldiers
carrying their heavy packs, the Riflemen eighty
rounds of ammunition.   But the battle of Talavera
was thundering in our ears, and created a spirit in
the Brigade which cast away all idea of fatigue.   We
reached the sanguinary field at daylight after the
battle [29 July], greeted as if we were demi-gods by
all the gallant heroes who had gained *such* a victory.
We took up the outposts immediately, and some
of us Riflemen sustained some heavy skirmishing.
The field was literally covered with dead and dying.
The bodies began to putrefy, and the stench was
horrible, so that an attempt was made to collect
the bodies and burn them.   Then, however, came a
stench which literally affected many to sickness.
The soldiers were not satisfied with this mode of
treating the bodies of their dead comrades, and the
prosecution of the attempt was relinquished.   After
our stay at Talavera [29 July—3 Aug.], during
which we were nearly starved, the army commenced
its retreat, passing the bridge of Arzobispo in the
most correct and soldier-like manner, our Brigade
forming the rear-guard.   The army retired on
Deleytosa, the Light Brigade remaining in a
position so as to watch the bridge of Almaraz.
Here for three weeks we were nearly starved
[6 Aug.—20 Aug.], and our position received the
name of Doby Hill.*   We marched every evening

* Cp. E. Costello, *Adventures of a Soldier*, p. 36: "For bread
we took the corn from the fields, and, having no proper means of

and bivouacked so as to occupy the passage of the Tagus, and at daylight returned to our hill. Honey was plentiful, but it gave dysentery. My mess—Leach's Company (Leach, Smith, Layton, and Bob Beckwith)—were not as badly off as our neighbours. We had a few dollars, and as I could speak Spanish, I rode into the lines of the Spanish troops, where I could always purchase some loaves of bread at a most exorbitant price. With this and some horrid starved goats we lived tolerably for soldiers in hard times. The army retired into quarters—the headquarters to Badajos, our Division (which had added to it Sir Rufane Donkin's Brigade, the 45th, 87th, and 88th Regiments) to Campo Mayor [11 Sept.], where sickness and mortality commenced to an awful extent. On our reaching the frontier of Portugal, Castello de Vidi, wine was plentiful, and every man that evening had his skin full.

During the period we were at Campo Mayor [11 Sept.—12 Dec.], the Hon. Captain James Stewart and I got some excellent greyhounds. We were always out coursing or shooting, and were never sick a day ; our more sedentary comrades many of them distressingly so. The seven right-hand men of Leslie's Company died in the winter of this year.

winnowing and grinding it, were obliged, as a substitute, to rub out the ears between our hands and then pound them between stones to make it into dough, such as it was. From this latter wretched practice, we christened the place ' Dough Boy Hill,' a name by which it is well remembered by the men of our Division." Cp. p. 321, below.

While at Campo Mayor the convalescents of my Light Brigade were ordered to our old fortress, called Onguala, on the immediate frontier of Portugal, and opposite to Abuchucha, the frontier of Spain. They consisted of forty or fifty weakly men. I was first for Brigade duty, and I was sent in command, with a Lieut. Rentall of the 52nd Regiment and my brother Tom, who was sick. I knew this country well, for we had had some grand battues there, and shot red deer and wild boars. So soon, therefore, as I was installed in my command, lots of comrades used to come from Campo Mayor to breakfast with me and shoot all day. On one occasion Jack Molloy, Considine, and several fellows came, and while out we fell into the bivouac of a set of banditti and smugglers. We hallooed and bellowed as if an army were near us. The bandits jumped on their horses and left lots of corn-sacks, etc., in our hands; but on discovering our numbers, and that we fired no balls (for we had only some Rifle buttons pulled off my jacket), being well armed, they soon made us retreat. This, after my friends returned to Campo Mayor, so disconcerted me that I made inquiry about these same rascals, and ascertained there were a body of about twenty under a Catalan, the terror of the country. I immediately sent for my sergeant (a soldier in every sense of the word) to see how many of our convalescents he could pick out who could *march at all*. He soon returned. He himself and ten men, myself, Rentall, and my sick brother Tom (who *would* go) composed my army. I got a guide, and ascertained that there were several haunts of these bandits ; so off I started. We moved on a small chapel (many of which lone spots there are in all Roman Catholic countries), at which there was a large stable. On approaching we heard a shot fired, then a great and lawless shouting, which intimated to us our friends of the morning were near at hand. So Pat Nann and I crept on to peep about. We discovered the fellows were all inside a long stable, with a railed gate shut, and a regular sentry with his arms in his hand. They were all about and had lights, and one very dandy-looking fellow with a smart dagger was cutting tobacco to make a cigar. Pat and I returned to our party and made a disposition of attack, previously ascertaining if the stable had a back door, which it had not. I then fell in our men very silently, Mr. Rentall being much opposed to our attack, at which my brother Tom blew him up in no bad style of whispering abuse, and our men went for the gate. The sentry soon discovered us and let fly, but hit no one. The gate was fast and resisted two attempts to force it, but so amazed were the bandits, they [never] attempted to get away their horses, although their arms were regularly piled against the supports of the roof of the stable, and we took twelve banditti with their captain, a fine handsome fellow, horses, etc. His dagger I sent to my dear father. I sent my prisoners on the next day to Campo Mayor, galloping ahead myself, in an awful funk lest General Craufurd

should blow me up.   However, I got great credit
for my achievement in thus ridding the neighbourhood of a nest of robbers ; and the captain and five
of his men (being Spaniards) were sent to Badajos
and sentenced to the galleys for life, being recognized as old offenders.   The remainder received
a lesser punishment. My men got forty Spanish
dollars each prize money, the amount I sold the
horses for.   I bought for forty dollars the captain's
capital horse.   The men wanted me to keep him as
my share, but I would not.   Dr. Robb, our surgeon,
gave sixty Spanish dollars for a black mare.   Thus
ended the Battle of the Bandits.

CHAPTER IV.

CAMPAIGN OF 1810—THE 1ST GERMAN HUSSARS.

In the winter of this year [12 Dec. 1809] we marched towards the northern frontier of Portugal. We marched towards Almeida, and were cantoned in villages to its rear—Alameda, Villa de Lobos, Fequenas, not far from the Douro. Here too was good shooting and coursing; but I was not permitted to be idle. We moved into Spain [19 Mar. 1810], and at Barba del Puerco had a most brilliant night attack, in which Colonel Beckwith greatly distinguished himself.

At Villa de Ciervo a detachment of one sergeant and twelve Hussars (1st German) were given me by General Craufurd to go right in among the French army, which had moved on Ciudad Rodrigo and then retired. Many are the hairbreadth escapes my Hussars and I had, for we were very daring; we were never two nights in the same place. One night at Villa de Ciervo, where we were watching a ford over the Agueda, two of my vedettes (two Poles elegantly mounted) deserted to the enemy. The old sergeant, a noble soldier, came to me in great distress. "O mein Gott, upstand and jump up

your horse; *she* will surely be here *directly !*"   I was
half asleep, with my horse's reins in my hand, and
roared out, "Who the devil is *she ?*"   "The Fran-
zosen, mein Herr.   Two d——d schelms have
deserted." So we fell back to the rear of the village,
sitting on our horses the remainder of the night,
every moment expecting the weakness of our party
would cause an attempt to cut us off.   At daylight
we saw fifty French dragoons wending their way on
the opposite bank to the ford.   I immediately got
hold of the *padre* and *alcalde* (priest and magistrate),
and made them collect a hundred villagers and
make them shoulder the long sticks with which
they drive their bullock-carts and ploughs, which
of course at a distance would resemble bayonets.
These villagers I stationed in two parties behind
two hills, so that the "bayonets" alone could be
seen by the enemy.   Then with my sergeant and
ten Hussars (two having deserted) I proceeded to
meet the enemy, first riding backwards and forwards
behind a hill to deceive him as to my numbers.
The French sent over the river about half their
number.   I immediately galloped up to them in
the boldest manner, and skirmished advancing.
The enemy were deceived and rapidly retired, and
I saved the village from an unmerciful ransacking,
to the joy of all the poor people.

At this period General Craufurd had officers at
two or three of the most advanced vedettes where
there were beacons, who had orders to watch the
enemy with their telescopes, and, in case of any

movement, to report or fire the beacon. I was on this duty in rather a remote spot on the extreme left of our posts. The vedette was from the 1st Hussar picquet. These men would often observe a patrol or body of the enemy with the naked eye which was barely discernible through a telescope, so practised were they and watchful. Towards the evening my servant ought to have arrived with my dinner (for we officers of the look-out could take nothing with us but our horse and our telescope), but he must have missed his way, and as my appetite was sharpened by a day's look-out, I began to look back, contrary to the vedette's idea of due vigilance. He asks, " What for Mynheer so much look to de rear ? " I, sad at the fast, " Hussar, you are relieved every two hours. I have been here since daylight. I am confounded hungry, and am looking out for my servant and my dinner." " Poor yonge mans ! but 'tis notings." " Not to you," said I, " but much to me." " You shall see, sir. I shall come off my horse, you shall up clim, or de French shall come if he see not de vedette all right." Knowing the provident habits of these Germans, I suspected what he was about. Off he got ; up get I *en vedette*. With the greatest celerity, he unbuckled his valise from behind his saddle, and took out a piece of bacon (I had kept up a little fire from the sticks and bushes around me), from a cloth some ground coffee and sugar, from his haversack some biscuit, and spread on the ground a clean towel with knife, fork, and a little tin cup.   He had water in his canteen—his cooking-tin.   He made me a cup of coffee, sliced some bacon, broiled it in the embers, and in ten minutes coffee, bacon, biscuit were ready and looked as clean as if in a London tavern.   He then says, " Come off."   Up he mounts, saying, " Can eat.   All you sall vant is de schnaps."   I fell to, and never relished any meal half so much ; appetite was perfect, and the ingenious, quick and provident care of the Hussar added another to the many instances I had witnessed of this regiment to make them be regarded, as indeed they were, as exemplary soldiers for our emulation.

My servant soon after arrived.   The contents of his haversack I transferred to my kind friend the Hussar's, and half the bottle of wine, on which the Hussar remarked, " Ah, dat is good ; the schnaps make nice ; " and my servant put up his valise again for him.   I was highly amused to observe the momentary glances the Hussar cast on me and my meal, for no rat-catcher's dog at a sink-hole kept a sharper look-out to his front than did this vedette. In the whole course of my service I never was more amused, and nothing could be more disinterested than the Hussar's conduct, which I never forgot.

CHAPTER V.

CAMPAIGN OF 1810—BATTLE OF THE COA.

SOON after this the French invested Ciudad Rodrigo, and regularly commenced the siege. The
Light Division (into which fell the three regiments
43rd, 52nd, and two Battalions of Rifles, 1st and
3rd Portuguese Caçadores, the latter under Elder, a
most brilliant Rifle officer), 1st Hussars, 14th Light
Dragoons, 16th Light Dragoons occupied Gallegos,
Exejo, etc., our advanced post being at Marialva, on
the road to Ciudad Rodrigo. During the whole
siege our alerts were innumerable, and at Marialva we
had several very smart skirmishes, but so able were
Craufurd's dispositions, we never lost even a vedette.

The French were in the habit of patrolling
over the Agueda with cavalry and infantry, about
30 Dragoons and 200 foot. General Craufurd
determined to intercept one of these patrols [10
July], and [moved out with] the cavalry, 1st Hussars,
14th and 16th Light Dragoons, and Light Division.
It may now be asked, Was it necessary to take
out such a force to intercept so small a party?
Certainly. Because the enemy might have crossed
the Agueda to support the patrols. We were all

moved to where directed, the infantry were halted, some of the cavalry moved on. At grey daylight the patrols of the enemy appeared, their Dragoons some way in advance of the infantry. The patrol was very incautiously conducted (not like our 1st Hussars), and the Dragoons were taken in a moment. The infantry speedily retired to an eminence above the ford and formed square. Craufurd ordered them to be attacked by the cavalry, and several right good charges were made; but the French were steady, the dead horses in their front became a defence, and our cavalry never made the slightest impression. Craufurd never moved one of *us*. The charges of cavalry ceased for a few seconds— the fields around were high-standing corn. The gallant fellow in command gave the word, "Sauve qui peut." In a moment all dispersed, ran through the standing corn down to the banks of the river, and were saved without the loss of a man. The officer was promoted on his arrival in his camp.

Our loss was very considerable. Poor Colonel Talbot of the 14th (commanding) killed, and a lot of men. I and Stewart, Adjutant of the Rifle Brigade, asked leave to go ahead, and we saw it all. Indeed, it was in sight of the whole division. Had two Companies of ours only been moved to threaten the ford, the enemy would have laid down their arms. Such a piece of soldiering as that morning presented the annals of war cannot produce.*

* Cp. Cope, p. 55 : "Why Craufurd did not use his guns or let loose the Riflemen at the French infantry, seems inexplicable."

While we were at a village called Valde Mula, in the neighbourhood of Fort Concepcion, that most perfect little work was blown up [21 July]. It was the neatest fortification I ever saw (except the Moro in the Havana subsequently), and the masonry was beautifully executed.

After the fall of Ciudad Rodrigo, which made a brilliant defence, our advanced line fell back to the Dos Casas, and in front of Alameda we had a brilliant affair with the French, in which Krauchenberg 1st Hussars and McDonald Royal Artillery greatly distinguished themselves. The 3rd Caçadores were this day first under fire, and behaved *nobly*. After this our advanced posts were retired behind the Dos Casas to cover Almeida. While Massena prepared his army to invade Portugal and besiege Almeida, we were daily on the alert and had frequent skirmishes. General Craufurd, too, by a variety of *ruses* frequently made the whole French army turn out.

In the early morning of the 24th of July (I was on picquet with Leach and my Company that night) the enemy moved forward with 40,000 men. Our force, one Brigade of Horse Artillery, three Regiments of cavalry, five of infantry, were ordered by the Duke to remain as long as possible on the right bank of the Coa, where there was a bridge over the river on the road from Almeida into Portugal to Celerico and Pinhel, posting ourselves between the fortress and the bridge, so as to pass over so soon as the enemy advanced in force. In place of doing this, Craufurd took up a position to our right of Almeida, and but for Colonel Beckwith our whole force would have been sacrificed. Fortunately a heavy rain had fallen, which made the Coa impassable except by the bridge, which was in our possession, and the enemy concentrated his force in one rush for the bridge [24 July].

During the Peninsular War there never was a more severe contest. The 43rd lost 17 officers and 150 men, my Regiment 10 officers and 140 men. When we passed the bridge my section was the rear-guard of the whole, and in a rush to drive back the enemy (with whom we were frequently absolutely mixed), my brother Tom and I were both severely wounded, and a Major Macleod, a noble fellow, afterwards killed at Badajos, put me on his horse, or I should have been taken. The enemy made several attempts to cross, but old Alister Cameron, Captain in the Rifle Brigade, had posted his Company in a ruined house which commanded the bridge, and mainly contributed to prevent the passage of the enemy, who made some brilliant attempts. The bridge was literally piled with their dead and they made breastworks of the bodies. On this day, on going to the rear wounded, I first made the acquaintance of my dear friend Will Havelock,* afterwards my whipper-in, who was joining the 43rd fresh from England, with smart chako and jacket. I had a ball lodged in my ankle-joint, a most painful wound. We were sent to Pinhel,

---

* Elder brother of Sir Henry Havelock. See p. 297.

where the 3rd Division was seven leagues from
the action, the nearest *support* (?). Sir Thomas
Picton treated us wounded *en princes*.

The wounded were ordered to the rear, so as
to embark on the Mondego at Pinhel. In collecting transport for the wounded, a sedan chair
between two mules was brought, the property of
some gentleman in the neighbourhood, and, fortunately for me, I was the only person who could ride
in it, and by laying my leg on the one seat and
sitting on the other, I rode comparatively easy to
the poor fellows in the wretched bullock-cars, who
suffered excruciating agony, poor brother Tom
(who was very severely wounded above the
knee) among the rest. This little story will
show what wild fellows we were in those days.
George Simmons' (1st Rifles) bullocks at one
stage had run away. As I was the spokesman,
the surgeon in charge came to me in great distress. I sent for the village magistrate, and actually
fixed a rope in my room to hang him if he did
not get a pair of bullocks (if the Duke of W. had
known he would have hung *me*). However, the
bullocks were got, and off we started. The bullocks
were not broken, and they ran away with poor
George and nearly jolted him to death, for he was
awfully wounded through the thick of the thigh.
However, we all got down to Pinhel [31 July], and
thence descended the Mondego by boats, landing
every night. At one house a landlord was most
insolent to us, and Lieut. Pratt of the Rifles, shot

through the neck, got very angry. The carotid
artery must have been wounded, for it burst out in
a torrent of blood, and he was dead in a few
seconds, to our horror, for he was a most excellent
fellow. On the same bed with me was a Captain
Hull of the 43rd Regiment with a similar wound.
I never saw any man in such a funk.

On our reaching the mouth of the Mondego, we
were put on board a transport. In the ship with
me was a stout little officer, 14th Light Dragoons,
severely wounded, whose thigh afterwards dis-
gorged a French 6-lb. shot. On arrival in Lisbon
[7 Aug.] we were billeted in Buenos Ayres, poor Tom
and I in awful agony in our miserable empty house.
However, we got books, and I, although suffering,
got on well enough. But poor Tom's leg was in
such an awful state he was sent home. George
Simmons's wound healed.* My ball was lodged on
my ankle-joint, having partially divided the *tendo
Achillis*. However, we heard of the army having
retired into the celebrated lines of Torres Vedras,
and nothing would serve us but *join the Regiment*.
So our medical heroes very unwillingly sent us off to

* George Simmons writes in his diary for the 17th of September,
1810 : "I removed to Pedroso for the convenience of sea-bathing, my
thigh being much better, which enabled me, with crutches, to move
about. Lieutenant Harry Smith was also with me. I found great
benefit from the sea-bathing." Sir Harry Smith, writing to Major
George Simmons on the 16th of June, 1846 (soon after the battle of
Aliwal, when he had driven the Sikhs into the Sutlej), refers to
their bathing together at this time, though he says at Belem, not at
Pedroso (both places are close to Lisbon) : " Dear George,—We little
thought at Bellam [Belem], when hopping about there, I should become
a master of that art we were both 'girning' under, or a swimming
master for pupils in the Sutledge ! "

Belem, the convalescent department under Colonel
Tucker, 29th Regiment, a sharp fellow enough.
When I, George Simmons, and Charlie Eeles, 3rd
Battalion, just arrived sick from Cadiz, waited on
him to express our desire to join, he said, "Oh,
certainly ; but you must be posted to do duty with
convalescents going up the country." I was lame
and could not walk. George Simmons cantered on
crutches, and Charlie Eeles was very sick. However, *go* or *no go*, and so we were posted to 600
villains of every Regiment in the army under a long
Major Ironmonger of the 88th (afterwards of
Almeida celebrity, when the garrison escaped). We
marched in a day [7 Oct.]. On the first day's march
he pretended to faint. George Simmons, educated a
surgeon, *literally* threw a bucket of water over him.*
He recovered the faint, but not the desire to return ;
and the devil would have it, the command devolved
on me, a subaltern, for whom the soldiers of other
corps have no great respect, and such a task I never
had as to keep these six hundred rascals together.
However, I had a capital English horse, good at

---

* Simmons states in his diary that the Commandant was Major
Murphy (not Ironmonger), and writes that at the end of the second
day's march "another one hundred *heroes* had disappeared, which
made our Commandant raving mad. Smith called upon me to assist
him in a medical capacity. I had a bucket of spring water thrown
upon him, which did him good ; he had several fits, but this put an
end to them" (p. 111). According to the Army Lists, Major
Barnaby Murphy, 88th Regiment, was killed at Salamanca, July,
1812. Lieut.-Colonel W. Iremonger, 2nd Foot, retired 2 May,
1811 (? 12 May). There is no Ironmonger in the Army List. The
garrison of Almeida escaped on 11 May, 1811. In his despatch of
15 May, 1811, Wellington censures a Lieutenant-Colonel (name not
given), but it is for "imprudence," not cowardice.

riding over an insubordinate fellow, and a voice like thunder. The first bivouac I came to was the Guards (these men were very orderly). The commanding officer had a cottage. I reported myself. It was raining like the devil. He put his head out of the window, and I said, "Sir, I have 150 men of your Regiment convalescent from Belem." "Oh, send for the Sergeant-major," he very quietly said;— no "walk in out of the rain." So I roared out, "We *Light Division men* don't do duty with Sergeant-majors, nor are we told to wait. There are your men, every one—the only well-conducted men in 600 under my charge—and these are their accounts!" throwing down a bundle of papers, and off I galloped, to the Household man's astonishment. That day I delivered over, or sent by officers under me, all the vagabonds I had left. Some of my own men and I reached our corps that night at Arruda, when old Sydney Beckwith, dear Colonel, said, "You are a mad fool of a boy, coming here with a ball in your leg. Can you dance?" "No," says I; "I can hardly walk but with my toe turned out." "Can you be my A.D.C.?" "Yes; I can ride and eat," I said, at which he laughed, and was kind as a brother; as was my dear friend Stewart, or Rutu, as we called him, his Brigade Major, the actual Adjutant of the Regiment.

That very night General Craufurd sent for me, and said, "You have come from Sobral, have you not, to-day, and know the road?" I said, "Yesterday." "Well, get your horse and take this letter to the Duke for me when it is ready." I did not like the job, but said nothing about balls or *pains*, which were bad enough. He kept me waiting about an hour, and then said, "You need wait no longer; the letter won't be ready for some time, and my orderly dragoon shall take it. Is the road difficult to find?" I said, "No; if he keeps the chaussée, he can't miss it." The poor dragoon fell in with the French patrol, and was taken prisoner. When the poor fellow's fate was known, how Colonel Beckwith did laugh at my escape!

At Arruda we marched every day at daylight into position in the hills behind us, and by the ability of Craufurd they were made impregnable. The whole Division was at work. As Colonel Beckwith and I were standing in the camp one day, it came on to rain, and we saw a Rifleman rolling down a wine-cask, apparently empty, from a house near. He deliberately knocked in one of the heads; then— for it was on the side of a rapidly shelving hill— propped it up with stones, and crept in out of the rain. Colonel Beckwith says, "Oh, look at the lazy fellow; he has not half supported it. When he falls asleep, if he turns round, down it will come." Our curiosity was excited, and our time anything but occupied, so we watched our friend, when in about twenty minutes the cask with the man inside came rolling down the hill. He must have rolled over twenty times at least before the rapidity disengaged him from his round-house, and even afterwards, such was the impetus, he rolled over several times.

To refrain from laughing excessively was impossible, though we really thought the noble fellow must be hurt, when up he jumped, looked round, and said "I never had any affection for an empty wine-cask, and may the devil take me if ever I go near another —to be whirled round like a water-mill in this manner!" The fellow was in a violent John Bull passion, while we were nearly killed with laughing.

When Massena retired, an order came to the Light Division to move on De Litte, and to Lord Hill to do the same on our right at [Vallada ?]. This dispatch I was doomed to carry. It was one of the utmost importance, and required a gallop. By Jove, I had ten miles to go just before dark, and when I got to Colborne's position, who had a Brigade under Lord Hill, a mouse could not get through his works. (Colborne was afterwards my Brigadier in the Light Division, and is now Lord Seaton.) Such a job I never had. I could not go in front of the works—the French had not retired; so some works I leaped into, and led my noble English horse into others. At last I got to Lord Hill, and he marched immediately, night as it was. How I got back to my Division through the night I hardly know, but horse and rider were both done. The spectacle of hundreds of miserable wretches of French soldiers on the road in a state of *starvation* is not to be described.

We moved *viâ* Caccas to Vallé on the [Rio Mayor], where our Division were opposite Santarem. The next day [20 Nov.] the Duke came up and

ordered our Division to attack Santarem, which
was bristling on our right with abattis, three or four
lines. We felt the difficulty of carrying such heights,
but towards the afternoon we moved on. On the
Duke's staff there was a difference of opinion as to
the number of the enemy, whether one *corps d'armée*
or two. The Duke, who knew perfectly well
there were two, and our move was only a recon-
naissance, turned to Colonel Beckwith. " Beckwith,
my Staff are disputing whether at Santarem there is
one *corps d'armée* or two ? " " I'll be d——d if I
know, my Lord, but you may depend on it, a great
number were required to make those abattis *in one
night*." Lord Wellington laughed, and said, " You
are right, Beckwith ; there are two *corps d'armée*." *
The enemy soon showed themselves. The Duke, as
was his wont, satisfied himself *by ocular demonstration*, and the Division returned to its bivouac.
Whilst here, Colonel Beckwith was seized with a
violent attack of ague.

Our outposts were perfectly quiet, although
sentries, French and English, were at each end of
the bridge over the Rio Mayor, and vedettes along
each bank. There was most excellent coursing on
the plains of Vallé, and James Stewart and I were
frequently out. Here I gave him my celebrated
Spanish greyhound, Moro, the best the world ever
produced, with a pedigree like that of an Arab
horse, bred at Zamora by the Conde de Monteron ;
but the noble dog's story is too long to tell here.

* Cp. Kincaid, *Random Shots*, pp. 101, 102.

In one year Stewart gave me him back again to run a match against the Duke of Wellington's dog. But the siege of Ciudad Rodrigo prevented our sports of that description. Colonel Beckwith going to Lisbon, and I being his A.D.C., it was voted a capital opportunity for me to go to have the ball cut out from under the tendon Achillis, in the very joint. I was very lame, and the pain often excruciating, so off I cut.

Soon after we reached Lisbon, I was ordered to Buenos Ayres to be near the surgeons. A board was held consisting of the celebrated Staff Surgeon Morell, who had attended me before, Higgins, and Brownrigg. They examined my leg. I was all for the operation. Morell and Higgins recommended me to remain with a stiff leg of my own as better than a wooden one, for the wounds in Lisbon of late had sloughed so, they were dubious of the result. Brownrigg said, "If it were my leg, out should come the ball." On which I roared out, "Hurrah, Brownrigg, you are the doctor for me." So Morell says, "Very well, if you are desirous, we will do it *directly*." My pluck was somewhat cooled, but I cocked up my leg, and said, "There it is; slash away." It was five minutes, most painful indeed, before it was extracted. The ball was jagged, and the tendonous fibres had so grown into it, it was half dissected and half torn out, with most excruciating torture for a moment, the forceps breaking which had hold of the ball. George Simmons was present, whose wound had broken out and obliged him to go to Lisbon.* The surgeon wanted some linen during the operation, so I said, "George, tear a shirt," which my servant gave him. He turned it about, said, "No, it is a pity; it is a good shirt;" at which I did not —— him a few, for my leg was aching and smoking from a wound four or five inches long. Thank God Almighty and a light heart, no sloughing occurred, and before the wound was healed I was with the regiment. Colonel Beckwith's ague was cured, and he had joined his Brigade before I could move, so when I returned to Vallé he was delighted to see his A.D.C.

* He was at Lisbon from 3 Dec. to 4 Feb., when he returned to his Regiment with Colonel Beckwith (*A British Rifleman*, pp. 124, 135).

CHAPTER VI.

CAMPAIGN OF 1811.

I FOUND the army in hourly expectation to move, and the Captain of my Company—Leach—was gone sick to the rear, so I said to my Colonel, " I must be no longer A.D.C., sir. However grateful I am, my Company wants me." "Ah, now you can walk a little, you leave me! Go and be d——d to you; but I love you for the desire." Off I started, and the very next day we marched [6 Mar. 1811], Massena retreating out of Portugal, and many is the skirmish we had. My leg was so painful, the wound open, and I was so lame. When others could lie down I was on horseback, on a dear little Spanish horse given me by James Stewart, afterwards an animal of still greater renown.

At Pombala I had with my Company a very heavy skirmish [11 Mar.]. At Redinha my Company was in the advance [12 Mar.], supported by Captain O'Hare's. A wood on our front and right was *full* of Frenchmen. The Light Companies of the 3rd Division came up. I asked, "Are you going to attack that wood?" A Captain of the 88th Light Company, whom I knew, quite laughed at my question. I said very quietly, "You will be beat back, and when you are, I will move on the edge of the wood and help you." How he laughed! My prediction was very soon verified: he was wounded, and picked up by my Company, which I moved on the right flank of the French and stopped them immediately. I sent to my support, O'Hare, to move up to me. The obstinate old Turk would not, and so I was obliged to come back, and had most unnecessarily five or six men wounded.

The Plain of Redinha is a fine field for military display, and our lines formed to attack Ney's rearguard were magnificent. The enemy had many guns in the field, with prolonged lines, an excellent mode for retreat on such ground, and no rearguard was ever drawn off in more masterly style, while I thought our attack in lines was heavy, slow, and not half so destructive as a rush of many contiguous columns would have been. The enemy had to retire over a bridge through the village of Redinha, and we Riflemen sorely pressed them on their left. A line of French infantry, concealed behind an alataza (or tower) on a hill good for the purpose, were lying down as my Company and the one commanded by that wonderful Rifleman, Willie Johnstone, got within twenty yards of them. To our astonishment, up jumped the line, fired a volley (they did not hit a man), and went about. At them we all went like devils, a regular foot race, except for me and my little horse

Tiny, from which I could not dismount. In the pursuit he carried me down a rock twelve feet high, and Johnstone and I got to the bridge and cut off half a Battalion of French. So many Legions of Honour I scarcely ever saw in a group, but the eagle was off! We *never* told what we had done, though we enjoyed the fun, but it is an anecdote worthy of record in Napier's *History*.

We were engaged with the enemy every day. The next turn up was at Condesia [Condeixa]; the next at Casal Nova [14 Mar.], where we had as heavy a skirmishing fight as ever occurred. We Light Division gentlemen had our full complement of fighting, for the French were obliged to hold a village to give their column time to retire, and if the Duke's orders had been obeyed, our Division ought not to have attacked until the 3rd and 4th Divisions were well up on the Frenchmen's left. I lost several men that day, as did all our Companies, and particularly the 52nd. Poor Major Jack Stewart,* a dear little fellow, a friend of mine, was shot through the lungs and died in three days, (Beckwith's Brigade-Major, Lieut. James Stewart, was in three days [28 Mar., near Freixadas] killed off the very same little English horse, called Tom); Strode, a Lieutenant, received his death-wound while talking to me, etc. That night I was on picquet. The enemy were retiring all night, but their sentries and ours were in sight. At daylight a thick fog came

---

* Cope says Major John Stewart was killed in this fight near Casal Nova, and Lieut. Strode mortally wounded (14 March).

on. Beckwith's Brigade, with him at its head, moved up to where I was posted. He said, "Come, Harry, get your Company together, and fall in at the head of the column." At this moment two of the 16th Dragoons rode back, and Beckwith said, "Where do you come from?" "We have patrolled a league and a half in the front, and seen naught." "A league and a half, my friend," says old Sydney, "in a thick fog is a d——d long way. Why, Harry, you said the vedettes were close to you." "So they are," I said, "and you will be fired at the moment you advance." We had not gone fifty yards when "Pop! pop!" Oh, how old Sydney laughed! "A league and a half!" But the fog was so thick we could not move, and the enemy, hearing our column on their rear, being clear, moved off.

In a few days, as we had got well up to the French rear-guard and were about to attack, a General Order was received, to my astonishment, appointing me Brigade Major * to the 2nd Light Brigade, not dear old Sydney's. *He* expected it, since he and Colonel Pakenham (dear Sir Edward!) were trying to do something for me on account of my lame leg. Beckwith says, "Now give your Company over to Layton, and set off immediately

* The duties of a Major of Brigade are given in a letter of Sir W. Gomm, Sept. 19, 1808: "The pay and rank are the same as those of Aide-de-camp. The officer has the rank of Major during the time he holds the employment, and he is not considered as generally belonging to the General's family so much as the Aide-de-camp. The situation is more independent" (Carr-Gomm's *Life of Sir W. Gomm*, 1881, p. 106).

to Colonel Drummond," who commanded the
Brigade. Hardly had I reached it, when such a
cannonade commenced, knocking the 52nd about in
a way I never saw before and hardly since. We
were soon all engaged, and drove the French, with
very hard fighting, into and over the river, with a
severe loss in killed, prisoners, and drowned. A
very heavy fight it was, ending just before dark.
I said to my Brigadier, " Have you any orders for
the picquets, sir ? " He was an old Guardsman, the
kindest though oddest fellow possible. " Pray, Mr.
Smith, are you my Brigade Major ? " " I believe so,
sir." " Then let me tell you, it is your duty to post
the picquets, and mine to have a d—d good dinner
for you every day." We soon understood each
other. He cooked the dinner often himself, and I
commanded the Brigade.

Our next great fight was a bitter one, Sabugal
[3 April]. I shall never forget the German 1st
Hussars, my old friends, moving on that day ; their
singing was melodious. Sir W. Erskine commanded
the cavalry and Light Division, a near-sighted old
ass, and we got *meléed* with Reynier's *corps d'armée*
strongly posted on heights above Sabugal, and
attacked when the Duke intended we should have
moved round their left to Quadraseyes, as the 5th,
4th, and 3rd Divisions were to attack their front in
the centre of their position. However, we began,
and never was more gallantry mutually displayed
by friend and foe than on this occasion, particularly
by dear old Beckwith and his 1st Brigade. Some

guns were taken and retaken several times. A
French officer on a grey horse was most gallant.
Old Beckwith, in a voice like thunder, roared out
to the Riflemen, " Shoot that fellow, will you ? "
In a moment he and his horse were knocked over,
and Sydney exclaimed, " Alas! you were a *noble
fellow.*"

My Brigadier, as I soon discovered, left the
command to me, so I led away, and we came in for
a pretty good share in preventing Reynier's turning
the left of Beckwith's Brigade. Fortunately, the
5th Division got into action just in time, for the
French at the moment were squeezing us awfully.
The Light Division, under the shout of old Beckwith, rushed on with an impetuosity nothing could
resist, for, so checked had we been, our bloods were
really up, and we paid off the enemy most awfully.
Such a scene of slaughter as there was on one hill
would appal a modern soldier. The night came on
most awfully wet, and the 5th and Light Division
were sent back to Sabugal for shelter. Most dilapi-
dated the place was, but the roofs were on, and
Sir W. Gomm, A.Q.M.G. of the 5th, and I divided
the town between us, our poor wounded lying out
in the rain and cold all night. The next morning
was fine, and as the sun rose we marched over the
field of battle. Our soldiers' blood was then cool,
and it was beautiful to hear the remarks of sympathy
for the distress of the numerous dying and wounded
all around us. Oh, you kings and usurpers should
view these scenes and moderate ambition !

This evening [4 April] we had a long march into Quadraseyes, but did not see a vestige of the enemy all day, nor of our commissariat either. We were literally starving. That old rogue Picton had seized the supplies of the Light Division for his 3rd. If he be now in the Purgatory that we condemned him to, he is to be pitied.

We closely pursued the French over the frontier, but never had a real slap at them. Almeida, which was garrisoned by their troops, was invested by the 5th Division, while the Light Division moved into its old lines, Gallegos, Marialva, Carpio, and Espeja. From the French garrison of Ciudad Rodrigo the enemy frequently came out. The Duke had gone into the Alemtejo, and Sir Brent Spencer commanded—a regular old woman, who allowed the French to commit all sorts of extravagances under our noses, when a rapid move on their rear from Espeja would have punished them. Sir W. Erskine commanded the advance Cavalry and Light Division.

I was at breakfast one morning with Sir William Erskine, who, early in the morning, with his staff had taken out a small party to reconnoitre Ciudad Rodrigo. The enemy immediately sent over a detachment of cavalry to check the advance, and a great argument occurred between Sir William and his A.A.G., Macdonald, whether the enemy crossed one or two squadrons. During the discussion in came Sir William's orderly, a clever old dragoon of the 1st German Hussars. "Ah!" says Sir William, "here is my old orderly; he can tell

us.   Hussar, how many squadrons of the enemy
crossed the Agueda this morning?"   With a body
as stiff and erect as a statue, and a salute with
an arm braced as if in the act of cutting down his
enemy, "Just forty-nine mans, no more; I count
him."   The laugh was against both disputants.

Now occurred the dreadful disaster of the escape
of the French garrison of Almeida.   I shall never
forget the mortification of our soldiers or the admiration of our officers of the brilliancy of such an
attempt, the odds being a hundred to one against
success.   My long friend Ironmonger, then of the
Queen's, into whose face George Simmons threw
the bucket of water when marching, as before
described, from Belem,* was grievously to blame.

Massena's army were rapidly recovering.   They
had received reinforcements, and were preparing to
throw into Ciudad Rodrigo a large convoy of provisions.   For this, it was necessary for them to put
us back, and the present moment seemed a favourable one, as it was the intention ultimately to
withdraw the French army to Salamanca and the
neighbouring large towns, so that no demand might
be made on the ample supplies required for Ciudad
Rodrigo.   At this moment Soult was making a
formidable demonstration in the Alemtejo and Estremadura, our attempt on Badajoz had failed, and a
large portion of our army had moved towards the
south; it was therefore a fair opening for Massena
to drive us over the Coa.

* See p. 34.

However, the dear Duke of Wellington took a braver view of the situation, and concentrated his army behind Fuentes D'Oñoro, and there fought that celebrated battle which lasted a day and a half [5 May]. General Craufurd joined us here on the day of the general action. The soldiers received him with every demonstration of joy. The officers at that time execrated him. I did not; he had appointed me his A.D.C., though I would not go to him, and he was always most kind and hospitable to me.

On the morning of this day old Sydney again distinguished himself, for the enemy from Poza Velha * turned our right flank and licked our cavalry (14th Light Dragoons and Royals) awfully, bringing 4000 fresh fellows against them. There never was a more heavy fight than for several hours in the village of Fuentes. Here I saw the 79th Regiment, in an attack on the head of a French column coming up the road, bayonet eight or nine French officers and upwards of 100 men, the only real bayonet conflict I ever witnessed. After the battle of Fuentes d'Oñoro, the French retired unmolested, for we were glad to get rid of them. As they had such a formidable body of cavalry, on that open country we literally could not molest them.

At this time almost all our army moved into the Alemtejo *via* Arronchas, where, on Sir John Moore's advance to Salamanca, I had a nice quarter which I occupied four different times during the war. The

---

* Simmons (p. 170) has "Paya Velha."

poor family were always delighted to see me. On our advance into the Alemtejo we heard of the bloody battle of Albuera [16 May], and many of us rode on to see the field, which was well demonstrated by the lines of dead bodies, a most sanguinary conflict, and beautifully and truly described by Napier.

I must here record a most ridiculous night alarm the Light Division had, although leagues from any enemy, on their march into the Alemtejo. A drove of bullocks galloped over our men asleep in the bivouac, and for some time the officers could hardly persuade our best soldiers they were not French cavalry. My Brigadier, Drummond, was sleeping under a tree on his little portable iron bedstead. The light of a fire showed him, to my amusement, in his shirt (not a very long one), endeavouring to climb into the tree. I fell in his guard, and manfully charged *nothing* up a road leading to our camp, while General Craufurd lay on his back laughing to hysterics, poor fellow. Drummond soon after died at Guinaldo, in my arms, of a putrid sore throat, and Craufurd was killed in the storm of Ciudad Rodrigo.

During all this summer our army was assembled watching Soult, who neither attacked us nor we him. Never did we spend a more inactive summer. The enemy from Ciudad Rodrigo moved on Castillo Branco, and threatened thereby our left flank and line of communication over the Tagus. When Soult could no longer feed his assembled army, he retired,

and our Light Division were rapidly moved on
Castillo Branco, the remainder of the army of the
north following.

Our army this autumn was cantoned, as near as it
could be fed, on the frontiers to watch Ciudad Rodrigo, which the Duke contemplated besieging. After
the death of General Drummond, Major-General
Vandeleur was appointed to my Brigade, a fine,
gentleman-like old Irish hero. We were quartered
at Martiago, and our Division, some at El Bodon,
others at Zamora, Guinaldo, etc. It was a very hot
autumn, but towards the end of the year, when the
rains commenced, there was capital coursing.

General Craufurd this year, in one of his mad
freaks, reported that the Light Division was in
want of clothing, etc., and it must go to the
rear. The Duke ordered us to march one cold
night over the Agueda to Larade, not far from
Guinaldo, for his inspection. A great scene
occurred. Craufurd had not arrived before the
Duke rode down the line, and the Duke laughed
and said, "Craufurd, you are late." "No, my
Lord; you are before your time. *My watch* is to
be depended on." (I was riding a brown mare
which I gave £120 for to Charlie Rowan, who
had been thrown by her, after buying her from
General Craufurd because *he* could not ride her. The
mare charged the Duke, I on her back. "Hallo,
Smith," says the Duke, "your horse masters you.")
The Duke, to *our* delight, says to General Craufurd,
"I never saw the Light Division look better or

more ready for service. March back to your quarters; I shall soon require you in the field." About this time Marmont moved up to Ciudad Rodrigo with an enormous convoy of provisions, and he compelled the Duke to assemble, and the brilliant affair of cavalry and squares of infantry behind El Bodon took place [24 Sept.].

About this time we had some heavy and laborious manœuvring, night marches, etc. During these movements we marched a dark night's march from Guinaldo, and, as the road was wet and far from good, we had several checks in the column, when I heard a conversation between a 16th Light Dragoon and one of the German 1st Hussars, neither of whom had abstained from the ingredient which formed the subject. 16th Dragoon: "I say, Hussar, I likes it strong and hot and sweet, and plenty of ——. How do you like it?" Hussar: "I likes him raw."

Marmont, having accomplished his object, fell back, and we returned to our old cantonments. The Duke of Wellington's dispatch dated "Quadrasies, Sept. 29," so fully details all these operations and shows the beauty of the manœuvres so distinctly, I may confine myself to what occurred the evening General Pakenham's brigade had such a formidable brush at Aldea de Ponte.

The 4th Division was to return at dusk, as was the Light. I was lying in bivouac, talking to General Craufurd and John Bell, when a dragoon rode up with a note from General Cole, requesting

Craufurd to send an officer as a guide to lead his division to the heights of Rendo at dusk. I said, "Oh, John Bell will go, of course." "No," says John; "Harry Smith knows the road best." So I was ordered to go. Before I reached Cole it was dark. I found his Division moving : they were all right. I reported myself to him—the first time I had ever spoken to him. Colonel Brooke, brother of the "Shannon" Brooke, his Q.M.G., was with him. "Oh," says Cole, "sent by Craufurd, are you? Do you know the road?" We Light Division gentlemen were proper saucy fellows. I said, "I suppose I should not have been sent if I had not." "Ugh," says Cole, as hot as pepper. Here I may remark upon the difficulty there is at night to know roads, even for one well acquainted with them. Fires lighting, fires going out, the covering of the country with troops—such things change the face of nature, and a little anxiety adds to the difficulty. Cole, a most anxious man, kept saying, "Are you sure you know the road, sir?" etc., etc., etc. At last I said, "General Cole, if you will let me alone, I will conduct your Division; if you thus attract my attention, I cannot." It was an anxious moment, I admit. I was just at a spot where I might miss the road, a great road which I knew was near. I galloped ahead to look for it, and oh, how General Cole did blow me up! I found my road, though, and so soon as the head of the column had fairly reached it, I said, "Good night, General," and in a moment was in full speed,

while he was hallooing to me to come back. I had
some difficulty in finding my own Division, which
was moving parallel with the force. When I told
Craufurd of my first acquaintance with that hot
Irishman Cole, how he laughed! Poor dear Sir
Lowry! I was afterwards A.Q.M.G. to him after
the battle of Waterloo, and served under him as
Commandant of Cape Castle and Senior Member
of Council when he was Governor, and many is the
laugh we have had at our first acquaintance.

On one of our marches from the Alemtejo to
the north, in a house where General Drummond
and I were quartered at Idanha a Nova, a very
facetious Portuguese gentleman showed us a sort
of a return of the British, so incorrect that General
Drummond laughed at it; but Charlie Rowan, our
A.A.G. (now the great policeman in London *), who
was dining with General Drummond, told this
anecdote at the Duke's table at Guinaldo, and I
was sent back about 150 miles to fetch my friend.
I could speak Portuguese as well as English. I
therefore persuaded our hero to accompany me to
the Duke without telling why, but a more un-
pleasant ride than this, in charge of my friend and
all alone, without groom, etc., I never had, and many
was the blessing I bestowed on Charlie Rowan's
tongue. I delivered my friend to the Adjutant-
General at Guinaldo, and had twenty-four miles to
join my General at Robledillo.

* Colonel Rowan (from 1848 Sir Charles Rowan, K.C.B.) was
Chief Commissioner of the Metropolitan Police Force from its institution in 1829 till 1850. He died in 1852.

CHAPTER VII.

CAMPAIGN OF 1812 : STORMING OF CIUDAD RODRIGO.

As the winter approached we had private theatricals.
The Duke appointed so many days for horse races,
greyhound matches, etc., and the very day they
were to come off, which was well known to the
French army, we invested Ciudad Rodrigo, namely,
on the 8th of January, 1812, and that very night
carried by storm the outworks called Fort San
Francisco, up to which spot it took the French
several days to approach. We broke ground, and
thus the siege commenced.

When the detachments of the Light Division
Brigades were parading, my Brigade was to furnish
400 men. I understood four Companies, and when
Colonel Colborne (now Lord Seaton) was counting
them, he said, "There are not the complement of
men." I said, "I am sorry if I have mistaken."
"Oh, never mind; run and bring another Company." I mention this to show what a cool, noble
fellow he is. Many an officer would have stormed
like fury. He only thought of storming Fort

San Francisco, which he carried in a glorious
manner.*

The siege was carried on by four Divisions—
1st, 3rd, 4th, and Light, cantoned as near Ciudad
Rodrigo as possible. One Division was on duty at
a time, and each had to ford the Agueda the day it
was for duty. The Light was at El Bodon. We
had a distance of nine miles to march every fourth
day, and back on the fifth, so that we had only three
days' halt. The frost was excessive, and there was
some little snow, but fortunately the weather was
fine above head.

The Light Division stormed the little breach
on the evening of the 19th of January (nine
o'clock). I was supping with my dear friend
Captain Uniacke, and brother Tom, his only subaltern not wounded. When I parted from Uniacke
—he was a noble, light-hearted fellow—he says,
"Harry, you will be a Captain before morning."
Little, poor fellow, did he think he was to make the
vacancy. I was senior subaltern of the 95th, and
I went to General Craufurd and volunteered the
forlorn hope that was given to Gurwood. Craufurd
said, "Why, you cannot go; you, a Major of

* Costello (p. 140) tells how, after the taking of Fort San Francisco,
many of the French wounded prisoners were stripped naked by the
Portuguese Caçadores. One of them, a sergeant, on being marched
in, and seeing his officer in the same plight with himself, "ran to
embrace him, and, leaning his head on his shoulder, burst into tears
over their mutual misery. Captain Smith, the General's aide-de-
camp, being present, generously pulled forth his pocket-handkerchief
and wrapped it round the sergeant's totally naked person, till further
covering could be obtained."

Brigade, a senior Lieutenant, you are sure to get a Company. No, I must give it to a younger officer." This was to me a laborious night. Just as my Brigade had to march, I discovered the Engineer officer had not brought up the ladders, fascines, and bundles of hay, and old George Simmons was sent for them.

In ascending the breach, I got on a ravelin at the head of the 43rd and 52nd, moving in column together. Colborne pulled me down again, and up the right breach we ascended. I saw the great breach, stormed by the 3rd Division, was ably defended, and a line behind a work which, as soon as we rushed along the ramparts, we could enfilade. I seized a Company of the 43rd and rushed on the flank, and opened a fire which destroyed every man behind the works. My conduct caused great annoyance to the Captain, Duffy, with whom I had some very high words; but the Company obeyed me, and then ran on with poor Uniacke's Company to meet the 3rd Division, or rather clear the ramparts to aid them, when the horrid explosion took place which killed General Mackinnon of the 3rd Division on the spot and many soldiers, awfully scorching others. I and Uniacke were much scorched, but some splinters of an ammunition chest lacerated him and caused his death three days after the storm. Tom, my brother, was not hurt.

I shall never forget the concussion when it struck me, throwing me back many feet into a lot of charged fuses of shells, which in the confusion

I took for shells. But a gallant fellow, a Sergeant MacCurrie, 52nd Regiment, soon put me right, and prevented me leaping into the ditch. My cocked hat was blown away, my clothes all singed ; however the sergeant, a noble fellow, lent me a catskin forage-cap, and on we rushed to meet the 3rd Division, which we soon did. It was headed by a great, big thundering Grenadier of the 88th, a Lieutenant Stewart, and one of his men seized me by the throat as if I were a kitten, crying out, " You French ——." Luckily, he left me room in the windpipe to d—— his eyes, or the bayonet would have been through me in a moment.

Gurwood got great credit here unfairly. Willie Johnstone * and poor Uniacke were the two first on the ramparts, Gurwood having been knocked down in the breach and momentarily stunned, which enabled them to get before him. However, Gurwood's a sharp fellow, and he cut off in search of the Governor, and brought his sword to the Duke, and Lord Fitzroy Somerset buckled it on him in the breach. Gurwood made the *most* of it.

We had many officers of rank wounded. George Napier, of the 52nd, lost an arm ; the General of Brigade, Vandeleur, was wounded severely in the shoulder ; and Colonel Colborne, of the 52nd, received an awful wound, but he never quitted his Regiment until the city was perfectly

* There is an interesting account of this heroic soldier in the *United Service Journal* for 1837, Part I. p. 354, by J. K. (John Kincaid), written after Johnstone's death at the Cape.

ours, and his Regiment all collected. A musket-
ball had struck him under the epaulette of his
right shoulder, and broken the head of the bone
right off in the socket.   To this the attention of the
surgeons was of course directed.   Some months
after Colborne complained of a pain four inches
below where the ball entered, and suppuration took
place, and by surgical treatment the bone was
gradually exposed.   The ball, after breaking the
arm above, had descended and broken the arm four
inches below, and was firmly embedded in the bone.
The pain he suffered in the extraction of the ball
was more even than his iron heart could bear.   He
used to lay his watch on the table and allow the
surgeons five minutes' exertions at a time, and
they were three or four days before they wrenched
the ball from its ossified bed.   In three weeks from
that day Colborne was in the Pyrenees, and in command of his Regiment.   Of course the shoulder
joint was anchylosed, but he had free use of the
arm below the elbow.

After this siege we had a few weeks' holiday,
with the exception of shooting some rascals who
had deserted to the enemy.   Eleven knelt on one
grave at Ituero.   It is an awful ceremony, a
military execution.   I was Major of Brigade of
the day.   The Provost-Marshal had not told the
firing off, so that a certain number of men should
shoot one culprit, and so on, but at his signal the
whole party fired a volley.   Some prisoners were
fortunate enough to be *killed*, others were only

wounded, some untouched. I galloped up. An unfortunate Rifleman called to me by name—he was awfully wounded—" Oh, Mr. Smith, put me out of my misery," and I literally ordered the firing-party, when reloaded, to run up and shoot the poor wretches. It was an awful scene.

> " Blood he had viewed, but then
> It flowed in combat . . ."

CHAPTER VIII.

CAMPAIGN OF 1812 : THE STORMING OF BADAJOS—
HARRY SMITH'S MARRIAGE.

AT this period of the year (February, March) the coursing in this part of Spain is capital, and by help of my celebrated dog Moro and two other excellent ones, I supplied the officers' mess of every Company with hares for soup. We had a short repose, for the army moved into Estremadura for the purpose of besieging Badajos. We Light, 3rd and 4th Divisions, thought, as we had taken Ciudad Rodrigo, others would have the pleasure of the trenches of Badajos, but on our reaching Elvas [17 Feb., 1812] we were very soon undeceived, and we were destined for the duty,—to our mortification, for soldiers hate sieges and working-parties. The Guards work better than any soldiers, from their habits in London. Badajos was invested by the 3rd, 4th, and Light Divisions on the Spanish side, or left bank of the river, and by the 5th Division * on the Portuguese side, or right bank. On the night of the 17th March, St. Patrick's Day, the Light Division broke ground

* Not till 24 March (Napier, iv. 105).

under a deluge of rain, which swelled the
Guadiana so as to threaten our bridge of boats.
Our duties in the trenches were most laborious
during the whole siege, and much hard fighting we
had, sorties, etc.   The night [26 Mar.] the outworks La Picurina was carried by my dear friend Sir
James Kempt, part of the 3rd Division (which was
his) were to compose the storming party.   The Light
Division, the working party, consequently were sent
to the Engineer Park for the ladders.   When they
arrived, General Kempt ordered them to be planted
(Sir H. Hardinge, D.Q.M.G. of the Portuguese
army, was here distinguished).   The boys of the
3rd Division said to our fellows, "Come, stand out
of the way ; " to which our fellows replied, "D——
your eyes, do you think we Light Division fetch
ladders for such chaps as you to climb up ?   Follow
us"—springing on the ladders, and many of them
were knocked over.   A notorious fellow, a Sergeant
Brotherwood, a noble fellow on duty, told me this
anecdote.   The siege was prosecuted with the same
vigour from without with which it was repelled from
within.

After some hours in the trenches, when we
returned I invariably ate and went out coursing,
and many is the gallant course I had, and many
the swift hare I and my dog Moro brought home
from the right bank of the Guadiana.   One day
James Stewart, I, and Charlie Eeles set off, having
three hours off duty, to look for a hare or two
at a celebrated spot where the hares ran very

strong because there was a rabbit warren which saved them. Moro, of course, was of the party. We soon found an unusually strong hare, and, although the greyhounds fetched round a dozen times, she still worked her way for the warren. I was riding a great stupid Irish horse bought from General Vandeleur, called Paddy, and as it was important for the soup to kill this hare, however unsportsmanlike on quiet occasions it would be deemed, I rode to head her from the warren. My stupid beast of a horse put his foot into a hole and rolled over me. Stewart and Eeles picked me up, but I was insensible. Although I have generally managed on such occasions to get away from the horse, the animal had rolled over me, and when I came to myself I was sitting on Eeles' knee, my arms tied up with a whip-thong, and James Stewart, with a blunt-looking penknife, trying to bleed me, an operation I quickly prohibited by starting on to my legs. Moro killed his hare, though, without my help.

On the night of the 6th April the 3rd Division were to storm the citadel, the 4th and Light the great breach, the 5th the Olivença Gate, and to escalade, if possible. The command of the Light Division had devolved on Colonel Barnard. Vandeleur was wounded, and stayed at Portalegre, and poor Beckwith had gone to the rear with violent ague; he never joined us again, noble soldier that he was.

This escalade has been so frequently described,

I shall only say that when the head of the Light
Division arrived at the ditch of the place it was
a beautiful moonlight night. Old Alister Cameron,
who was in command of four Companies of the
95th Regiment, extended along the counterscape to
attract the enemy's fire, while the column planted
their ladders and descended, came up to Barnard
and said, " Now my men are ready ; shall I begin ? "
" No, certainly not," says Barnard. The breach and
the works were full of the enemy, looking quietly at
us, but not fifty yards off and most prepared, although
not firing a shot. So soon as our ladders were all
ready posted, and the column in the very act to
move and rush down the ladders, Barnard called
out, " *Now*, Cameron ! " and the first shot from us
brought down such a hail of fire as I shall never
forget, nor ever saw before or since. It was most
murderous. We flew down the ladders and rushed
at the breach, but we were broken, and carried no
weight with us, although every soldier was a hero.
The breach was covered by a breastwork from
behind, and ably defended on the top by *chevaux-
de-frises* of sword-blades, sharp as razors, chained
to the ground ; while the ascent to the top of the
breach was covered with planks with sharp nails in
them. However, devil a one did I feel at this
moment. One of the officers of the forlorn hope,
Lieut. Taggart of the 43rd, was hanging on my
arm—a mode we adopted to help each other
up, for the ascent was most difficult and steep. A
Rifleman stood among the sword-blades on the

top of one of the *chevaux-de-frises*. We made
a glorious rush to follow, but, alas! in vain. He
was knocked over. My old captain, O'Hare, who
commanded the storming party, was killed. All
were awfully wounded except, I do believe, myself
and little Freer of the 43rd. I had been some
seconds at the *revêtement* of the bastion near the
breach, and my red-coat pockets were literally filled
with chips of stones splintered by musket-balls.
Those not knocked down were driven back by this
hail of mortality to the ladders. At the foot of
them I saw poor Colonel Macleod with his hands
on his breast—the man who lent me his horse when
wounded at the bridge on the Coa. He said,
"Oh, Smith, I am mortally wounded. Help me
up the ladder." I said, "Oh no, dear fellow!"
"I am," he said; "be quick!" I did so, and came
back again. Little Freer and I said, "Let us throw
down the ladders; the fellows shan't go out." Some
soldiers behind said, "D—— your eyes, if you do
we will bayonet you!" and we were literally forced
up with the crowd. My sash had got loose, and
one end of it was fast in the ladder, and the bayonet
was very nearly applied, but the sash by pulling
became loose. So soon as we got on the glacis,
up came a fresh Brigade of the Portuguese of the
4th Division. I never saw any soldiers behave with
more pluck. Down into the ditch we all went again,
but the more we tried to get up, the more we were
destroyed. The 4th Division followed us in marching up to the breach, and they made a most

uncommon noise. The French saw us, but took
no notice. Sir Charles Colville, commanding the
4th Division (Cole having been wounded at Albuera),
made a devil of a noise, too, on the glacis. Both
Divisions were fairly beaten back; we never carried
either breach (nominally there were two breaches).

After the attacks upon the breaches, some time
before daylight Lord Fitzroy Somerset came to our
Division. I think I was almost the first officer
who spoke to him. He said, "Where is Barnard?"
I didn't know, but I assured his Lordship he was
neither killed nor wounded. A few minutes after
his Lordship said that the Duke desired the Light
and 4th Divisions to storm again. "The devil!"
says I. "Why, we have had enough; we are all
knocked to pieces." Lord Fitzroy says, "I dare
say, but you must try again." I smiled and said,
"If we could not succeed with two whole fresh
and unscathed Divisions, we are likely to make a
poor show of it now. But we will try again with
all our might." Scarcely had this conversation
occurred when a bugle sounded within the breach,
indicating what had occurred at the citadel and
Puerto de Olivença; and here ended all the fighting.
Our fellows would have gone at it again when
collected and put into shape, but we were just as
well pleased that our attempt had so attracted the
attention of the enemy as greatly to facilitate that
success which assured the prize contended for.

There is no battle, day or night, I would
not willingly react except this. The murder of

our gallant officers and soldiers is not to be believed. Next day I and Charlie Beckwith, a brother Brigade-Major, went over the scene. It was *appalling*. Heaps on heaps of slain,—in one spot lay nine officers. Whilst we were there, Colonel Allen of the Guards came up, and beckoned me to him. I saw that, in place of congratulating me, he looked very dull. " What's the matter ?" I said. " Do you not know my brother in the Rifles was killed last night ? " " God help him and you ! no, for I and we all loved him." In a flood of tears, he looked round and pointed to a body. "There he lies." He had a pair of scissors with him. "Go and cut off a lock of his hair for my mother. I came for the purpose, but I am not equal to doing it."

The returns of killed and wounded and the evident thin appearance of our camp at once too plainly told the loss we had sustained. O memorable night of glory and woe ! for, although the 4th and Light were so beaten, our brilliant and numerous attacks induced the governor to concentrate all his force in the breaches ; thus the 3rd escaladed the citadel, and the 5th got in by the Olivença gate. Although we lost so many stout hearts, so many dear friends and comrades, yet not one staff officer of our Division was killed or wounded. We had all been struck. My clothes were cut by musket-balls, and I had several contusions, particularly one on my left thigh.

Now comes a scene of horror I would willingly

bury in oblivion.   The atrocities committed by our
soldiers on the poor innocent and defenceless inhabitants of the city, no words suffice to depict.
Civilized man, when let loose and the bonds of
morality relaxed, is a far greater beast than the
savage, more refined in his cruelty, more fiend-like
in every act ; and oh, too truly did our heretofore
noble soldiers disgrace themselves, though the
officers exerted themselves to the utmost to re-
press it, many who had escaped the enemy being
wounded in their merciful attempts ! Yet this scene
of debauchery, however cruel to many, to me has
been the solace and the whole happiness of my life
for thirty-three years.   A poor defenceless maiden
of thirteen years was thrown upon my generous
nature through her sister, as described so ably in
Johnny Kincaid's book, of which this is an extract—

"I was conversing with a friend the day after, at the
door of his tent, when we observed two ladies coming from
the city, who made directly towards us ; they seemed both
young, and when they came near, the elder of the two
threw back her *mantilla* to address us, showing a remarkably handsome figure, with fine features ; but her sallow,
sun-burnt, and careworn, though still youthful, countenance
showed that in her 'the time for tender thoughts and
soft endearments had fled away and gone.'

"She at once addressed us in that confident, heroic
manner so characteristic of the high-bred Spanish maiden,
told us who they were—the last of an ancient and honourable house—and referred to an officer high in rank in
our army, who had been quartered there in the days of her
prosperity, for the truth of her tale.

"Her husband, she said, was a Spanish officer in a distant part of the kingdom ; he might, or he might not, still be living.   But yesterday she and this her young sister were able to live in affluence and in a handsome house ; to-day they knew not where to lay their heads, where to get a change of raiment or a morsel of bread. Her house, she said, was a wreck ; and, to show the indignities to which they had been subjected, she pointed to where the blood was still trickling down their necks, caused by the wrenching of their ear-rings through the flesh by the hands of worse than savages, who would not take the trouble to unclasp them !

" For herself, she said, she cared not ; but for the agitated and almost unconscious maiden by her side, whom she had but lately received over from the hands of her conventual instructresses, she was in despair, and knew not what to do ; and that, in the rapine and ruin which was at that moment desolating the city, she saw no security for her but the seemingly indelicate one she had adopted—of coming to the camp and throwing themselves upon the protection of any British officer who would afford it ; and so great, she said, was her faith in our national character, that she knew the appeal would not be made in vain, nor the confidence abused.   Nor was it made in vain !   Nor could it be abused, for she stood by the side of an angel !   A being more transcendingly lovely I had never before seen—one more amiable I have never yet known !

" Fourteen summers had not yet passed over her youthful countenance, which was of a delicate freshness—more English than Spanish ; her face, though not perhaps rigidly beautiful, was nevertheless so remarkably handsome, and so irresistibly attractive, surmounting a figure cast in nature's fairest mould, that to look at her was to love her ; and I did love her, but I never told my love, and in the mean time another and a more impudent fellow stepped in and won her! But yet I was happy, for in him she found such a one as her loveliness and her misfortunes claimed—a man of honour, and a husband in every way worthy of her!

"That a being so young, so lovely, and so interesting, just emancipated from the gloom of a convent, unknowing of the world and to the world unknown, should thus have been wrecked on a sea of troubles, and thrown on the mercy of strangers under circumstances so dreadful, so uncontrollable, and not have sunk to rise no more, must be the wonder of every one. Yet from the moment she was thrown on her own resources, her star was in the ascendant.

"Guided by a just sense of rectitude, an innate purity of mind, a singleness of purpose which defied malice, and a soul that soared above circumstances, she became alike the adored of the camp and of the drawing-room, and eventually the admired associate of princes. She yet lives, in the affections of her gallant husband, in an elevated situation in life, a pattern to her sex, and everybody's *beau ideal* of what a wife should be." *

* *Random Shots by a Rifleman*, by Sir John Kincaid, pp. 292–296. I venture to quote the rest of Kincaid's interesting passage : "Thrown upon each other's acquaintance in a manner so interesting, it is not to be wondered at that she and I conceived a friendship for each other, which has proved as lasting as our lives—a friendship which was cemented by after-circumstances so singularly romantic that imagination may scarcely picture them ! The friendship of man is one thing —the friendship of woman another ; and those only who have been on the theatre of fierce warfare, and knowing that such a being was on the spot, watching with earnest and increasing solicitude over his safety alike with those most dear to her, can fully appreciate the additional value which it gives to one's existence.

"About a year after we became acquainted, I remember that our Battalion was one day moving down to battle, and had occasion to pass by the lone country-house in which she had been lodged. The situation was so near to the outposts, and a battle certain, I concluded that she must ere then have been removed to a place of greater security, and, big with the thought of coming events, I scarcely even looked at it as we rolled along, but just as I had passed the door, I found my

I confess myself to be the "more impudent fellow," and if any reward is due to a soldier, never was one so honoured and distinguished as I have been by the possession of this dear child (for she was little more than a child at this moment), one with a sense of honour no knight ever exceeded in the most romantic days of chivalry, an understanding superior to her years, a masculine mind with a force of character no consideration could turn from her own just sense of rectitude, and all encased in a frame of Nature's fairest and most delicate moulding, the figure of an angel, with an eye of light and an expression which then inspired me with a maddening love which, from that period to this (now thirty-three years), has never abated under many and the most trying circumstances. Thus, as good may come out of evil, this scene of devastation and

hand suddenly grasped in hers. She gave it a gentle pressure, and, without uttering a word, had rushed back into the house again, almost before I could see to whom I was indebted for a kindness so unexpected and so gratifying.

"My mind had, the moment before, been sternly occupied in calculating the difference which it makes in a man's future prospects—his killing or being killed, when 'a change came o'er the spirit of the dream,' and throughout the remainder of that long and trying day I felt a lightness of heart and buoyancy of spirit which, in such a situation, was no less new than delightful.

"I never until then felt so forcibly the beautiful description of Fitz-James's expression of feeling, after his leave-taking of Ellen, under somewhat similar circumstances—

> "'And after oft the knight would say,
> That not when prize of festal day
> Was dealt him by the brightest fair
> That e'er wore jewel in her hair,
> So highly did his bosom swell
> As at that simple, mute, farewell.'"

spoil yielded to me a treasure invaluable; to me who, among so many dear friends, had escaped all dangers; to me, a wild youth not meriting such reward, and, however desirous, never able to express half his gratitude to God Almighty for such signal marks of His blessing shown to so young and so thoughtless a being. From that day to this she has been my guardian angel. She has shared with me the dangers and privations, the hardships and fatigues, of a restless life of war in every quarter of the globe. No murmur has ever escaped her. Bereft of every relative, of every tie to her country but the recollection of it, united to a man of different though Christian religion, yet that man has been and is her all, on whom have hinged the closed portals of hope, happiness, and bliss; if opened, misery, destitution, and bereavement, and every loss language can depict summed up in *one* word, "*He* is lost to me." But, O my God, Thou hast kindly spared us for each other; we have, through Thy grace, been but little separated, and we have, in unison of soul, received at Thy holy altar the Blessed Sacrament of the Body and Blood of Christ.* May we, through His mediation, be still spared to each other in this life, and in the life to come be eternally united in Heaven!

After the disorganization our troops had rushed into, it became the duty of every officer to exert

---

* From the time of their first residence at the Cape in the thirties, Juana Smith conformed to the Church of England, and was in consequence disowned by her remaining Spanish relatives.

himself, and nobly did Colonel Barnard set about the task, and ably supported was he by every officer in the Division. We had not marched for the north two days when our soldiers were, like Richard, "themselves again." When the French garrison were marched to the rear, my Brigade furnished an escort to the next Division *en route* to Elvas. I paraded upwards of four thousand very orderly, fine-looking fellows. Many of the officers praised the gallantry of our men, and all said, "Why break ground at all with such soldiers? Had you stormed on the rainy night of the 17th March, you would have taken the place with half the loss." This is creditable to us, but the Duke of Wellington would have been by no means borne out in such an attempt.

However, as all this writing is to show rather my individual participation in these scenes of glory and bloodshed, I must dwell a little upon the joy of my marriage. I was only twenty-two, my wife just on the verge of fourteen.* But in southern climates Nature more early develops herself and attains maturity. Every day was an increase of joy. Although both of us were of the quickest tempers, we were both ready to forgive, and both intoxicated in happiness. All my dearest friends — Charlie Beckwith, John Bell, Johnstone, Charlie Eeles, Jack Molloy, etc.—were saying to themselves, "Alas! poor Harry Smith is lost, who was the

---

* He was really twenty-four, but he seems never to have known his own age. His wife (born 27 March, 1798) was just past fourteen.

example of a duty-officer previously.   It is only natural he must neglect duty now." I assured them all that the contrary would be the case, for love would incite me to exertions in hopes of preferment, the only mode I had to look to for a comfortable maintenance ; and my wife's love, aided by her good sense, would see I was never neglecting her if engaged in the performance of my duty.   Conscientiously did I act up to my feeling then, and no one ever did or ever could say, I was out of my place night or day.

My duty was my duty—I gloried in it ; my wife even still more so, and never did she say, "You might have been with me," or complain if I was away.   On the contrary, after many a day's fatiguing march, when I sought her out in the baggage or awaiting me, her first question invariably was, "Are you sure you have done all your duty ?"   *Then* I admit my attention was unbounded, and we were happy—oh, how happy, often amidst scenes of distress and privation that would have appalled stouter hearts, not devoted like ours ! And oh, when I reflect on God's mercy to us both ! In a succession of the most brilliant battles for years I was never even wounded, and, although I say it, no man ever exposed himself in every way more as a soldier, or rode harder as a sportsman. Wonderful, most wonderful, have been my hair-breadth escapes from falls of horses under and over me all over the world.

CHAPTER IX.

BUT to the thread of my narrative. Hardly had
we reached the frontier of Portugal [24 April,
1812], our old haunts, Ituero, Guinaldo, etc., when
our army moved on again for Spain, and fought the
Battle of Salamanca. Before this battle we had
an immense deal of marching and manœuvring.
The armies of Marmont and Wellington were close
to each other for several days, so that a trifling
occurrence would have brought on a general action,
and we were frequently under cannonade.

My wife could not ride in the least at first, and
oh, the difficulty I had! although she had frequently
ridden a donkey on her pilgrimage to Olivença,
once to avoid the siege of Badajos, and at other
times to her grandmother's at Almendrajos.*

---

* Her relations are numerous. She was in three sieges of her
native city : in one her wounded brother died in her arms. She was
educated in a convent, and is a lineal descendant of Ponce de Leon,
the Knight of Romance, and certainly she, as a female, inherits all his
heroism. Her name, Juana Maria de Los Dolores de Leon, at once
gives the idea of Hidalgo consanguinity, and she is of one of the
oldest of the notoriously old *Spanish*, not Moorish, families. After
Talavera, when the Duke's headquarters were at Badajos, and my wife
was a child, Colonel Campbell and Lord Fitzroy Somerset were

However, I had one of my saddles turned into a side-saddle most ably by a soldier of Ross's Troop of Horse Artillery, and at first made her ride a great brute of a Portuguese horse I had; but she so rapidly improved, took such pains, had so much practice and naturally good nerves, that she soon got ashamed of her Portuguese horse, and wanted to ride my Spanish little fellow, who had so nobly carried me at Redinha and in many other fights. I always said, "When you can ride as well as you can dance and sing, you shall," for in those accomplishments she was perfect. In crossing the Tormes [21 July], the very night before the battle of Salamanca (there are quicksands in the river), her Portuguese horse was so cowardly he alarmed me, and hardly had we crossed the river when a clap of thunder, louder than anything that can be described, burst over our heads. The Portuguese horse was in such a funk, she abjured *all Portuguese*, and insisted hereafter on riding her own gallant countryman, as gallant as any Arab. He was an Andalusian, which is a thorough-bred descendant of the Moosul horse, which is literally an Arab. The next day she mounted her Tiny, and rode him ever afterwards over many an eventful field, until the end of the war at Toulouse. She

billeted in her sister's house. That was in the palmy days of their affluence, when they derived a considerable income from their olive groves. These, alas! were all cut down by the unsparing hand of the French, and the sisters' income seriously reduced. An olive tree requires great care and cultivation, nor does it bear well until twenty or thirty years old.—H.G.S.

had him afterwards at my father's house. The affection between them was of the character of that between spaniel and master. The dear, gallant horse lived to twenty-nine years of age, and died a happy pensioner on my brother Charles's estate.

It is difficult to say who was the proudest on the morning of the battle [22 July], horse, wife, or Enrique (as I was always called). She caracoled him about among the soldiers, to their delight, for he was broken in like a Mameluke, though very difficult to ride. (The soldiers of the whole Division loved her with enthusiasm from the events so peculiar in her history, and she would laugh and talk with all, which a soldier loves. Blackguards as many of the poor gallant fellows were, there was not a man who would not have laid down his life to defend her, and among the officers she was adored, and consulted on all occasions of baggage-guard, etc.) Her attendant, who also had a led horse in case of accident, with a little tent and a funny little pair of lanterns, my dear, trusty old groom West, as the battle began, took her to the rear, much to her annoyance, and in the thunder of cannon, the pride of equestrianism was buried in anxiety for him on whom her all depended. She and West slept on the field of battle, he having made a bed for her with the green wheat he had cut just in full ear. She had to hold her horse all night, and he ate all her bed of green wheat, to her juvenile amusement; for a creature so gay and vivacious, with all her sound sense, the earth never produced.

Next morning soon after daylight she joined me on the march. I was at that time so afflicted with boils, I could hardly live on horseback. I had eleven immense ones at the time on my legs and thighs, the excruciating pain of which is not to be described. Our surgeon, old Joe Bowker, insisted on my going to Salamanca, and one particular boil on the bone of the inside of my knee proved a more irresistible argument. So to Salamanca I had to go, my brother Tom doing my duty. I stayed fourteen days at Salamanca, a time of love and excitement, although, so distressed was the army for money, we lived almost on our rations, except for a little assistance from the lady of our house in coffee, etc. Wade, Sir Lowry Cole's A.D.C., lent me one dollar out of forty which he had received to support his General (who had been severely wounded in the battle), and his staff. In such times of privation heroism is required which our countrymen little dream of.

At the end of the fourteen days I had as many boils as ever, but, boils and all, off we started, and rode some terrible distances for three or four days. We overtook the Division, to the joy of the soldiers, before we crossed the Guadarama Pass [11 Aug.]. There had been no fighting in my absence, thank God.

We soon reached the neighbourhood of Madrid. No city could be better laid out for pomp and show, and the Duke's entry [13 Aug.] was a most brilliant spectacle. My vivacious wife used to enjoy her native capital, and in her admiration treated London and Paris as villages in comparison. We spent a very happy time. It was a great amusement to improve our wardrobe for the walk on the elegant Prado of an evening, in which no love among the Spanish beauties showed to greater advantage than my Estremenha, or native of Estremadura. During our stay in the vicinity of Madrid we made several agreeable acquaintances, among others the vicar of one of the many rich villages around Madrid, Vicalbaro, a highly educated and clever fellow, a great sportsman and excellent shot, with a morbid hatred to a Frenchman. Upon our moving forward beyond Madrid as far as the beautiful and *clean* city Alcala [23 Oct.], I was brought in contact with the celebrated and unfortunate General Elio, whom I had known in South America at Monte Video. He was very conversational, and we had a long talk as to that colonial war; but, as I was acting as interpreter for my friend James Stewart, the A.Q.M.G. of our Division, who was making arrangements of march with Elio, conversation on the past turned into plans for the future. We moved forwards towards our right to Arganda [27 Oct.]. At this period the Duke had gone to Burgos, and Lord Hill commanded. We soon felt the loss of our decided and far-seeing chief, and we made marches and counter-marches we were unaccustomed to. At ten at night, at Arganda, Major-General Vandeleur received an order from General Alten, who remained in Alcala, to march immediately back to Alcala with the whole Division. Vandeleur sent for me and told me to order the assembly to sound. I remonstrated and prayed him to wait until two hours before daylight, for every soldier in the Division had more or less indulged in the wine for which Arganda was celebrated. The good general had been at the shrine of Bacchus too, and was uncontrollable. Blast went the assembly, and staggering to their alarm-posts went the soldiers. Such a scene of good-natured riot I had never seen in my own Division. With the Duke we generally had a sort of hint we might be wanted, and our tried soldiers would be as steady as rocks. Oh, such a dark night's march as we had back to Alcala! Vandeleur repented of his obstinacy, and well he might.

We halted the next day at Alcala. Here, although it was now October, it was evident to me that a long retreat to the frontier was about to be undertaken, and I got from a Spanish officer, called Labrador, his fine large Andalusian horse in exchange for an Irish brute I had bought from General Vandeleur. He gave me three Spanish doubloons to boot, a fortune in those days, particularly to me.

These three doubloons were given to my vivacious Spanish wife, who put them up most carefully in my portmanteau, among my few shirts. On the march the motion of the mule had shaken them out of place, the doubloons were gone, and all our fortune! Her horror, poor girl, is not to be described. She knew it was our all, and her delight when I gave the treasure into her charge was now more than eclipsed by the misery of the loss. I only laughed, for in those days hardships and privations were so common, they were missed when comparative affluence supplied their place.

We marched [30 Oct.] to Madrid, or rather its suburbs, where the poor inhabitants were in indescribable distress, seeing that they were again to be abandoned to French clemency and contributions. While our troops were halted, waiting for orders whether to bivouac or whether to retire, to our astonishment up came the Vicar of Vicalbaro. He took me on one side, and told me most pathetically that he had made himself so obnoxious to the French, he feared to stay, and had come to crave my protection. This I gladly promised. While I described to him the hardships a winter retreat would impose upon him and us, he said gallantly, " I am young and healthy like yourselves ; what you suffer, I can. My only fear is that I may inconvenience you and my young countrywoman, your wife." I laughed, and called her. She was all fun, notwithstanding the loss of the doubloons, and began to quiz him ; but in the midst of her raillery he observed, as he said to me afterwards, her soul of kindness, and the Padre was installed in my establishment, while my old comrades laughed and said, " Harry Smith will do, now he has a father confessor," by which name the Padre always went— " Harry Smith's confessor." The hour or two of halt was occupied by the Padre in buying a pony, which he soon effected, and his marching establishment, a few shirts, with an immense *capa*, or cloak, almost as much as the pony could carry.

It rained in torrents, and we marched to Aravaca, some miles to the rear of the capital, where we found Lord Hill's headquarters in possession of every hole in the village, which was a very small one. General Vandeleur, who was still suffering from his wound at Ciudad Rodrigo, found a Captain of the Waggon Train in possession of a small house. In walks the General to a nice clean little room with a cheerful fire. "Who are you, sir?" says the General. "I am Captain ——, of the Royal Waggon Train, attached to Lord Hill, and this house is given me for my quarters." "I, sir, am General Vandeleur, and am d——d glad to see you in my quarters for *five minutes*." The poor Captain very quietly packed up his traps and went —I know not where.

I, my young wife, the Padre, all my greyhounds and dogs, about thirteen, got into a little hole about six feet square, and were glad enough to get out of the rain, for, though my wife had her little tent, that, pitched on exceedingly wet ground, was a horrid shelter for any one. Owing to the kindness of our Provost-Marshal (Mr. Stanway), I got my horses also under a kind of out-office. We marched the next day to the foot of the Guadarama Pass, where our soldiers, when dismissed in bivouac, had a fine hunt after a wild boar, which they killed. The sunshine brightened, and when I returned from a variety of duties I found the young wife as neat as a new pin in her little tent, her habit and all her things which had got wet in yesterday's rain hung out to dry. So after breakfast I proposed to decorate my person (shave I need not, for as yet that operation was unnecessary), and *the* portmanteau was opened, the delinquent from which our doubloons had escaped. Some of the shirts were wet from the rain, and in searching for a dry one, out tumbled the three doubloons, which had been shaken into the folds of the shirt by the motion of the mule, and so lost. Oh, such joy and such laughing! We were so rich. We could buy bread and chocolate and sausages and eggs through the interest of the Padre (for we found the holy friar could get things when, however much money was exhibited, it proved no talisman), and our little fortune carried us through the retreat even to Ciudad Rodrigo, where money was paid to us.

This retreat was a very severe one as to weather, and although the enemy did not actually press us, as he did the column from Burgos, we made long marches and were very broad awake, and lost some of our baggage and stores, which the wearied bullocks obliged us to abandon. On reaching Salamanca, my wife, with the foresight of age rather than youth, expended some of the doubloons in buying me two pairs of worsted stockings and a pair of worsted mits, and the same for herself, which I do believe saved her from sickness, for the rain, on the retreat from Salamanca, came in torrents.

CHAPTER X.

CAMPAIGN OF 1812: RETREAT TO THE LINES OF
TORRES VEDRAS—WINTER OF 1812–13.

THE army concentrated again under the dear Duke
of Wellington, and took up its old victorious
position on the Arapiles [14 Nov.], but not
with the same prospects. Soult, an able fellow,
had nearly double our force, and so soon as our
rear was open the army was in full march on
Ciudad Rodrigo. It rained in torrents, and the
roads rose above the soldiers' ankles. Our supplies
were *nil*, and the sufferings of the soldiers were
considerable. Many compared this retreat with that
of Coruña, at which I then laughed, and do now.
The whole distance from Ciudad Rodrigo is only
forty-four miles. On one day to Coruña we marched
thirty-seven miles, fighting every yard, and the cold
was intense; on this retreat it was cold, but no *frost*
in the atmosphere.

In crossing the Huebra [17 Nov.], at San
Muños, the enemy pressed our rear-guard very
sharply, and we had some very heavy skirmishing.
Sir E. Paget, by his own obstinacy in not believing
the French Dragoons had intervened upon our line

of march, was taken prisoner, and our rear-guard (my Brigade) driven from the ford. They had to take to the river as well as they were able, the soldiers leaping from a steep bank into it.

The sense and strength of my wife's Spanish horse were this day put to the test, for she had nothing for it but to make him leap into the river from the high bank, which the noble animal did, all fours like a dog. The poor Padre attempted the same, with the result that he and pony floated down the stream, and the pony was drowned, but his large Spanish *capa* or cloak kept him afloat, and he was dragged out by some of our soldiers. His holiness began now to think I had not exaggerated the hardships of a soldier's life. When well out of the river, he quietly asked my poor old West for a horse I always had ready to jump on in case my own were killed. West very quietly said, "Never lend master's other fighting horse, not to nobody." My wife interceded for the poor Padre, but had the same refusal. Old West says, "We shan't march far; the river bothered us, it will stop the French. Our Riflemen don't mean to let those fellows over. Night and the walk will warm you."

I, seeing the distress my poor wife was likely to be in, had told her particularly to stay with the 52nd, thinking they would move into bivouac, while the Riflemen held the bed of the river where we had crossed, to which alone my attention was drawn. There was a ford, however, lower down the river, to which the 52nd were suddenly ordered. It was impassable, but in the enemy's attempt to cross, a heavy skirmish ensued, in which poor Captain Dawson was killed and forty or fifty men wounded; my wife in the thick of it, and the friar.

As soon as the ford was ascertained impassable, I was sent to bring back the 52nd, when, to my astonishment and alarm, I found my young wife drenched with leaping in the river, as much as from the torrents of rain above. The poor Padre might have been drawn for "the Knight of the Woeful Countenance." I brought the whole into our wet and miserable bivouac, and gave some Portuguese of my Brigade a dollar for a large fire, when, cold and shivery as she was, she laughed at the Padre. We had nothing to eat that night, as our mules were sent on, and there was this young and delicate creature, in the month of November in the north of Spain, wet as a drowned rat, with nothing to eat, and no cover from the falling deluge. Not a murmur escaped her but once. I had had no sleep for three nights, our rear being in a very ticklish position. In sitting by the fire I had fallen asleep, and fell between the fire and her. She had previously been roasted on one side, a cold mud on the other. This change of temperature awoke her, and for the only time in her life did she cry and say I might have avoided it. She had just woke out of her sleep, and when cold and shivery our feelings are acute. In a moment she exclaimed, " How foolish! you must have been nice and warm, and to know that is enough for me."

I took the Padre a mule; the rain broke, the little rivulet would soon be fordable, and at daylight the next morning we expected a regular squeeze from the enemy. To amend matters, too, in place of our moving off before daylight and getting a start, we were to follow the 1st Division, and this did not move. General Alten sent repeatedly to poor dear Sir William Stewart (who gave me my commission), to represent the prospect he had of a brush which ought to be avoided, when up rides to Charlie Beckwith, our A.Q.M.G., the Honourable Arthur Upton, saying, " My *dear-e* Beckwith, you could not inform me where I could get a *paysano* (a peasant) ? The 1st Division can't move; we have no guide." " Oh, d——," says Charlie, " is that it ? We will do anything to get you out of our way. Come to Harry Smith. He has a paysano, *I know.*" I always had three or four poor fellows in charge of a guard, so requisite are guides with light troops. I gave him his paysano, and by this time the sun was an hour high at least. To our delight, in place of a *fight retreating*, which partakes neither of the pomp nor majesty of war, but of nothing but hard and often inglorious losses, we saw the French army dismissed, all drying their clothes, and as little in a state to attack as we were desirous of their company. We had a clear, cold, but unmolested long march, and fell in with some stores coming. Yesterday the soldier's life was one of misery, to-day all joy and elasticity !

Just as the rear-guard had moved off the ground,

I heard the voice of a soldier familiar to me calling
out, "Oh, Mr. Smith!" (The Rifle soldiers ever
called me "Mr. Smith.") "Don't leave me here."
I rode up. As gallant a Rifleman as ever breathed,
by name O'Donnell, lay there with his thigh fractured
the day before by a cannon-shot. I was grieved
for him. I had no means to assist him but one
which I deemed it impossible he could avail himself
of—the tumbril of a gun. He said, "Oh, I can
ride." I galloped to Ross, who literally sent back
with me a six-pounder, and took the poor fellow on
the tumbril, the gunner cheerfully giving him his
place. It was grievous to see poor O'Donnell
hoisted up with his thigh smashed. We got him
there, though, and he said, "I shall do now." He
died in two hours. I shall ever feel grateful to
Ross; few men could have done it, but his guns
were drawn by noble horses, and he was, and is, a
SOLDIER.

Over the bivouac fire this night the Padre
became eloquent and sentimental. "When you
told me at Madrid what were the hardships and
privations of a soldier's life in retreat, pursued by
a vigorous enemy, I considered I had a very correct
idea; I now see I had no conception whatever.
But what appears to me so extraordinary is that
every one acts for himself alone. *There* you see a
poor knocked-up soldier sitting in the mud, unable
to move; *there* come grooms with led horses. No
one asks the sick man to ride, no one sympathizes
with the other's feelings—in short, every one appears

to struggle against difficulties for himself alone."
I could see the Padre had not forgotten my old
man West's refusal of my second war-horse.

On the day following [19 Nov.], the weather
was clear but bitterly cold. We reached the
suburbs of Ciudad Rodrigo, happy enough to know
that for this campaign the fighting was over.
Although some of our troops had a long march
before them into Portugal, we Light Division
gentlemen were close at home. Many of our
stoutest officers were sick, John Bell, Charlie Eeles,
etc., and we had many wounded to look after. The
Padre and my cheerful, light-hearted wife were
cooking in a little house all day long. The Padre
was a capital cook, and equally good when the food
was prepared. I went out coursing every day, and
some of our regiment fellows, notwithstanding the
"retreat" and its hardships, went out duck-shooting,
up to their middles in water, Jonathan Leach among
the rest.

My brigade was ordered into our old villages of
Alameda, Fuentes d'Oñoro, Guinaldo, and to march
viâ San Fehus el dicio, there to cross the Agueda.
The weather was very rainy and cold, but my
vivacious little wife was full of animation and happiness, and the Padre usually cooking.

Fuentes d'Oñoro was to be the head-quarters
of our Brigade. General Vandeleur took up his
quarters in the Curé's house, around which in the
battle had been a sanguinary conflict. I was at the
other end of the village for the sake of an excellent

stable. It belonged to the father of the beautiful
Maria Josefa, who fled from her father's house with
a commissary, was infamously treated by him, returned to her father's house, and was received by
the good old man kindly, although with nearly a
broken heart. Songs were sung about her all over
Spain, and she was universally condemned, pitied,
and pardoned. I put the Padre in this house, told
him the tale of woe, and, to his credit, he did everything a Christian clergyman ought, to urge on the
parents pardon of the ill-used penitent. Nor did
he plead in vain, the poor thing was forgiven by
every one but herself. The Padre requested my
generous-hearted wife to see her, and this was a
consolation to poor Maria Josefa worth a general
action to behold.

My billet was some little distance from the
stable, and while there my landlord married a
second wife. The inhabitants of this part of Spain
are very peculiar and primitive in their manners,
dress, and customs; they are called Charras. The
dress of the women is most costly, and a marriage
feast exceeds any feast that I ever saw, or that has
been described by Abyssinian Bruce. We had fun
and much feasting for three days. One of the
ceremonies is that during a dance in which the
bride is, of course, the *prima donna*, her relatives
and friends make her presents, which she receives
while dancing in the most graceful, though rustic,
attitudes. The presents are frequently considerable
sums in gold, or gold and silver ornaments of singular

workmanship. All relatives and friends give something, or it is regarded as a slight. My wife, who learned to dance the rustic measure on purpose, presented a doubloon in the most elegant and graceful manner, to the delight of her compatriots around, although, being an Estremenha, she was regarded by these primitive, but hospitable and generous, creatures, as half a foreigner. The bride has a knife in her uplifted hand, upon it an apple, and the smaller presents are presented by cutting the apple, and placing in the cut the money or ornament.

In this part of Spain the pigs are fed most delicately; they are driven first into woods of cork trees, which produce beautiful, sweet acorns, then into woods of magnificent chestnut trees, the keeper getting into the trees and flogging down the acorns and chestnuts with an immense long whip. The pigs thus fed yield a meat different from the usual meat of the animal. They are of a beautiful breed, become exceedingly fat, and the season of killing them and making black puddings and sausages for the year's supply is one of continual feasting. The peasants also cure the meat along each side of the backbone called *loma de puerco*. This they do in a very peculiar manner with salt, red pepper, and of course a *soupçon* of garlic in a thick slice; and, notwithstanding the little garlic, when simply boiled, it is the most delicious food, for breakfast particularly, that even a French cook could boast of.

During our stay at Fuentes, many were the rides my wife took on her horse Tiny to our friends in the different villages. At last, however, an order came to our Brigade head-quarters to vacate Fuentes d'Oñoro, as it was required for a part of the head-quarters establishment not far off at Freneda, and we moved to Guinaldo, to our deep regret. The Padre a few days before had taken his departure for his living at Vicalbaro. Two most magnificent mules, and his servant, came for him. We parted with mutual regret, but I am sorry to say he only wrote to us twice afterwards, and once to ask a favour for some individual.

At this time I was sporting mad. The Duke had a capital pack of fox-hounds. James Stewart, my chum, our A.Q.M.G., had an excellent pack of harriers to which I acted as whipper-in. After a very severe run, swimming two rivers, my Andalusian, which produced the doubloons at Alcala, died soon after he got back to his stable. Mr. Commissary Haines, at head-quarters, had a beautiful pack of little beagles. I was too proud to look at them. I had the best greyhounds in the world,—" Moro," and some of his almost equally celebrated sons.

CHAPTER XI.

CAMPAIGN OF 1813: BATTLE OF VITTORIA.

AT Guinaldo we soon saw it was requisite to prepare for another campaign, and without any previous warning whatever, we received, about twelve at night, an order to march, which we did at daylight [21 May, 1813], and marched nineteen successive days without one halt.

I commenced this campaign under very unfortunate circumstances as far as my stud was concerned. I had five capital horses, and only two fit for work. Tiny, my wife's noble little horse, had received a violent injury from the pulling down of the bullock-manger (an immensely heavy timber, with mere holes in it for the ox's muzzle), when the extreme end and sharp point fell on his off fore-hoof, and he was so lame he could hardly travel to Vittoria. This was an awful loss to my wife. General Vandeleur now and then mounted me, or I should have been badly off indeed. James Stewart gave me a celebrated English hunter called " Old Chap." He had picked up a nail in his hind foot, and was not fit to ride for months, and an English mare had thrown out a ring-bone. (I must observe that winter quarters to my stud was no holiday.)

The march from Guinaldo to Palencia and thence to Vittoria was exceedingly interesting; the weather delightful; supplies, the mainspring of happiness in a soldier's life, plentiful; and never was any army (although the Duke had so censured us after the retreat from Burgos) inspired with such confidence in their leader, and such dependence on their own prowess. All was cheerfulness, joy, and anticipation. On reaching Toro [2 June], we found the bridge over the Douro destroyed. The river was full and barely fordable for cavalry and baggage animals. The bridge was partially repaired, some boats collected, and by boats our artillery, baggage, and material crossed, some of the infantry in boats, some scrambling over the bridge. The Douro, a magnificent and deep flowing river, was much up for the time of year. The passage was a most animating spectacle; it would have been a difficulty to an inexperienced army. With us, we were ordered to cross, and it was a matter of fun and excitement. No halt of Divisions, the river was crossed, and the day's march completed. My wife's dear Spaniard being lame, she rode a thoroughbred mare, which I gave £140 for, an elegant animal, but it no more had the sagacity of Tiny than a cur has that of a foxhound, and the day before we reached Palencia, upon a greasy bank, the mare slipped up and fell upon my poor wife and broke a small bone in her foot. This was to me an awful accident; heretofore health and happiness facilitated all; now, but for her natural vivacity and devotion, such was the pain, she must have remained at Palencia, and we must have separated. The bare idea aroused all her energy, and she said, " Get me a mule or an ass, and put a Spanish saddle for a lady on it ; my feet will rest upon the foot-board, and go I will ! " Dozens of officers were in immediate requisition, some trying mules to find a very easy one, others running from shop to shop to get a good easy and well-cushioned saddle. There was no difficulty. The word " stay behind " was the talisman to move pain, and the mule was put in progress next morning with that success determination ever ensures, for " Where there's a will, there's a way."

The whole of the Duke's army passed this day through the narrow main street of rather a pretty city, Palencia [7 June]. From a little after daylight, until past six in the evening, there was a continued stream of men—cavalry, artillery, infantry, and baggage, without a moment's interruption the whole day. To view this torrent of life was a sight which made an indelible impression upon a beholder.

But to my wounded wife. At the end of the march, the Brigade head-quarters went, as usual, into the village near the bivouac. Oh, the ceremony of her dismounting, the quantity of officers' cloaks spread for her reception ; the "Take care! Now I'll carry the leg," of the kind-hearted doctor ! Talk of Indian attention ! Here were a set of fellows ready to lay down their lives even to alleviate momentary pain.

As we approached Burgos, the scene of previous failure, we Light, 3rd, and 4th Divisions expected the reluctant honour of besieging it, and so flushed with hope were we to meet the enemy in an open field and not behind bastions, curtains, embrasures, and defences, we fairly wished Burgos at the devil.

The day we were moving upon it [13 June] (the Duke knew it would not be defended), to our delight, one, two, three, four terrific explosions took place, and well did we know the enemy had blown Burgos to where we wished it. The universal joy was most manifest, for, if we had besieged it, former failure would have excited these crack Divisions to get into it with the determination they had ever previously evinced, but the blowing it up happily got us out of the difficulty to our hearts' content.*

My wife's foot gradually improved, and in a few days she was on her horse again, and *en route* in the column ; for the soldiers, although generally averse to be interfered with by horses on the line of march, were ever delighted to get her to ride with their Company. Seeing her again on her horse was a great relief to my mind, for, in her peculiar and isolated position, the bare surmise of our separation was horrid, and, if I must have left her behind, the fact of a true Catholic allying herself to a heretic would, among bigoted inhabitants, have secured her anything but tender attention.

* *Vide* Duke's letter, Nov. 23, 1812, to Lord Liverpool, in his Grace's letter to Marshal Beresford, Oct. 31, " You see what a scrape we have been in, and how well we have got out of it."—H.G.S.

Our Division at San Millan, near Vittoria [18 June], intercepted the route of one of the French Columns as it was retiring into their position at Vittoria, and had as brilliant a fight entirely of our own as any one throughout the campaign. Some of the 1st Hussars also had a severe brush. Our Division halted the next day [20th], but the army never did, from the day of breaking up its cantonments until they fought the battle of Vittoria. It was a most wonderful march, the army in great fighting order, and every man in better wind than a trained pugilist.

At the Battle of Vittoria [21 June] my Brigade, in the middle of the action, was sent to support the 7th Division, which was very hotly engaged. I was sent forward to report myself to Lord Dalhousie, who commanded. I found his lordship and his Q.M.G., Drake, an old Rifle comrade, in deep conversation. I reported pretty quick, and asked for orders (the head of my Brigade was just getting under fire). I repeated the question, "What orders, my Lord?" Drake became somewhat animated, and I heard His Lordship say, "Better to take the village," which the French held with twelve guns (I had counted by their fire), and seemed to be inclined to keep it. I roared out, "Certainly, my Lord," and off I galloped, both calling to me to come back, but, as none are so deaf as those who won't hear, I told General Vandeleur we were immediately to take the village. There was no time to lose, and the 52nd Regiment deployed into

line as if at Shorncliffe, while our Riflemen were
sent out in every direction, five or six deep, keeping
up a fire nothing could resist. I galloped to the
officer commanding a Battalion in the 7th Division
(the 82nd, I think). "Lord Dalhousie desires you
closely to follow this Brigade of the Light Division."
"Who are you, sir?" "Never mind that; disobey
my Lord's order at your peril." My Brigade, the
52nd in line and the swarms of Riflemen, rushed
at the village, and although the ground was intersected in its front by gardens and ditches, nothing
ever checked us until we reached the rear of the
village, where we halted to reform—the twelve
guns, tumbrils, horses, etc., standing in our possession. There never was a more impetuous onset—
nothing could withstand such a burst of determination. Before we were ready to pursue the enemy
—for we Light Division ever reformed and got
into order before a second attack, thanks to poor
General Bob Craufurd's most excellent tuition —
up came Lord Dalhousie with his Q.M.G., Drake,
to old Vandeleur, exclaiming, "Most brilliantly
achieved indeed! Where is the officer you sent
to me for orders?" "Here I am, my lord." Old
Drake knew well enough. "Upon my word, sir,
you receive and carry orders quicker than any
officer I ever saw." "You said, 'Take the village.'
My lord, there it is," I said, "guns and all." He
smiled, and old Drake burst into one of his grins,
"Well done, Harry."

We were hotly engaged all the afternoon

pursuing the French over very broad ditches. Until we neared Vittoria to our left, there was a plain free from ditches. The confusion of baggage, etc., was indescribable. Our Brigade was moving rapidly on, when such a swarm of French Cavalry rushed out from among the baggage into our skirmishers, opposite a company of the 2nd Battalion Rifle Brigade, commanded by Lieutenant Tom Cochrane, we thought they must have been swept off. Fortunately for Tom, a little rough ground and a bank enabled him to command his Company to lie down, and such a reception they gave the horsemen, while some of our Company were flying to their support, that the French fled with a severe loss. Our Riflemen were beautiful shots, and as undaunted as bulldogs. We knew so well, too, how to support each other, that scarcely had the French Dragoons shown themselves when Cochrane's rear was supported, and we had such mutual confidence in this support that we never calculated on disaster, but assumed the boldest front and bearing.

A rather curious circumstance occurred to me after the first heights and the key of the enemy's central position was carried. I was standing with Ross's Brigade of guns sharply engaged, when my horse fell as if stone dead. I jumped off, and began to look for the wound. I could see none, and gave the poor animal a kick on the nose. He immediately shook his head, and as instantly jumped on his legs, and I on his back. The artillerymen all said it was the current of air, or, as they call it,

the wind, of one of the enemy's cannon-shot.   On
the attack on the village previously described,
Lieutenant Northey (52nd Regiment) was not
knocked off as I was, but he was knocked down
by the wind of a shot, and his face as black as if he
had been two hours in a pugilistic ring.

The fall of my horse had been observed by
some of our soldiers as they were skirmishing
forward, and a report soon prevailed that I was
killed, which, in the course of the afternoon, was
communicated to my poor wife, who followed close
to the rear on the very field of battle, crossing the
plain covered with treasure.   Her old groom, West,
proposed to carry off some on a led horse.   She
said, " Oh, West, never mind money.   Let us look
for your master."   She had followed the 1st Brigade
men, the 2nd having been detached, unobserved by
her, to aid the 7th Division.   After the battle, at
dusk, my Brigade was ordered to join the 1st
Brigade, with General Alten's head-quarters.   I
had lost my voice from the exertion of cheering
with our men (not cheering them *on*, for they
required no such example), and as I approached
the 1st Brigade, to take up the ground for mine,
I heard my wife's lamentations.   I immediately
galloped up to her, and spoke to her as well as
I could, considering the loss of my voice.   " Oh,
then, thank God, you are not killed, only badly
wounded."   " Thank   God," I   growled, " I   am
neither," but, in her ecstasy of joy, this was not
believed for a long while.

After putting up my Brigade (we required no picquets, the Cavalry were far in our front in pursuit of the flying enemy) we, that is, my General and Staff, repaired to a barn, where we got in our horses and some forage, and lay down among them. It was dark ; we had no lights, and sleep after such a day was as refreshing as eating, even if we had any means. At daybreak our luggage had arrived, and we were busy preparing some breakfast. Hardly did the kettle boil when " Fall in !" was the word. Just as we were jumping on our horses, my young wife, her ears being rather quick, said, " I am sure I hear some one moaning, like a wounded man." We looked round, and I saw there was a loft for hay over our barn. I immediately scrambled up with assistance, for the ladder, like Robinson Crusoe's, had been hauled up. When I reached the landing-place, such a scene met my eye ! Upwards of twenty French officers, all more or less severely wounded, one poor fellow in the agony of death, and a lady, whom I recognized as Spanish, grieving over him. At first the poor fellows funked. I soon assured them of every safety and protection, and put my wife and the poor Spanish lady, her countrywoman, in communication. All we could spare, or, rather, all our breakfast, was given to the wounded, for march we must. The General sent his A.D.C. for a guard ; we did all we could at the moment, and the poor fellows were grateful indeed. The Spanish lady had a most beautiful little pug dog, a thoroughbred one, with a very extraordinary collar of bells about its neck. She insisted upon my wife's accepting the dog as a token of gratitude for our kindness. The little animal was accepted immediately, and named "Vittoria"; we jumped on our horses, and parted for ever, gratified, however, at having had it in our power to render this slight assistance to the poor fellows wounded and in distress. The dog became afterwards a celebrated animal in the Division, universally known and caressed, and the heroine of many a little anecdote, and hereafter at Waterloo must claim half a page to itself. It was the most sensible little brute Nature ever produced, and it and Tiny became most attached friends.

On this day's march our soldiers could scarcely move—men, in such wind and health as they were —but the fact is they had got some flocks of the enemy's sheep, and fallen in with a lot of flour; they had eaten till they were gorged like vultures, and every man's haversack was laden with flour and raw meat, all of which, except a day or two's supply, the Generals of Brigade were obliged to order to be thrown away. We were soon, however, close on the heels of the enemy, and the first shot revived the power to march. The retreat of the enemy was marked by every excess and atrocity and villages burning in every direction. Oh, my countrymen of England, if you had seen the twentieth part of the horrors of war I have, readily would you pay the war-taxes, and grumble less at the pinching saddle of National Debt! The seat of war is hell upon earth, even when stripped of the atrocities committed in Spain and Portugal, and everywhere else, I believe, except dear old England, by the French Army.

We Light Division had the pleasure, ere we reached Pamplona, to take the enemy's only remaining gun.*

* Cope, p. 141.

CHAPTER XII.

CAMPAIGN OF 1813: ADVANCE TO VERA.

THE night before we reached Pamplona [24 June], the enemy, rather unexpectedly to us, drove in the picquets of my Brigade in a very sharp skirmish, although we were as ever prepared, and the Division got under arms. This convinced us that the whole army, except the garrison at Pamplona, was in full retreat into France. It is a peculiar custom of the French unexpectedly to put back your picquets when they are about to retire; that is, when the ground admits no obstacle of bridge, river, or village, intervening. The object of such forward moves I have never heard satisfactorily given.

On this evening a stout French gentleman came in to our advanced post, saying he wanted to see the Duke. I took him to General Vandeleur. He dined with us, and a most jawing, facetious fellow he was. At first we regarded him as a spy, which he afterwards told General Vandeleur he was, and in the employ of the Duke. He could not proceed that night, for we did not know in the least where head-quarters were, and the night was excessively dark; so the French gentleman, whom I wished at the devil, was given in charge to *me*. If he had had any inclination to escape I defied him, for I put some of our old vigilant Riflemen around him, so that not a man could get in or out of the room I had put him in. We afterwards heard my friend was a man of great use to the Duke, and one of King Joseph's household.

The next day [25 June] we Light Division passed Pamplona, leaving it by a very intricate road to our right, and were cantoned in the village of Offala. It was necessary to keep a look-out towards Pamplona, and my General, Vandeleur, and I, rode to look where to post our picquets. I had a most athletic and active fellow with me as a guide, very talkative, and full of the battle of Vittoria. He asked me what was the name of the General before us. I said, "General Vandeleur." I heard him muttering it over to himself several times. He then ran up to the General, and entered into conversation. The General soon called me to him, for he could not speak a word [of Spanish]. "What's the fellow say?" "He is telling all he heard from the Frenchmen who were billeted in his house in the retreat. He is full of anecdote." He then looked most expressively in Vandeleur's face, and says, "Yes, they say the English fought well, but had it not been for one General *Bandelo*, the French would have gained the day." "How the devil did this fellow know?" says Vandeleur. I never undeceived the General, and he fancies to this day his Brigade's being sent to assist the 7th Division was the cause of the Frenchmen's remark. My guide, just like a "cute" Irishman or American, gave me a knowing wink.

This very fellow turned out to be owner of the house my wife and baggage and I got into—the General's Aide-de-camp, as was often the case, having shown her into one near the General. After I had dressed myself, he came to me and said, "When you dine, I have some capital wine, as much as you and your servants like; but," he says, "come down and look at my cellar." The fellow had been so civil, I did not like to refuse him. We descended by a stone staircase, he carrying a light. He had upon his countenance a most sinister expression. I saw something exceedingly excited him : his look became fiend-like. He and I were alone, but such confidence had we Englishmen in a Spaniard, and with the best reason, that I apprehended no personal evil. Still his appearance was very singular. When we got to the cellar-door, he opened it, and held the light so as to show the cellar; when, in a voice of thunder, and with an expression of demoniacal hatred and antipathy, pointing to the floor, he exclaimed, "There lie four of the devils who thought to subjugate Spain! I am a Navarrese. I was born free from all foreign invasion, and this right hand shall plunge this stiletto in my own heart as it did into theirs, ere I and my countrymen are subjugated!" brandishing his weapon like a demon. I see the excited patriot as I write. Horror-struck as I was, the instinct of self-preservation induced me to admire the deed exceedingly, while my very frame quivered and my blood was frozen, to see the noble science of war and the honour and chivalry of arms reduced to the practices of midnight assassins. Upon the expression of my admiration, he cooled, and while he was deliberately drawing wine for my dinner, which, however strange it may be, I drank with the gusto its flavour merited, I examined the four bodies. They were Dragoons—four athletic, healthy-looking fellows. As we ascended, he had perfectly recovered the equilibrium of his vivacity and naturally good humour. I asked him how he, single-handed, had perpetrated this deed on four armed men (for their swords were by their sides). " Oh, easily enough. I pretended to love a Frenchman " (or, in his words, ' I was an Afrancesado '), " and I proposed, after giving them a good dinner, we should drink to the extermination of the English." He then looked at me and ground his teeth. " The French rascals, they little guessed what I contemplated. Well, we got into the cellar, and drank away until I made them so drunk, they fell, and my purpose was easily, and as joyfully, effected." He again brandished his dagger, and said, " Thus die all enemies to Spain." Their horses were in his stable. When the French Regiment marched off, he gave these to some guerrillas in the neighbourhood. It is not difficult to reconcile with truth the assertion of the historian, who puts down the loss of the French army, during the Spanish war, as 400,000 men, for more men fell in this midnight manner than by the broad-day sword, or the pestilence of climate, which in Spain, in the autumn, is excessive.

The next day we marched a short distance to a beautiful village, or town, rather,—Villalba, where we halted a day, and expected to remain three or four.   It was on a Sunday afternoon, and some of the recollection of the Sunday of our youth was passing across the mind of the lover of his family and his country—the very pew at church, the old peasants in the aisle ; the friendly neighbours' happy faces ; the father, mother, brothers, sisters ; the joys, in short, of home, for, amidst the eventful scenes of such a life, recollection will bring the past in view, and compare the blessings of peace with the horror, oh! the cruel horror, of war!   In the midst of this mental soliloquy, my dear wife exclaims, "Mi Enrique, how thoughtful you look!" I dare not tell her that my thoughts reverted to my home. Hers being a desolate waste, the subject was ever prohibited, for her vivacious mind, and her years of juvenile excitement, could never control an excess of grief if the words, "your home," ever escaped my lips.

My reverie was soon aroused by the entrance of a soldier, without ceremony—for every one was ever welcome.   "Sir, is the order come?"   "For what?" I said.   "An extra allowance of wine?" "No," he said, "for an extra allowance of marching. We are to be off directly after these French chaps, as expects to get to France without a kick from the

Light Division." I was aware he alluded to General Clausel's division that was retiring by the pass over the Pyrenees, called La Haca. It is most singular, but equally true, that our soldiers knew every move in contemplation long before any officer. While we were in conversation, in came the order; away went all thoughts of home, and a momentary regret on quitting so nice a quarter was banished in the excitement of the march.

In twenty minutes our Division was in full march to try and intercept Clausel's Division. That night we marched most rapidly to Tafalla, next day to Olite, thence brought up our right shoulder towards Sanguessa. This was a night-march of no ordinary character to all, particularly to me and my wife. Her Spanish horse, Tiny, was so far recovered from his lameness that she insisted on riding him. On a night-march we knew the road to be difficult. In crossing the Arragon [30 June], although the bridge was excellent, on this march by some singular accident (it was very dark and raining) an interval occurred in our column — a thing unprecedented, so particular were we, *thanks to Craufurd's instructions*—and the majority of the Division, in place of crossing the bridge, passed the turn and went on a league out of the direction. My Brigade was leading. Two Battalions came all right, and I stayed more at the head of the column than was my wont, to watch the guides. So dark and intricate was the road we were moving on, I proposed to the General to form up, and see that our troops were all right. After the two first Battalions formed, I waited a short time in expectation of the next, the 2nd Battalion of the Rifle Brigade. I hallooed, seeing no column, when a voice a long way off answered. It was that of the most extraordinary character, the eccentric Colonel Wade. I galloped up, and said, "Colonel, form up your Battalion, so soon as you reach the Brigade." " By Jesus," he said, "we are soon formed ; I and my bugler are alone." I, naturally somewhat excited, asked, " Where's the Regiment ? " "Upon my soul, and that's what I would like to ask you." I then saw some mistake must have happened. I galloped back in the dark to the bridge, saw no column whatever, but heard voices far beyond the bridge. The column, after passing it in the dark, had discovered the error and were coming back. Meanwhile, my wife heard me hallooing and came towards me. I had dismounted, and was leading my horse a little way off the road up the left bank of the Arragon ; the rain was falling in torrents, the bank of the river gave way under me, and a flash of lightning at the moment showed me I was falling into the bed of the river about thirty feet below. I had firmly hold of my bridle — the avalanche frightened my noble horse (the celebrated " Old Chap," the hunter that James Stewart gave me); he flew round and dragged me from inevitable perdition. My wife and old West were close behind at the moment, and she witnessed the whole, equally to her horror and satisfaction. Then such a tale of

woe from herself. The uneven ground at night
had so lamed her dear little horse, Tiny, that he
could not carry her. She got off in the rain and
dark, herself still excessively lame from the broken
bone in the foot, and literally crawled along, until
the rocky road improved, and West again put her
upon her faithful Tiny. I could devote neither
time nor attention to her. Day was just beginning
to break. I directed her to the bivouac, and most
energetically sought to collect my Brigade, which,
with the daylight, I soon effected. When I got
back, I found my wife sitting, holding her umbrella
over General Vandeleur (who was suffering dreadfully from rheumatism in the shoulder in which he
had been wounded at the storm of Ciudad Rodrigo),
recounting to him her night's adventures and laughing heartily. The weather totally precluded any
possibility of our molesting Clausel, and we were
ordered to march to Sanguessa, which we did the
following day, and Charlie Gore, General Kempt's
A.D.C., gave a ball [1 July], where there was as
much happiness as if we were at Almack's, and
some as handsome women, the loves of girls of
Sanguessa.

That night's march was the most extraordinary
thing which ever occurred to our organized Light
Division. We all blamed each other, but the fact
is, the turn of the road to the bridge was abrupt,
the night dark, the road so narrow that staff-officers
could not ride up and down the flank of the column ;
it may be regarded as "an untoward event." From

Sanguessa we made rather long marches for the Valle of San Estevan, through a most beautiful country covered in a great measure with immense chestnut trees. After we had halted a day or two [7–14 July] in this valley, of which the beauty is not to be conceived, we marched on towards Vera by a road along the banks of the river Bidassoa. At Vera, the enemy had fortified a large house very strongly, and their picquets were upon its line. On our advance, we put back the enemy's picquets, but not without a sharp skirmish, and we held the house that afternoon.

In front of the mountain of Santa Barbara was a very steep hill, which the enemy held in force, but a dense fog of the mountains prevented us seeing each other. Colonel Barnard, with the 1st Battalion Rifle Brigade, was sent to dislodge them [15 July]. They proved to be three or four times his numbers. His attack, however, was supported, and as he himself describes it, "I hallooed the fellows off in the fog." We had a good many men and officers, however, severely wounded. The next day, or in the night, the enemy abandoned the fortified house of the large village of Vera in their front, retired behind the village, and firmly established themselves on the heights, while we occupied Vera with some sick officers, our picquets being posted beyond. The enemy's vedettes and ours for many days were within talking distance, yet we never had an alert by night or by day.

CHAPTER XIII.

CAMPAIGN OF 1813: IN THE PYRENEES—GENERAL
SKERRETT—COMBAT OF VERA—FIGHT AT THE
BRIDGE, AND DEATH OF CADOUX.

JUST before we reached Vera, my dear friend
and General, Vandeleur, was moved to a Cavalry
Brigade, and General Skerrett, a very different
man, was sent to us, with a capital fellow for an
A.D.C.—Captain Fane, or, as usually designated,
"Ugly Tom." I, who had been accustomed to go
in and out of my previous Generals' tents and
quarters as my own, and either breakfast or dine as
I liked, was perfectly thunderstruck when it was
intimated to me I was to go only when asked ; so
Tom the A.D.C. and we lived together, to the
great amusement of my wife, who was always play-
ing Tom some trick or other.

During our halt in this position, the siege of
San Sebastian was going on. Soult, an able officer,
who had been appointed to the command of the
beaten French force, soon reorganized it, and in-
stilled its old pride of victory, and inspired all again
with the ardour and vivacity of French soldiers.
The siege of San Sebastian was vigorously

prosecuted. Pamplona was closely invested, and, from want of provisions, must inevitably ere long surrender.   Soult, therefore, had a brilliant opportunity either to raise the siege of San Sebastian, or to throw supplies in to Pamplona, or to do both, if great success attended his operations.   This opportunity he ably availed himself of, by making a rapid movement to our right to the Pass of Roncesvalles of knightly fame, and obliging the Duke of Wellington to concentrate a great part of his army to protect Pamplona, or, rather, to ensure its strict blockade, while the siege of San Sebastian was for the time suspended, awaiting supplies which were on their passage from England.   My Division, the Light, was kept between the two, as were Lord Dacre's "horsemen light," to "succour those that need it most," * and we had some very harassing marches, when it was discovered Soult had penetrated the Pyrenees and was resolved on a general action.   This he fought on the 27th and 28th July, with the Frenchman's usual success, a good thrashing.†

The Light Division made a terrible night march on this occasion, one of the most fatiguing to the soldiers that I ever witnessed.   On the Pyrenees, as on other mountains, the darkness is indescribable.   We were on a narrow mountain path,

---

* " Lord Dacre, with his horsemen light,
  Shall be in rearward of the fight,
  And succour those that need it most."
                              Marmion, VI. xxiv.

† At the battles of the Pyrenees.

frequently with room only for one or two men, when a soldier of the Rifle Brigade rolled down a hill as nearly perpendicular as may be. We heard him bumping along, pack, rifle, weight of ammunition, etc., when from the bottom he sang out, "Halloa there! Tell the Captain there's not a bit of me alive at all; but the devil a bone have I broken; and faith I'm thinking no soldier ever came to his ground at such a rate before. Have a care, boys, you don't follow. The breach at Badajos was nothing to the bottomless pit I'm now in."

After the battles of the Pyrenees, our Division was pushed forward with great rapidity to intercept the retreat of one of the *corps d'armée*, and General Kempt's—the 1st—Brigade had some very heavy fighting [at Jansi, 1 Aug.]; while at [Echallar], poor General Barnes, now no more, in command of a Brigade of the 7th Division, made one of the boldest and most successful attacks on five times his number, but one in which bravery and success far exceeded judgment or utility.

We moved on again, and on one of our marches came to some very nice cottages, one of which fell to the lot of myself and Tom Fane, the A.D.C. The poor peasant was a kind-hearted farmer of the mountains, his fields highly cultivated, his farm-yard supplied with poultry; every domestic comfort his situation in life demanded was his—poor fellow, he merited all. He killed some ducks for our supper, his garden supplied beautiful peas, and we had a supper royalty would have envied with our appetites. My wife had spread her cloak on the floor—she was perfectly exhausted—and was fast asleep. I awoke her, she ate a capital supper, but the next morning upbraided me and Tom Fane for not having given her anything to eat; and to this day she is unconscious of sitting at our supper-table. Judge by this anecdote what real fatigue is. The next morning we could hardly induce our host to receive payment for his eggs, his poultry, his bread, bacon, peas, milk, etc., and he would insist on giving my wife a beautiful goat in full milk, which was added to the boy Antonio's herd.* We marched with mutual feelings of newly-acquired but real friendship. Three days afterwards, we returned to the very same ground, and we again occupied our previous dear little mountain retreat, but the accursed hand of war had stamped devastation upon it. The beautiful fields of Indian corn were all reaped as forage, the poultry yard was void, the produce of our peasant's garden exhausted, his flour all consumed—in a word, he had nothing left of all his previous plenty but a few milch goats, and that night he, poor thing, supped with us from the resources of our rations and biscuit. He said the French had swept off everything the English did not require. The latter paid for everything, and gave him *bons* or receipts for the Indian corn reaped as forage, which he knew some day or commissary would take up and pay. I never pitied man more, and in the midst of his affliction it w

* See pp. 129, 130.

beautiful to observe a pious resignation and a love for his country, when he exclaimed, " Gracias a Dios, you have driven back the villainous French to their own country."

> " O fortunatos nimium, sua si bona norint,
> Agricolas . . . procul discordibus armis."

We returned to our line on this side of Vera, and the siege of San Sebastian was again vigorously resumed. We Light Division, with the 3rd and 4th, were out of that glory, which we did not regret, although the Duke never took the town until he sent to these three Divisions for volunteers for the storming party [31 Aug.]. Then we soon took it; but in candour I should state that the breaches were rendered more practicable than when first stormed, the defences destroyed, and the enemy's means of defence diminished. It was, however, still a tough piece of work, in which we lost some valuable officers and soldiers. The enemy made a forward movement [the same day, 31 Aug.] for the purpose of reinforcing the garrison, and in the morning put back our picquets, and we anticipated a general action. However, the whole of the enemy moved to the Lower Bidassoa, and crossed in force. The day was very rainy, and the river was so full the French were compelled to retreat rapidly; in fact, so sudden was the rise of the river, many were obliged to retire by the bridge in our possession, as described by Napier.

I have only, therefore, to relate an incident

which occurred between me and my new General—
who, I soon discovered, was by nature a gallant
Grenadier, and no Light Troop officer, which requires
the eye of a hawk and the power of anticipating the
enemy's intention—who was always to be found off
his horse, standing in the most exposed spot under
the enemy's fire while our Riflemen were well concealed, as stupidly composed for himself as inactive
for the welfare of his command.*   When the enemy
put back our picquets in the morning, it was evidently
their intention to possess themselves of the bridge,
which was curiously placed as regarded our line of
picquets.   Thus—

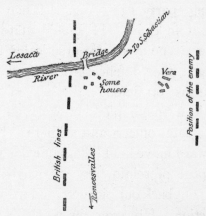

* Sir R. D. Henegan writes thus of Col. Skerrett, in describing the
defence of Tarifa: "The commanding-officer of this expedition,
although unimpeachable in the courageous bearing of a soldier, was
wanting in the bold decision which, in military practice, must often
take the lead of science and established rules."—Henegan's *Seven
Years' Campaigning* (1846), vol. i. p. 234. Colonel T. Bunbury,
Reminiscences of a Veteran, i. p. 116, gives a similar account:
"Skerrett as an individual was brave to rashness; but I should have
doubted it had I not so frequently witnessed proofs of his cool
intrepidity and contempt of danger. At the head of troops, he was
the most undecided, timid, and vacillating creature I ever met with."

We did not occupy Vera, but withdrew on our own side of it, and I saw the enemy preparing to carry the houses near the bridge in the occupation of the 2nd Battalion Rifle Brigade. I said, "General Skerrett, unless we send down the 52nd Regiment in support, the enemy will drive back the Riflemen. They cannot hold those houses against the numbers prepared to attack. Our men will fight like devils expecting to be supported, and their loss, when driven out, will be very severe." He laughed (we were standing under a heavy fire exposed) and said, "Oh, is that your opinion?" I said—most impertinently, I admit,—"And it will be yours in five minutes," for I was by no means prepared to see the faith in support, which so many fights had established, destroyed, and our gallant fellows knocked over by a stupidity heretofore not exemplified. We had scarcely time to discuss the matter when down came a thundering French column with swarms of sharpshooters, and, as I predicted, drove our people out of the houses with one fell swoop, while my General would move nothing on their flank or rear to aid them. We lost many men and some officers, and the enemy possessed the houses, and consequently, for the moment, possessed the passage of the bridge. From its situation, however, it was impossible they could maintain it, unless they put us farther back by a renewed attack on our elevated position. So I said, "You see now what you have permitted, General, and we must retake these houses, which we ought never to have lost." He quietly said, "I believe you are right." I could stand this no longer, and I galloped up to Colonel Colborne, in command of that beautiful 52nd Regiment, now Lord Seaton, who was as angry as he soon saw I was. "Oh, sir, it is melancholy to see this. General Skerrett will do nothing; we must retake those houses. I told him what would happen." "I am glad of it, for I was angry with you." In two seconds we retook the houses, for the enemy, seeing our determination to hold them, was aware the nature of the ground would not enable him to do so unless he occupied the position we intended to defend, and his effort was as much as not to see whether we were in earnest, or whether, when attacked in force, we should retire. The houses were retaken, as I said, and the firing ceased the whole afternoon.

The evening came on very wet. We knew that the enemy had crossed the Bidassoa [31 Aug.], and that his retreat would be impossible from the swollen state of the river. We knew pretty well the Duke would shove him into the river if he could; this very bridge, therefore, was of the utmost import-ance, and no exertion should have been spared on our part so to occupy it after dark as to prevent the passage being seized. The rain was falling in torrents. I proposed that the whole of the 2nd Battalion Rifle Brigade should be posted in the houses, the bridge should be barricaded, and the 52nd Regiment should be close at hand in support.

Skerrett positively laughed outright, ordered the whole Battalion into our position, but said, "You may leave a picquet of one officer and thirty men at the bridge." He was in the house on the heights he had previously occupied. I had a little memo-randum-book in my pocket; I took it out for the first time in my life to note my General's orders. I read what he said, asking if that was his order. He said, "Yes, I have already told you so." I said most *wickedly*, "We shall repent this before day-light." He was callous to anything. I galloped down to the houses, ordered the Battalion to retire, and told my brother Tom, the Adjutant, to call to me a picquet of an officer and thirty men for the bridge. Every officer and soldier thought I was mad. Tom said, "Cadoux's company is for picquet." Up rode poor Cadoux, a noble soldier, who could scarcely believe what I said, but began to abuse me for not supporting them in the morning. I said, "Scold away, all true; but no fault of *mine*. But come, no time for jaw, the picquet!" Cadoux, noble fellow, says, "My company is so reduced this morning, I will stay with it if I may. There are about fifty men." I gladly consented, for I had great faith in Cadoux's ability and watchfulness, and I told him he might rest assured he would be attacked an hour or two before daylight. He said, "Most certainly I shall, and I will now strengthen myself, and block up the bridge as well as I can, and I will, if possible, hold the bridge until supported; so, when the attack commences, instantly send the whole

Battalion to me, and, please God, I will keep the bridge." It was then dark, and I rode as fast as I could to tell Colborne, in whom we had all complete faith and confidence. He was astonished, and read my memorandum. We agreed that, so soon as the attack commenced, his Battalion should move down the heights on the flank of the 2nd Battalion Rifle Brigade, which would rush to support Cadoux, and thus we parted, I as sulky as my hot nature would admit, knowing some disaster would befall my dear old Brigade heretofore so judiciously handled.

In the course of the night, as we were lying before the fire, I *far from asleep,* General Skerrett received a communication from General Alten to the purport "that the enemy were retiring over the swollen river; it was, therefore, to be apprehended he would before daylight endeavour to possess himself of the bridge; that every precaution must be taken to prevent him." I, now being reinforced in opinion, said, "Now, General, let me do so." As he was still as obstinate as ever, we were discussing the matter (I fear as far as I am concerned, very hotly) when the "En avant, en avant! L'Empereur récompensera le premier qu'avancera," was screeched into our very ears, and Cadoux's fire was hot as ever fifty men's was on earth. "Now," says I, "General, who is right?" *I* knew what the troops would do. My only hope was that Cadoux could keep the bridge as he anticipated. The fire of the enemy was very severe, and

the rushes of his columns most determined; still Cadoux's fire was from his post. Three successive times, with half his gallant band, did he charge and drive back the enemy over the bridge, the other half remaining in the houses as support. His hope and confidence in support and the importance of his position sustained him until a melancholy shot pierced his head, and he fell lifeless from his horse.*
A more gallant soul never left its mortal abode. His company at this critical moment were driven back; the French column and rear-guard crossed, and, by keeping near the bed of the river, succeeded in escaping, although the Riflemen were in support of poor Cadoux with as much rapidity as *distance* allowed, and daylight saw Colborne where he said he would be.

I was soon at the bridge. Such a scene of mortal strife from the fire of fifty men was never witnessed. The bridge was almost choked with

---

* Cope's account of Cadoux's death (pp. 149, 150), derived, he tells us, from Colonel Thomas Smith, is rather different. According to this, Skerrett sent to desire Cadoux to evacuate his post. Cadoux refused, saying that he could hold it. At 2 a.m. the French made a rush, but Cadoux, by his fire from the bridge-house, kept the head of the advancing column in check. Skerrett now peremptorily ordered Cadoux to leave the bridge-house. Cadoux could only comply, but remarked that " but few of his party would reach the camp." And as a matter of fact every officer present was either killed or wounded (Cadoux being killed), besides 11 sergeants and 48 rank and file out of a total strength of 100 men. Until the party left the bridge-house, Cadoux had not lost a man except the double sentries on the bridge, who were killed in the rush made by the French. Accordingly, while Harry Smith in the text blames Skerrett for leaving Cadoux in an almost impossible position without support, Thomas Smith's charge against Skerrett is that he recalled Cadoux when he was well able to hold his own.

the dead; the enemy's loss was enormous, and
many of his men were drowned, and all his
guns were left in the river a mile or two below
the bridge. The number of dead was so great,
the bodies were thrown into the rapid stream in
the hope that the current would carry them, but
many rocks impeded them, and when the river
subsided, we had great cause to lament our pre-
cipitancy in hurling the bodies, for the stench
soon after was awful. The Duke was awfully
annoyed, as well he might be, but, as was his
rule, never said anything when disaster could not be
amended. I have never told my tale till now.
Skerrett was a bilious fellow (a gallant Grenadier, I
must readily avow), and I hope his annoyance so
affected his liver it precipitated a step he had
desired—as his father was just dead, and he was heir
to an immense property—to retire home on sick-
leave. You may rely on it, I threw no impediment
in his way, for when he was gone, Colonel Colborne
was my Brigadier, whom we all regarded inferior to
no one but the Duke. Many is the conversation he
and I have had over the lamentable affair which
killed poor Cadoux. I really believe, had he survived, he would have held the bridge, although the
enemy attacked it in desperation, and although each
time the column was driven back, a few men in the
dark succeeded in crossing, and these fellows, all
practised soldiers, posted themselves under cover on
the banks of the river below the bridge, and caused
the loss our people sustained, that of noble Cadoux

among the rest, with impunity. Cadoux's manner
was effeminate, and, as a boy, I used to quiz him.*
He and I were, therefore, although not enemies, not
friends, until the battle of Vittoria, when I saw him
most conspicuous. He was ahead of me on his
gallant war horse, which he took at Barossa with
the holsters full of doubloons, as the story went. I
was badly mounted that day, and my horse would
not cross a brook which his was scrambling over.
I leaped from my saddle over my horse's head (I
was very active in those days), seized his horse by
the tail, and I believe few, if any, were as soon in the
middle of the Frenchmen's twelve guns as we were
in support of the 7th Division. From that day we
were comrades in every sense of the term, and I
wept over his gallant remains with a bursting heart,
as, with his Company who adored him, I consigned
to the grave the last external appearance of Daniel
Cadoux. His fame can never die.

The enemy retired into their previous position,
as did we, and San Sebastian was ours. We were
in this line for some time, daily watching the enemy
making works with extraordinary vigour and diligence, which we knew ere long we should have the
glory (the pleasure, to most of us) to run our heads

---

* In the *Recollections of Rifleman Harris* (1848), we have an
account of Cadoux which tallies closely with that of the text: "I remember there was an officer named, I think, Cardo, with the Rifles. He was
a great beau ; but although rather effeminate and ladylike in manners,
so much so as to be remarked by the whole Regiment at that time,
yet he was found to be a most gallant officer when we were engaged
with the enemy in the field. He was killed whilst fighting bravely in
the Pyrenees, and amongst other jewellery he wore, he had a ring on
his finger worth one hundred and fifty guineas."

against, for such was the ardour and confidence of
our army at this moment, that, if Lord Wellington
had told us to attempt to carry the moon, we should
have done it.

During the occupation of our present position, I
found the Basque inhabitants on the Spanish side,
and those on the French side of the Pyrenees,
carried on a sort of contraband trade, and that
brandy and claret were to be had.   One day, therefore, upon General Skerrett's complaining to me he
could get no wine or sheep, I told him I could get
him both.   My smugglers were immediately in
requisition.   They got me eight sheep and one
dozen of claret.   I was disappointed at the small
supply—accustomed to hospitable old Vandeleur's
consumption—and I told my new General. He said
he was exceedingly obliged to me ; he should be glad
of one sheep and two bottles of wine.   It did not
make a bad story through the Brigade.   I and
the A.D.C., Tom Fane, however, managed to con-
sume all.

One day (the man may now be conceived)
Skerrett gave a great dinner, and the *liberal* Barnard and Colborne, commanding Regiments in the
Division, were asked to dine.   Tom Fane and I
were amused, for we knew he had but little to give
them to eat and less to drink, and where were the
materials to come from ?   And Barnard loved a
good dinner, with at least two bottles of good wine.
To my astonishment, when I waited on him, as
I usually did every morning, for orders, he was

dressed. I said, "Where are you going, General?" (To me he was ever a most affable, and rather an amusing, fellow.) He said, "To head-quarters at Lesaca." So Tom and I supposed he would come back laden with supplies. (At head-quarters there was an excellent sutler, but the prices were, of course, beyond any moderate means.) So Tom, A.D.C., was on the look-out for his return. He soon arrived with a bottle of sherry in each pocket of his military blue coat, viz. two, and says, "Fane, tell Smith, as my wine stock is not large, to be cautious of it." Tom did tell me, and, when we met in the dining-room, the joke was too good not to tell such noble and liberal fellows as Barnard and Colborne. Down we sat to, oh! such a dinner; our soldiers in camp lived far better. So Barnard says, "Being so near the French, we shall have plenty of cooks in camp soon; come, Smith, a glass of wine," and I think we drank the pocket two bottles in about as many minutes; when Barnard, as *funny a fellow* and as *noble a soldier* as ever lived, says, "Now, General, some more of this wine. We camp fellows do not get such a treat every day." Barnard had a French cook, taken at the battle of Salamanca, and lived like a gentleman. "Barnard," Skerrett says, looking like a fiend at me, "that is the last, I very much regret to say, of an old stock" (Barnard winked at me); "what I must now give you, I fear, won't be so good." It was produced; it was trash of some sort, but not wine. "No," says Barnard, "that won't do, but let us have some brandy." We

got some execrable coffee, and here ended the only
feast he ever gave while in command of my Brigade.
Poor Skerrett, he soon inherited £7000 a year, not
long to enjoy it.   He was killed in the most brilliant,
and at the same time the most unfortunate, affair
that ever decorated and tarnished British laurels, at
Bergen Op Zoom.

CHAPTER XIV.

CAMPAIGN OF 1813: COLONEL COLBORNE—SECOND
COMBAT OF VERA.

IN our Division, generally speaking, the officers
of each Company had a little mess of their own, an
arrangement indispensable, so much detached were
we on picquets, etc. Some of us lived most comfortably, and great interchange of hospitality existed.
We all had goats, and every mess had a boy, who
was in charge of them on the march and in quarters,
and milked them. On the march the flock of each
Regiment and Brigade assembled and moved with
their goat-herds, when each drove his master's goats
to his quarters. We observed extraordinary regularity with these goats, and upon inquiry we found
out the little fellows organized themselves into
regular guards. They had a captain, quite a little
fellow of dear old Billy Mein's (52nd Regiment);
their time of duty was as regular as our soldiers';
they had sentries with long white sticks in their
hands, and Mein's little boy held a sort of court-
martial, and would lick a boy awfully who neglected
his charge. My little boy's name was Antonio, and
when he was for guard, I have seen him turn out

unusually smart, with his face and hands washed.
This little republic was very extraordinary, and quite
true to the letter as I have drawn it. Mein's little
captain told it all to my wife, who took great
interest in them after she was acquainted with their
organization, and the captain often consulted her.
When our army was broken up after Toulouse, and
all the Portuguese Corps of course marched back
into Portugal, and the followers with them, we all
of us gave our goats to the poor little boys to whom
we had been so much indebted. My little fellow
had a flock of fifteen. Many are probably great
goat-proprietors now from this basis for future
fortune.

Our Brigade was now commanded by Colonel
Colborne, in whom we all had the most implicit
confidence. I looked up to him as a man whose
regard I hoped to deserve, and by whose knowledge
and experience I desired to profit. He had more
knowledge of ground, better understood the posting
of picquets, consequently required fewer men on
duty (he always strengthened every post by throwing obstacles—trees, stones, carts, etc.—on the road,
to prevent a rush at night), knew better what the
enemy were going to do, and more quickly anticipated his design than any officer; with that coolness
and animation, under fire, no matter how hot, which
marks a good huntsman when he finds his fox in his
best country.

The French were now erecting works, upon a
position by nature strong as one could well devise,

for the purpose of defending the Pass of Vera, and
every day Colonel Colborne and I took rides to look
at them, with a pleasant reflexion that the stronger
the works were, the greater the difficulty we should
have in turning them out—an achievement we well
knew in store for us.   On Oct. 7, the Duke resolved
to cross the Bidassoa, and push the enemy at once
into his own country, San Sebastian having been
taken.   Now had arrived the time we long had
anticipated of a regular tussle with our fortified
friends on the heights of Vera.   The Duke's dispatch,
Oct. 9, 1813, No. 837, tells the military glory of the
exploit.   My object is the record of anecdotes of
myself and my friends.   On the afternoon of the
7th, about two o'clock, we were formed for the
attack, and so soon as the head of the 4th Division
under that noble fellow, Sir Lowry Cole, appeared
in sight, we received the command to move forward.
We attacked on three different points.   Advancing
to the attack, Colborne, who had taken a liking to
me as an active fellow, says, " Now, Smith, you see
the heights above us ? "   " Well," I said, " I wish
we were there."   He laughed.   " When we are,"
he says, " and you are not knocked over, you shall
be a Brevet-Major, if my recommendation has any
weight at head-quarters."   Backed by the performance
of our Brigade, next day off he posted to Lord Fitzroy Somerset, and came back as happy as a soldier
ever is who serves his comrade.   " Well, Major
Smith, give me your hand."   I did, and my heart
too (although not as a blushing bride).   Kind-hearted

Colonel Barnard heard of this, went to Lord Fitzroy
Somerset, asking for the Brevet for one of his
Captains, remarking that I should be made a Major
over the heads of twenty in my own Regiment.
This startling fact obliged Lord Fitzroy to lay the
matter before the Duke, who, I am told, said, " A
pity, by G—! Colborne and the Brigade are so
anxious about it, and he deserves anything. If
Smith will go and serve as Brigade-Major to another
Brigade, I will give him the rank after the next
battle." Colborne's mortification was so great that
I banished mine altogether by way of alleviating his
disappointment. There was such a demonstration
of justice on the part of his Grace, and so did I love
the fellows whose heads I should have jumped over,
that, honestly and truly, I soon forgot the affair.
Colborne said, " Go and serve with another
Brigade." " No," says I, "dear Colonel, not to be
made of *your* rank. Here I will fight on happily,
daily acquiring knowledge from your ability."

The 1st Caçadores, under poor Colonel Algeo,
moved so as to threaten the enemy's left, and
intercept or harass the retreat of the troops in the
redoubt (which the noble 52nd were destined to
carry at the point of the bayonet without one check),
and the 2nd Battalion of the 95th and the 3rd
Caçadores moved to the enemy's right of this
redoubt for a similar purpose. This Battalion was
fiercely opposed, but so soon as it succeeded in
putting back the enemy, Colonel Colborne, at the
head of the 52nd, with an eye like a hawk's, saw

the moment had arrived, and he gave the word "Forward." One rush put us in possession of the redoubt, and the Caçadores and 2nd Battalion 95th caused the enemy great loss in his retreat to the top of the pass where his great defence was made. The redoubt just carried was placed on the ridge of the ravine, and must be carried ere any advance could be made on the actual [position].

In this attack poor Algeo was killed. He rode a chestnut horse marked precisely as my celebrated hunter and war-horse, "Old Chap," which I rode on that day. My wife was looking on the fight from the very cottage window we had occupied so long, barely without the range of musketry, and saw this horse gallop to the rear, dragging for some distance the body by the stirrup. The impulse of the moment caused her with one shriek to rush towards it, and so did anxiety and fright add to her speed that my servant for some time could not overtake her. The horse came on, when she soon recognized it was poor Algeo's charger, not mine, and fell senseless from emotion, but soon recovered, to express her gratitude to Almighty God.

After this attack—and there never was a more brilliant one—the 4th Division was well pushed up the hill, and, so soon as our Brigade was reformed, we prepared for the great struggle on the top of the Pass of Vera. Colborne sent me to Sir Lowry Cole, to tell him what he was about to attempt, and to express his hope of a support to what he had just so vigorously commenced. General Cole was all animation, and said, " Rely on my support, and you will need it, for you have a tough struggle before you." On my return, we again advanced with a swarm of Riflemen in skirmishing order keeping up a murderous fire. Firing up a hill is far more destructive than firing down, as the balls in the latter case fly over. The 52nd Regiment, well in hand, with their bayonets sharp and glistening in the sun (for the afternoon was beautiful), were advanced under a most heavy fire, but, from the cause mentioned, it was not near so destructive as we expected. Still more to our astonishment, the enemy did not defend their well-constructed work as determinedly as we anticipated. Although they stood behind their parapets until we were in the act of leaping on them, they then gave way, and we were almost mixed together, till they precipitated themselves into a ravine, and fled down almost out of sight as if by magic.

On the opposite side of this ravine, a few of the Riflemen of General Kempt's Brigade were pushing forward with a noble fellow, Reid, of the Engineers, at their head. At the moment he did not know how full of the enemy the ravine was. Colonel Colborne and I were on horseback. We pushed on, a little madly, I admit, followed by those who could run fastest, until the ravine expanded and a whole column of French were visible, but we and Reid on the opposite side were rather ahead, while the enemy could not see from out the ravine. The few men who were there could not have resisted them, and certainly could not have cut them off, had they been aware. Colonel Colborne, however, galloped up to the officer at the head of the column with the bearing of a man supported by 10,000, and said to the officer in French, "You are cut off. Lay down your arms." The officer, a fine soldier-like looking fellow, as cool as possible, says, presenting his sword to Colonel Colborne, " There, Monsieur, is a sword which has ever done its duty," and then ordered his men to lay down their arms. Colborne, with the presence of mind which stamps the character of a soldier, said, " Face your men to the left, and move out of the ravine." By this means the French soldiers were separated from their arms. At this moment there were up with Colborne myself, Winterbottom, Adjutant of the 52nd Regiment, my brother Tom, Adjutant of the 95th, and probably ten soldiers, and about as many with Reid on the opposite ridge. Reid wisely did not halt, but pushed forward, which added to the Frenchman's impression of our numbers, and Colborne turns to me, " Quick, Smith ; what do you here ? Get a few men together, or we are yet in a scrape." The French having moved from their arms, Colborne desired the officer commanding to order them to sit down. Our men were rapidly coming up and forming, and, when our strength permitted, we ordered the enemy to march out of the ravine, and there were 22 officers and 400 men. Three pieces of cannon we had previously carried (*vide* the Duke's dispatch, Oct. 9, 1813, No. 837). Colonel Colborne, myself, and others were called madmen for our audacity. I never witnessed such presence of mind as Colborne evinced on this occasion, and when, like a *man* as he is, he returned the poor Frenchman's sword, "There," he says, "wear the sword, your pride; it is not yet disgraced." The fortune of war gave us the advantage over equal bravery.*

By this time our men had got well out of the Pyrenees into the plain of France below, and as night was rapidly approaching, I was sent on to halt them, ready for Colonel Colborne to take up his position. The prisoners were sent to the rear (what became of their arms I never knew) under charge of a Lieutenant Cargill, of the 52nd Regiment, a manly, rough young subaltern, who on his march, just at dusk, met the Duke, who says, "Halloa, sir, where did you get those fellows?" "In France. Colonel Colborne's Brigade took them." "How the devil do you know it was France?" "Because I saw a lot of our fellows coming into the column just before I left with pigs and poultry, which we had not on the Spanish side." The Duke turned hastily away without saying a word. The next morning Mr. Cargill reported this to Colonel Colborne, whom I hardly ever saw so angry. "Why, Mr. Cargill, you were not such a blockhead as to tell the Duke *that*, were you?" In very broad Scotch, "What for no? It was fact as death." It did not escape the Duke, who spoke to Colborne,

---

* Kincaid (*Random Shots*, p. 273) tells the story at second hand with his usual *esprit*.

saying, "Though your Brigade have even more than usually distinguished themselves, we must respect the property of the country." "I am fully aware of it, my lord, and can rely upon the discipline of my soldiers, but your lordship well knows in the very heat of action a little irregularity will occur." "Ah, ah!" says my lord, "stop it in future, Colborne." Nor had his Grace cause to complain of us.

This night we slept on our arms, and cold and miserable we were, for no baggage had been permitted to come to us. The next day we occupied the heights of Vera, our outposts remaining pushed forward, and head-quarters and our general hospital were established at Vera. My wife joined me very early, and I never before had seen her under such excitement, the effect of the previous day, when, as she conceived at the moment, she had seen me killed. She did not recover her usual vivacity for several days, and the report of a musket acted on her like an electric shock. We remained in this position several days.

One day I dressed myself in all my best to do a little dandy at head-quarters, to see some of my wounded comrades and officers, and to look into our hospitals. In galloping through the country, I heard a very melancholy and faint call, repeated once or twice without attracting my attention. When I turned towards it, it was repeated. I rode up and among several dead bodies of the enemy, I found the poor fellow who had called to me greatly exhausted. *Four days* had elapsed since the action, and he had both legs shot off high up. I dismounted and felt his pulse, which was still far from faint. Of course he prayed me to send succour. I promised to do so, and I proceeded to tie some of the bushes of the underwood to mark the spot, and continued to do so until I reached a mountain track leading to Vera. I now even hear the hideous moans he uttered when I turned from him, although I earnestly assured him of help. Away I galloped to the hospital, not to visit my own poor fellows, but to get a fatigue party and a stretcher, and off I set for my poor wounded enemy, whom, from the precautions taken, I easily found. Poor thing, from the belief that I had abandoned him, he was nearly exhausted. We got him on the stretcher, the party set off to the hospital, and I to my bivouac, for it was late and I was well aware the poor thing would be treated just as one of our own soldiers. I had literally forgotten the circumstance, when one day after we had advanced considerably into France, a month or five weeks after the man was picked up, a large convoy of disabled men, as an act of humanity, were sent to their own country from the rear. My Brigade was of course on the outpost, and it became my duty to go to the enemy's advanced post close to, with a letter and flag of truce. I was received as usual with great civility, and the convoy passed on. While I was talking to the French officers, a poor fellow on one of the stretchers called to me and the officer, and began a volley of thanks, which, if it had been of musquetry, would have been difficult to resist. I said, "I know nothing about you, poor fellow; that will do." "I know you; I owe my life to you; you fetched the party who carried me to hospital. Both stumps were amputated; I am now doing perfectly well, and I was treated like one of your own soldiers." I never saw gratitude so forcibly expressed in my life.

CHAPTER XV.

CAMPAIGN OF 1813 : BATTLE OF THE NIVELLE.

OUR Division was soon after pushed forward to
our right on a ridge somewhat in advance, and
fully looking upon the enemy's position. His right
extended from St. Jean de Luz, his left was on the
Nivelle, his centre on La Petite Rhune * and the
heights beyond that village. Our Division was in
the very centre opposite La Petite Rhune.

One morning Colonel Colborne and I were at
the advance vedette at daylight, and saw a French
picquet of an officer and fifty men come down to
occupy a piece of rising ground between our respective advanced posts, as to which the night before I
and a French staff-officer had agreed that neither
should put a picquet on it. (Such arrangements
were very commonly made.) Colonel Colborne said,
"Gallop up to the officer, wave him back, or tell
him he shall not put a picquet there." Having
waved to no purpose, I then rode towards him and
called to him. He still moved on, so I galloped
back. Colborne fell in our picquet, ordered up a

* Cope writes *Arrhune*. The Duke's Despatches have *Rhune*.

reserve, and fired five or six shots *over the heads* of
the Frenchmen.   They then went back immediately,
and the hill became, as previously agreed, neutral
ground.   I give this anecdote to show how gentlemanlike enemies of disciplined armies can be; there
was no such courtesy between French and Spaniards.

A few days previously to Nov. 10, the Battle
of the Nivelle, the Division took ground on the
ridge of hills in our occupation, and the extreme
right of the Division became the left.   Gilmour,
commanding the 1st Battalion of the Rifles, then
in the 1st Brigade, had built a very nice little mud
hut about ten feet square with a chimney, fireplace,
and a door made of wattle and a bullock's hide.
When my wife rode up, Gilmour had just turned
out.   The night was bitterly cold; it was November
in the Pyrenees.   Gilmour says, "Jump off, and
come into *your own castle*, which I in perpetuity
bequeath to you."   When I returned from my
Brigade and new line of picquets, etc., I found my
wife as warm and as snug as possible—dinner
prepared for me and Tom Fane, our horses all
bivouacked, our cold tent pitched, and our servants
established in it; all was comfort, happiness, and
joy, every want supplied, every care banished.
At night we retired to our nuptial couch, a hard
mattress on the floor, when a sudden storm of rain
came on.   In ten seconds it came down through
the roof of our black-earth sods, and, literally in a
moment, we were drenched to the skin and as
black as chimney-sweepers.   The buoyant spirits

of my wife, and the ridiculous position we were in, made her laugh herself warm. We turned the servants out of our tent, and never enjoyed the late comforts of our castle again.

The enemy, not considering this ground strong enough, turned to it with a vigour I have rarely witnessed, to fortify it by every means art could devise. Every day, before the position was attacked, Colonel Colborne and I went to look at their progress; the Duke himself would come to our outpost, and continue walking there a long time. One day he stayed unusually long. He turns to Colborne, " These fellows think themselves invulnerable, but I will beat them out, and with great ease." "That we shall beat them," says Colborne, "when your lordship attacks, I have no doubt, but for the ease——" " Ah, Colborne, with your local knowledge only, you are perfectly right; it appears difficult, but the enemy have not men to man the works and lines they occupy. They dare not concentrate a sufficient body to resist the attacks I shall make upon them. I can pour a greater force on certain points than they can concentrate to resist me." "Now I see it, my lord," says Colborne. The Duke was lying down, and began a very earnest conversation. General Alten, Kempt, Colborne, I, and other staff-officers were preparing to leave the Duke, when he says, "Oh, lie still." After he had conversed for some time with Sir G. Murray, Murray took out of his sabretache his writing-materials, and began to write the plan of attack for the whole army. When it was finished, so clearly had he understood the Duke, I do not think he erased one word. He says, "My lord, is this your desire?" It was one of the most interesting scenes I have ever witnessed. As Murray read, the Duke's eye was directed with his telescope to the spot in question. He never asked Sir G. Murray one question, but the muscles of his face evinced lines of the deepest thought. When Sir G. Murray had finished, the Duke smiled and said, "Ah, Murray, this will put us in possession of the fellows' lines. Shall we be ready to-morrow?" "I fear not, my lord, but next day." "Now, Alten," says the Duke, "if, during the night previous to the attack, the Light Division could be formed on this very ground, so as to rush at La Petite Rhune just as day dawned, it would be of vast importance and save great loss, and by thus precipitating yourselves on the right of the works of La Petite Rhune, you would certainly carry them." This Petite Rhune was well occupied both by men and works, and a tough affair was in prospect. General Alten says, "I 'dink' I can, my lord." Kempt says, "My Brigade has a road. There can be no difficulty, my lord." Colborne says, "For me there is no road, but Smith and I both know every bush and every stone. We have studied what we have daily expected, and in the darkest night we can lead the Brigade to this very spot." I was proud enough at thus being associated, but no credit was due to me. "Depend on me, my lord," says

Colborne. "Well then, Alten, when you receive your orders as to the attack, let it be so."

Just before starting on this night's march, [9 Nov.], having had many military arrangements to make before I got on my horse, I had got a short distance when I remarked that, although I knew a proper tough fight was in hand, I had forgotten to bid my "goodbye" to my wife, which habit (on my part, at least) had rendered about as formal as if going to London out of the country. Her feelings were acute enough on such occasions, so I went into my hut, and avowed my neglect. She looked very sad, and I said, "Hallo, what's the matter?" "You or your horse will be killed to-morrow." I laughed and said, "Well, of two such chances, I hope it may be the horse." We parted, but she was very sad indeed.

As we started for our position before the great, the important day [Battle of Nivelle, 10 Nov.], the night was very dark. We had no road, and positively nothing to guide us but knowing the bushes and stones over a mountain ridge. Colborne stayed near the Brigade, and sent me on from spot to spot which we both knew, when he would come up to me and satisfy himself that I was right. I then went on again. In this manner we crept up with our Brigade to our advanced picquet within a hundred and fifty yards of the enemy. We afterwards found Kempt's Brigade close to our right, equally successfully posted. When Colborne and I rode up to our most advanced picquet, of course by the rear, we found, to the delight of us both, the Sergeant, Crowther, and his men, all sitting round a fire, as alert as if on sentry themselves, with their rifles between their legs, the sentry a few paces in their front.   We had crept up by ourselves.   Without any agitation, they stood up very quietly to reconnoitre us, when Colborne spoke, and commended their vigilance.   [I and] Tom Fane, Skerrett's A.D.C., who nobly stayed with me rather than go to the rear, lay down for about two hours, when I could sleep, but Tom told me he could not. He had had a small flask of brandy, but, what with the cold and the necessity of keeping it out, the brandy was exhausted.   About an hour before daylight, by some accident, a soldier's musket went off. It was a most anxious moment, for we thought the enemy had discovered us, and, if they had not, such shots might be repeated, and they would ; but most fortunately all was still.   I never saw Colborne so excited as he was for the moment.   The anxious moment of appearing day arrived.   We fell in, and our attack was made on the enemy's position in seven columns, nor did we ever meet a check, but carried the enemy's works, the tents all standing, by one fell swoop of irresistible victory.   Napier, the author of the *History of the Peninsular War*, at the head of the 43rd, had his pantaloons torn by the ball, and singed by the fire, of one of the enemy from the parapet of their works.   Such was the attack and such the resistance, that a few prisoners whom we took declared that they and their officers were perfectly thunderstruck, for they had no conception any force was near them. The 4th Division had some heavy fighting on our right. *Vide* Napier and the Duke's despatch.* Ours was the most beautiful attack ever made in the history of war.

The key of the enemy's position was in our hands, and the great line was our next immediate object. We were speedily reformed, and ready for our attack on the enemy's line-position and strong field fortifications. In descending La Petite Rhune, we were much exposed to the enemy's fire, and when we got to the foot of the hill we were about to attack, we had to cross a road enfiladed very judiciously by the enemy, which caused some loss. We promptly stormed the enemy's works and as promptly carried them. I never saw our men fight with such lively pluck; they were irresistible; and we saw the other Divisions equally successful, the enemy flying in every direction. Our Riflemen were pressing them in their own style, for the French themselves are terrific in pursuit, when poor dear gallant (Sir Andrew) Barnard was knocked off his horse by a musket-ball through his lungs.†
When Johnny Kincaid (the author), his adjutant,

* St. Pé, Nov. 13, 1813.   No. 847.

† Cope's account (p. 155) represents Barnard as falling wounded in the attack on the redoubt described in the text below. But he seems here to have read George Simmons's rather carelessly. Though Simmons, in his Journal for Nov. 10, says Barnard was wounded "towards the end of this day's fighting" (p. 321), in his letter of Dec. 7, he makes it clear that it was before the final attack on the redoubt; in fact, as Barnard was "reconnoitring how to move to the best advantage" (p. 326). There is no discrepancy between this and the text above.

got up to him, he was nearly choked by blood in his mouth. They washed it out for him, and he recovered so as to give particular orders about a pocket-book and some papers he wished sent to his brother. He did not want assistance; the soldiers loved him; he was borne off to the rear, and, when examined by Assistant-Surgeon Robson, it was found that the ball had not passed through, but was perceptible to the touch. The surgeon had him held up, so that when he made a bold incision to let the ball out, its own weight would prevent its being repelled into the cavity of the chest. The ball was boldly and judiciously extracted, no fever came on, and in three weeks Barnard was at the head of a Brigade, with one wound still open, and in the passage of the Gave d'Oleron he plunged into the water, and saved the life of a soldier floating down the river.

But to the fight. Everything was carried apparently, and our Division was halted. Some sharp skirmishing was going on, and Colborne and I were standing with the 52nd Regiment, again ready for anything, on a neck of land which conducted to a strong-looking star redoubt, the only work the enemy still held, when Charlie Beckwith, the A.Q.M.G. of our Division, came up with orders from General Alten to move on. "What, Charlie, to attack that redoubt? Why, if we leave it to our right or left, it must fall, as a matter of course; our whole army will be beyond it in twenty minutes." "I don't know; your orders are to move on." "Am

I to attack the redoubt?" says Colborne. "Your orders are to move on," and off he galloped. Colborne turns to me, and says, "What an evasive order!" "Oh, sir," says I, "let *us* take the last of their works; it will be the operation of a few minutes," and on we went in a column of companies. As we neared the enemy, Colborne's brilliant eye saw they were going to hold it, for it was a closed work, and he says, "Smith, they do not mean to go until fairly driven out; come, let us get off our horses." I was just mounted on a beautiful thoroughbred mare, my "Old Chap" horse being somewhat done, and I really believed anything like *fighting* was all over. I said nothing, but sat still, and on we went with a hurrah which we meant should succeed, but which the garrison intended should do no such thing. My horse was struck within twenty yards of the ditch, and I turned her round so that I might jump off, placing her between me and the fire, which was very hot. As I was jumping off, another shot struck her, and she fell upon me with a crash, which I thought had squeezed me as flat as a thread-paper, her blood, like a fountain, pouring into my face. The 52nd were not beat back, but swerved from the redoubt into a ravine, for they could not carry it.* While lying under

* It is difficult to reconcile this story with that told by Colonel Gawler (quoted by Leeke, *Lord Seaton's Regiment at Waterloo*, vol. ii. p. 365). Speaking of the check received by Colborne and the 52nd in their advance on the redoubt, he goes on: "At this moment an interesting episode occurred. Baron Alten, seeing from the lower ridge the desperate nature of the effort, endeavoured to send an order to prevent further attempts. It was confided to the Brigade-Major,

my horse, I saw one of the enemy jump on the parapet of the works in an undaunted manner and in defiance of our attack, when suddenly he started straight up into the air, really a considerable height, and fell headlong into the ditch. A ball had struck him in the forehead, I suppose—the fire of our skirmishers was very heavy on the redoubt. Our whole army was actually passing to the rear of the redoubt. Colborne, in the most gallant manner, jumped on his horse, rode up to the ditch under the fire of the enemy, which, however, slackened as he loudly summoned the garrison to surrender. The French officer, equally plucky, said, " Retire, sir, or I will shoot you ! " Colborne deliberately addressed the men. " If a shot is fired, now that you are surrounded by our army, we will put every man to the sword." By this time I succeeded in getting some soldiers, by calling to them, to drag me from under my horse, when they exclaimed, " Well, d— my eyes if our old Brigade-Major is killed, after all." " Come, pull away," I said ; " I am not even wounded, only squeezed." " Why, you are as bloody as a butcher." I ran to Colborne just as he had finished his speech. He took a little bit of paper out, wrote on it, " I surrender unconditionally," and gave it to me to give the French officer, who laughed at the

Harry Smith. Trusting to the shifting character of the mark of a horseman in motion, he tried the desperate venture ; but it was impossible ; no single living creature could reach the 52nd under the concentrated fire from the forts. The horse was soon brought down, and Captain Smith had to limit his triumph to carrying off his good and precious English saddle, which he performed with his accustomed coolness, to the amusement of observing friends and enemies."

state of blood I was in. He signed it, and Colborne sent me to the Duke. When I rode up (on a horse just lent me), his Grace says, "Who are you?" "The Brigade-Major, 2nd Rifle Brigade." "Hullo, Smith, are you badly wounded?" "Not at all, sir; it is my horse's blood." "Well." I gave him the paper. "Tell Colborne I approve." The garrison began to march out just as my Brigade were again moved on, and General Downie was left to receive it with his Spaniards. The garrison was composed of the whole of the French 88th Regiment, complete in every respect. The Duke was sorry we had attacked, for the 52nd lost many men, and it never was the Duke's intention, as he saw what Colborne had previously observed. Some discussion afterwards took place as to the order Colborne received. However, I think now, as I did then, *move on* implied *attack.*

This was a most brilliant day's fighting, and showed how irresistible our army was. As the Duke foretold, the enemy had not men enough. We were never opposed to a formed body. The whole army was in occupation of their works, and when we penetrated, retired. A proclamation had been issued to show the French inhabitants we made war on their army, not on them, and never in an enemy's country was such rigid discipline maintained as by the British Army. It is scarcely to be credited. The day after the battle our baggage moved up, and my wife joined me, horror-struck at the state of my cocked hat, clothes, and only half-washed face. She would not believe I was not awfully wounded, and then reminded me of her prophecy, that either I or my horse would be killed the following day.

A curious coincidence occurred in respect to this horse. Shortly before the Battle of Salamanca [22 July, 1812] a great friend of mine, Lindsay,* of the 11th Dragoons, came and prayed me to take it in exchange for a magnificent brown mare I had bought from Charlie Rowan; he had often tempted me, but I resisted, but upon this occasion I yielded, so earnest was he for a Dragoon's charger; and he gave me sixty guineas to boot. In a few months he was killed off my gallant mare on the Bridge of Tudela on the Douro, and now his mare was killed under me as described. Lord Fitzroy Somerset bought his mare at the sale; his lordship afterwards sold her to me, and she went with me to Washington. I brought her back, gave her to a brother, and she bred many foals afterwards.

* Query, Lindsell?

CHAPTER XVI.

COMBAT OF THE 10TH DECEMBER—HARRY SMITH'S
DREAM AND THE DEATH OF HIS MOTHER.

THE following day we moved into a most beautiful country, intersected with hedgerows, and
the finest and sweetest second crop of hay I ever
saw, which our horses rejoiced in. We took up our
posts in front of Arbonne [15 Nov.], and the
following day had a sharp skirmish at our advanced
posts. We halted here a day or two, and then
moved on to a line more approaching Bayonne.
The first Brigade occupied the Chateau d'Arcangues
[17 Nov.], of which Johnny Kincaid recounts
some anecdotes; the second the Chateau of Castilleur, where Colonel Colborne packed the 52nd
Regiment as close as cards; and the 2nd Battalion,
95th Regiment, and the 1st and 3rd Caçadores also
had cover. Our posts were here very close upon
each other, and we had far more skirmishing and
alarms than usual.

Upon the morning of the 9th December, the 1st
and 7th Divisions came close up to our rear, which
led us to suppose something was going on. The
enemy in our front were alarmed, and stood to their

arms. Shortly after these Divisions moved to our right, for the purpose of crossing the river [Nive], and our Division moved on to drive back the enemy's picquets in the direction of Bayonne. To occupy his attention, our Riflemen formed up before the firing commenced close to the enemy's strongest post, on the high-road to Bayonne, where we had been watching each other for several days. When I and Beckwith, the A.Q.M.G., rode up and ordered our people to advance, not a shot was fired. The French saw we were going to attack, but did not withdraw their picquet. We beckoned to them to do so, but they would not take the hint. We then actually fired some shots over their heads. There was positively a reluctance on our part to shoot any man in so cold-blooded a manner. The moment a shot was fired the affair became general, and we drove in the French picquets, who rapidly retired, and we had little fighting all day. In the evening, having effected the demonstration required, the Division retired to its old ground, and we resumed our usual line of picquets.

On the following morning [10 Dec.], having a presentiment the enemy would create a considerable diversion upon the left of our army, I was with our most advanced picquets before daylight. I had not been there many minutes, when I was joined by Beckwith, and soon after up came Colborne. We said, "The enemy are going to attack us." Colborne said, "No; they are only going to resume their ordinary posts in our front." I said, "But look at the body in our immediate front, and a column far off, evidently moving on the 1st Division," which was on the extreme left. It was evident we should be attacked immediately, and I said so, but Colborne asserted it was no such thing. I prayed him to allow me to order my Brigade under arms. At last he consented, and, although I rode at the utmost speed, our troops were barely out in time, so furiously did the French drive us back. They took the Chateau of Castilleur from us, making at the same time a heavy attack on that of Arcangues. Much of our baggage fell into the enemy's hands, although they could not carry it off. My wife had barely time to slip on her habit and jump upon her horse ; her Vittoria pug-dog in the scuffle was left behind, so sharp was the fire on the Chateau. A bugler of the 52nd Regiment, however, knew pug, whipped him up, and put him in his haversack. This was nearer a surprise than anything we had ever experienced. For some time the enemy possessed our quarters and bivouac, and—what was of great importance to Tom Fane—rifled his portmanteau. They also carried off a goose which was fattening for our Christmas dinner. We soon repaid our friends with interest and retook our position, but it was one of as heavy attacks as I have ever witnessed.

In the afternoon of that day, the enemy made a most vigorous attack on Sir J. Hope, particularly at the Mayor's House of Biaritz,* sharply skirmishing

* Query, Bar.ouilhet? See Napier, Bk. xxiii. ch. ii., and the plan in Sir H. E. Maxwell's *Life of Wellington*, i. p. 358.

with us at the same time to occupy our attention. I thought then, and I think now, if my
Brigade had been moved on the left of the attack
on Sir J. Hope, it would have caused the enemy
great loss, as his flank was exposed, but the Duke
of Wellington knew better, and never attempted
hazardous and little affairs, but ever played a great
and safe game.

That evening the Regiments of Nassau and
Frankfort walked over to us from the French lines
into those of the 7th Division at Arbonne. Colonel
Beyring,* Count Alten's A.D.C., was said to have
been for some time with them, and it was evident
the Duke knew about their intention.

Upon the 11th [Dec.] we had some partial
skirmishing. The 2nd Battalion Rifle Brigade
struck their tents for the purpose of moving their
ground. The enemy were most alarmed, and took
up their ground to receive us. That night, when
our armies were dismissed, rations were served out.
In my life I never heard such a row as among the
French when preparing to cook. I was posting the
night's sentries, when I saw a French officer doing
the same. I went towards him, and we civilly
greeted each other. I said I wished to speak to
him. He came up with the greatest confidence and
good humour. I showed him my vedette, and then
remarked that his was too far in advance and might
create an alarm at night when relieving. He said

* Query, Baring? The name Beyring seems not to occur in the
Army Lists of 1813, 1814.

he did not see that, but to please me, if I would point out where I wished he should be, he would immediately move him—which he did. He presented his little flask of excellent French brandy, of which I took a sup, and we parted in perfect amity.

When I returned to Colborne, who was in the Chateau, I found him lying asleep before a fire just as he had got off his horse. I did not awake him, nor had I anything to eat. Sleep at night readily supplies the place of food, and hunger at night on that account is not nearly so acute and painful as in the morning, when your day's work is before you. Down I lay, without one thought in the world, from exhaustion. I had a long dream, its purport that the enemy had attacked my father's house (the front of which opened to the street, the back into a beautiful garden, by what we children called " The Black Door "). My father had my mother in his arms ; I saw them as plainly as ever I did in my life, he carrying her through the Black Door, at the moment calling out, " Now, some one shut the door ; she is safe and rescued." At the instant I sprang on my feet, and in our usual military words in cases of alarm, roared out in a voice of thunder, " Stand to your arms." Colborne was on his feet like a shot, the light of the fire showed me the room and my delusion, and I said, " Oh, sir, I beg your pardon ; I have been dreaming." He said, in his noble way, " Never mind, it is near daylight, and it shows that, asleep or awake, you are intent on your duty." He

SIR HARRY SMITH'S BIRTHPLACE, WHITTLESEY.

(The "Black Door" is seen to the right.)

From a photograph by A. Gray, Whittlesey, 1900.

lay down, and was asleep in a moment. I never felt so oppressed in my life, so vividly was depicted to my mind the scene described, and I took out of my pocket a little roster of duties and picquets bound in calf-skin, and noted down the hour and particulars of my dream. In a few days I received a letter from my afflicted father,* telling me my mother died on Sunday morning, Dec. 12, at one o'clock, at the very moment I cried out, "Stand to your arms." Such is the fact. When I lay down, I was tired and exhausted, as before expressed. I had not a thought in the world of home or anything, nor was I prepared for the probability of the event. I presume to make no remarks on such intimations from God alone, but the whole day I was heavy and oppressed, nor did I ever shake off the vivid impression until the receipt of the letter put me in possession of the loss I had sustained.

Her dying moments were perfectly composed ; to the last she blessed her two sons engaged in the wars of their country, and died saying, " Would I could have seen them after their dangers and good conduct !" Among all our relations and friends we receive kindness and attention and unbounded love, but the love of a mother is distinct in character ; youth in distress turns to the mother for sympathy and pardon ; in joy it desires to impart its feeling to the mother, who participates in it with the warmth of a mother's heart. The mother is the friend, the counsellor, the pardoner of offences,

* See Appendix II. The *hour* of the death is not stated in the letter.

and, happen what may, the mother ever clings to her offspring. When I first parted from my mother to join my Regiment, the French Army was assembled at Boulogne, and every day was full of news that the French were coming. We dined early that day, I and my father, who was kindly to accompany me to Brabourne Lees, in Kent. At dinner I held up manfully. Then I ran to the stable to part with a beautiful little horse I had reared almost from a foal—he was thorough-bred, and carried me hunting in such a style that no one could beat me. I threw my arms round Jack's neck, and had a good cry. I saw my poor mother observed what I had been doing, and a smile of approbation curled upon her placid lip. The awful moment now approached : the buggy was at the door. I parted with my dear brothers and sisters (five boys and five girls) tolerably well, my poor mother glad to observe in me a force of character which *she hoped* in greater and more eventful scenes I might evince. It came next to her turn. She seized me in her arms, and wept awfully. Suddenly, with an effort I shall never forget, her tears were dried, she held me at arm's length, and, gazing at me most intently, said, " I have two favours to ask of you : one is that you never enter a public billiard-room ; the next—our country is at war—if ever you meet your enemy, remember you are born a true Englishman. Now, God bless and preserve you, which I hope He will, and listen to the constant, the fervent prayers, I

will offer up for your welfare." I exclaimed, " Dear
mother, I promise !" God knows the first request
I have honestly fulfilled, the latter I hope I have—
at least, my superiors and comrades ever gave me
credit for a bold and courageous bearing. I returned to her beloved embrace after South America,
and got a commission for my brother Tom, and
again to her nearly naked and a skeleton after the
retreat to Coruña. I was covered with vermin,
and had no clothes but those on my back. *To her
alone* did I impart what, although I felt no disgrace, I did not want to be known. She dressed
me, and put me in a hot bath, and we preserved
our secret mutually inviolate. I soon again left her
for Talavera, restored to health by her care, never
to see her again, but our intercourse by letters was
constant. The last she received from me was after
we had carried the heights of Vera in such a brilliant
manner, and it told her that for my conduct I was
promised the brevet rank of Major. May every
soldier obey the fifth commandment as I did ! I
never was in a situation of appalling death, mortality,
and danger, but my mother's words rang in my
ears, " Remember you were born an Englishman."
My dear wife participated and sympathized in all
my grief, for I admit it was excessive, saying ever,
" I have lost father and mother, and my brother
died in my arms of his wounds. Your home and
relatives you have still left, while I live alone for
you,—my all, my home, my kindred."

The morning after my dream [12 Dec.] I was

very early at our advanced posts, and I saw some French soldiers coming on in a very unusual manner to attack us, while the mass of their force were dismissed in bivouac. The 1st Caçadores had the advance. I never saw the French so daring since the retreat to Coruña, and they were most excellent shots, and actually astonished our Caçadores. Colborne, hearing a smart firing, rode up, and stopped in the road opposite one of the barricades of our picquets. I said, " I don't know what the devil we have got in our front to-day. Don't stand there, you will be shot in a moment!" He laughed, but would not move. In a second a ball went through his cap just above his noble head. He moved then and laughed. " Look at the fellows," he says, " how viciously they come on; it is evident it is no general attack, for the troops in their bivouac are not under arms. They want this post." " Which," says I, " they will have in ten minutes, unless I bring up the 2nd Battalion Rifle Brigade," for our Caçadores were evidently not equal to their task. Colborne says, " Fetch them!" In a very short time our Riflemen came up. By this time the enemy had driven in everything beyond the barricade, and were prepared to assault it. Our 95th fellows had a few men wounded as they were coming up the road, before they could be extended, which made them as savage as the enemy, who were capering about the fields in our front as if drunk. Our fellows turned to, and soon brought them to repent any pranks or exposure. We took a few prisoners, and ascertained the Regiment was the 32nd Voltigeurs, a crack corps of Suchet's army which had joined the night before, when we heard all the noise going on in the bivouac. These gentlemen had ever previously been venturous and laughed at the tales of British prowess; that morning's lesson, however, seemed to have made converts of them, for I never after observed any extra feats of dancing; but Colborne and all of us were perfectly astonished when the fact was known, and our 2nd Battalion 95th Regiment were rather elated in having thus shown themselves such able instructors.

We were very much on the alert all day, and a few shots were exchanged. At night our picquets were strengthened, for we were not aware if our friends, the new Voltigeurs, intended a fresh prank. After these three days' fighting and vigilance, the enemy withdrew close to Bayonne, their and our advanced posts being nearly as before. Notwithstanding the loss of our goose, we had a capital Christmas dinner, at which, of course, we had the Commissary of the Brigade, and induced him to find us champagne, which many commissaries were able to do.

CHAPTER XVII.

CAMPAIGN OF 1814 : BATTLE OF ORTHEZ—ANECDOTE
OF JUANA SMITH.

FROM the Chateau of Castilleur we moved more
into the mountains to the rear and to our left of
Ustaritz, where we never saw the enemy [Jan.
1814]. Our time was spent in shooting, and ex-
ploring the mountains. While we were in this
position forage was very scarce, and we chopped
up the furze-bushes very small by way of hay.
It is astonishing how it agreed with the horses.
The natives use it in the same way for their cattle.

We remained in this position until the end of
February, when we moved, reaching Orthez on the
26th. Here our Division had one of the sharpest
skirmishes in a town which I ever saw. Orthez is
situated on both sides of the Gave de Pau and has
a bridge, which the enemy held with great jealousy.
On the afternoon of this day, the Duke and his
head-quarters came up. It was his intention to
have fought the battle that afternoon, had the 3rd
Division been able to reach its position in time. I
heard the Duke say, " Very well, Murray, if the
Division does not arrive in time, we must delay the

attack till to-morrow. However, I must have a sleep." He folded his little white cloak round him, and lay down, saying, "Call me in time, Murray." Murray awoke the Duke, saying, "It is too late to-day, my Lord." "Very well, then, my orders for to-morrow hold good."

At dark we withdrew all our posts out of Orthez but a picquet near the bridge in the town, and at daylight [27 Feb.] we crossed by a pontoon bridge below Orthez, and marched over difficult ground. We saw the enemy very strongly posted, both as regards the elevation and the nature of the ground, which was intersected by large banks and ditches, while the fences of the field were most admirably calculated for vigorous defence. As we were moving on the right of the 3rd Division, Sir Thomas Picton, who was ever ready to find fault with the Light, rode up to Colonel Barnard. "Who the devil are you?" knowing Barnard intimately. "We are the Light Division." "If you are Light, sir, I wish you would move a little quicker," said in his most bitter and sarcastic tone. Barnard says very cool, "Alten commands. But the march of infantry is quick time, and you cannot accelerate the pace of the head of the column without doing an injury to the whole. Wherever the 3rd Division are, Sir Thomas, we will be in our places, depend on it."

We were soon engaged, but less for some time than the troops to our right and left. I never saw the French fight so hard as this day, and we were actually making no advance, when the Duke came up, and ordered the 52nd Regiment to form line and advance. The Battalion was upwards of seven hundred strong. It deployed into line like clockwork, and moved on, supported by clouds of sharpshooters. It was the most majestic advance I ever saw. The French, seeing this line advance so steadily, were appalled ; their fire, which at first was terrific, gradually decreased as we neared. The Divisions on our right and left also moved on. The battle was won.

In this advance the 52nd suffered considerably. The present Duke of Richmond, then Lord March, a Captain in the corps, received a severe wound in the side ; the ball still annoys him. The Duke himself also got a crack on his knee, which lamed him for several days. When Lord March lay on the ground after the attack, I went to bring up Maling, Surgeon of the 52nd Regiment. As soon as he arrived, to my horror, he poked his forefinger into the wound to trace the course of the ball. At this moment up rode Lord Fitzroy Somerset, and Lord March's brother, Lord George Lennox, awfully affected, believing the wound mortal. Lord March said, " Maling, tell me if I am mortally wounded, because I have something I wish to impart to George." Maling said, " If you will be quiet, you will do very well." Maling did not think so. However, Lord March made a miraculous recovery. I never knew a finer young fellow, braver or cooler. In those days, he would not have opposed his kind patron, the Duke, as he did subsequently. That every peer and every other man should speak out his mind according to his conscience, I earnestly desire; but, as Duke of Richmond, he opposed the Duke of Wellington politically in a manner rather partaking of personal hostility than political consistency.* Every admirer of Lord March in the army, and he had many, lamented the course he pursued.

But to the fight. We drove the enemy in great confusion before us. On this occasion, I literally lost a Battalion of my Brigade, the 1st Caçadores, for two days, they got so mixed with the 6th Division. The night I found them, after much diligence, I and my Brigadier, Barnard, got into a little sort of inn, kept by an old soldier disabled in Bonaparte's Italian campaigns. He did not require to be told the wants of a soldier, but from habit and sympathy turned to like a "good 'un" to cook us some dinner. As he was hard at work, he said to Barnard, "Ah, the French are not always victorious, and I see war now is [not?] what it was when I served. The Cavalry give way first, then come the Artillery, and then follow the Infantry in disorder." He became in the course of the evening very eloquent over his own wine, and told us some

* Charles, from 1819 5th Duke of Richmond, after the introduction of the Catholic Emancipation Bill became a vigorous opponent of Wellington. Though reckoned an ultra-Tory, he joined the Reform Ministry in 1830, and afterwards supported Lord Melbourne. On the other hand, in 1845-6 (after the date when the remarks in the text were written), he was a leader of the opposition to corn-law abolition. He died within a few days of Sir Harry Smith, on 21st October, 1860.

very amusing stories. The next morning, when Barnard paid him for everything we had consumed, he was perfectly thunderstruck. I shall never forget his astonishment or his " Eh bien! monsieur, comme vous voulez."

The baggage reached us early the following day [1 March], and in the afternoon we forded the Adour, which was deep, rapid, and broad. My wife had ridden over the field of battle, and described it as covered with dead, dying, and wounded. She observed an extraordinary number of wounds in the head. These were due to the fact that, owing to the cover of the high banks before described, the head only was vulnerable or exposed. She saw one fine fellow of an Artilleryman with both his arms shot off, which he said occurred while he was ramming down the cartridge into his own gun. She offered him all she had in the eating or drinking way, but he most disdainfully refused all.

The same afternoon we made a long and rapid march on Mont de Marsan, where a Division of Cavalry and Marshal Beresford and his headquarters preceded us. We did not reach Mont de Marsan until some hours after dark. We were ordered to take up quarters for the night, but so full of Cavalry and head-quarters was the place, and all scattered over the town, not collected, as we Light Division used to be by streets and regiments as if on parade, we had great difficulty in getting in anywhere.

The night was showery, with sleet drifting, frosty and excessively cold. My poor wife was almost perished. We at last got her into a comfortable little house, where the poor Frenchwoman, a widow, lighted a fire, and in about half an hour produced some bouillon in a very handsome Sèvres slop-basin, saying this had been a present to her many years ago on the day of her marriage, and that it had never been used since her husband's death. She, therefore, wished my wife to know how happy she was to wait on the nation who was freeing France of an usurper. The widow was a true " Royaliste," and we were both most grateful to the poor woman. The next day we were ordered back to St. Sever, on the high-road to Toulouse, and parted with our widow with all mutual concern and gratitude, our baggage being left to follow. We had a very showery, frosty, and miserable long march over an execrable road, after which we and Barnard got into a little cottage on the roadside. At daylight the following morning we were expecting to move, but, having received no order, we turned to to breakfast, my wife relating to Barnard the kindness she had received the previous night and the history of the basin. To our horror in came my servant, Joe Kitchen, with the identical slop-basin full of milk. The tears rolled down my wife's cheeks. Barnard got in a storming passion. I said, " How dare you, sir, do anything of the sort ? " (he was an excellent servant.) " Lord, sir," he says, " why, the French soldiers would have carried off *the widow,* an' she had been young, and I thought it would be so nice for the goat's milk in the morning; she was very angry, though, 'cos I took it."

Barnard got on his horse, and rode to head-quarters. About ten o'clock he came back and said the Duke told him the army would not march until to-morrow. My wife immediately sent for the trusty groom, old West, and said, " Bring my horse and yours too, and a feed of corn in your haversack." She said to me, " I am going to see an officer who was wounded the day before yesterday, and if I am not back until late, do not be alarmed." Young as she was, I never controlled her desire on such occasions, having perfect confidence in her superior sense and seeing her frequently visit our wounded or sick. I went to my Brigade, having various duties, just before she started. It became dark, she had not returned, but Barnard would wait dinner for her, saying, " She will be in directly." She did arrive soon, very cold and splashed from hard riding on a very dirty, deep, and wet road. She laughed and said, " Well, why did you wait dinner ? Order it ; I shall soon have my habit off." Barnard and I exclaimed with one voice, " *Where have you been?* " "Oh," she says, "do not be angry, I am not taken prisoner, as you see. I have been to Mont de Marsan, to take back the poor widow's basin." I never saw a warm-hearted fellow so delighted as Barnard. " Well done, Juana, you are a heroine. The Maid of Saragossa is nothing to you." She said the widow cried exceedingly with joy, but insisted on her now keeping the basin for the milk, which my wife would on no account do. She had ridden that day thirty miles and had every reason to expect to meet a French patrol. I said, "Were you not afraid of being taken prisoner?" "No, I and West kept a good look-out, and no French dragoon could catch me on my Spanish horse, Tiny." She was tired from the excessive cold, but the merit of her act sustained her as much as it inspired us with admiration. The story soon got wind, and the next day every officer in the Division loaded her with praise. It was a kind and noble act which few men, much less a delicate girl of sixteen, would have done under all the circumstances. Our worthy friend, Bob Digby, of the 52nd Regiment, Barnard's A.D.C., overhearing my wife's orders to West, after she had started, most kindly followed and joined my wife on the road, for, as he said, he was alarmed lest she should fall in with a patrol.

CHAPTER XVIII.

CAMPAIGN OF 1814 : AT GÉE, NEAR AIRE—BATTLE OF
TARBES—BATTLE OF TOULOUSE—END OF THE WAR.

ON our advance [9 March, etc.], we were for
some days at a village called Gée,* near Aire,
where the 2nd Division, under Sir W. Stewart, had
a brilliant little affair.

But I must first interpose an anecdote. One of
his A.D.C.'s, his nephew, Lord Charles Spencer, a
Lieutenant of the 95th Regiment, was mounted on
a very valuable horse which he had paid more for
than he could afford, contrary to the advice of Sir
William. In driving the French through the town,
Lord Charles's horse was shot on the bank of a
large pond, into which he himself was thrown head
foremost. (The fire at this moment was very heavy,
and in a street more balls take effect than in the
open.) Sir William very quietly says, " Ha, there
goes my poor nephew and all his fortune," alluding
to the price he paid for his horse.

I have often heard Colonel Colborne (Lord
Seaton) affirm that if he were asked to name the
bravest man he had ever seen (and *no one* was a

* MS. Ghee.

better judge), he should name Sir William Stewart. Although he gave me my commission, I never saw him under fire. If he exceeded in bravery my dear friend, Sir Edward Pakenham, he was gallant indeed. Pakenham's bravery was of that animated, intrepid cast that he applied his mind vigorously at the moment to the position of his own troops as well as to that of the enemy, and by judicious foresight ensured success, but he never avoided a fight of any sort.

The village of Gée was to the right of the high-road to Toulouse, the River [Adour] running to our right. The Cavalry were posted on the main road, their advance vedettes looking on to the village of [Tarsac?] where the enemy were very alert and obstinate in resisting our approach.

On the day the army advanced,* the French Cavalry made a fierce resistance in the village, and when driven out, made some desperate charges on the chaussée, in one of which the officer in command was cut down while gallantly leading his Squadron. An officer of our 15th Hussars (I think Booth), having admired his gallant bearing, dismounted to his assistance. He said he believed he was not mortally wounded, and he requested to be carried to the Chateau in the village he had so gallantly fought for, where his father and family resided. This peculiar tale may be relied on, like everything

* According to G. Simmons' diary (p. 340), this attack on the French Cavalry took place on 16th March, two days before the advance of the Division. Simmons says the French captain "died soon after."

else, as I hope, which I have asserted. For several days it was the usual topic of conversation, and when any one came from the rear, inquiry was always made if the French Captain who was wounded and in his father's house, (we never knew his name), was doing well. We learnt afterwards that he perfectly recovered, but the sword wound had stamped him with a deep scar.

At Gée we had several alerts, and our baggage for some successive days was loaded for hours. On one of these occasions the old housekeeper of a large house which Barnard occupied, and whom he had paid for many a fat fowl and fish out of tanks, etc., came into the room where my wife remained waiting to join the troops, seized my wife and vowed she would put her to death, grasping her with a fiend-like strength. Fortunately, at this moment my servant returned to say the Division were not to march, and rescued my poor affrighted and delicate wife. We afterwards learnt that this violent woman, if anything excited her, was afflicted with temporary insanity, and she had been put in a rage below, and came up to vent her spleen on my poor wife. We were in this house for two or three days after, but my wife had been so alarmed she would never allow her servant to quit her. The latter was a powerful woman of the 52nd, rejoicing in the name of Jenny Bates.

While in this village, Charlie Beckwith, the Q.M.G., came to me and said, "Harry, I want a Company for picquet immediately." I named the

Corps, 1st Battalion 95th, who had one ready accoutred in waiting, as we always had in positions subject to alerts. It was out in five minutes, and Charlie Beckwith marched to point out where the officer commanding was to post it. I invariably went out with every picquet when possible. On this occasion I had other duty. In the afternoon I got on my horse to look for my picquet. I met Charlie Beckwith in the village. He said, "I will ride with you." We did not find the picquet where we expected—on our side of a bridge (beyond which was a comfortable village). Having heard no firing, we were not alarmed for the safety of the Company, still we could not find it. We rode to the bridge, the object of the officer's watch, saying, "There will surely be a sentry upon it." We rode up and found one certainly, but on the enemy's side. We asked where the Company was. The vedette was an Irishman. "By Jasus, the Captain's the boy. It was so rainy and cold on the plain, he harboured us all comfortably, like the man that he is, in the village." The French were in the habit of patrolling into this village in force, and, although the Captain had so posted himself as I do believe he would have been able to hold his own until the Division came up, it would have cost us a fight to rescue him from the far side of the bridge, which he ought never to have crossed. So the Captain got a blowing-up, and the Company had to make their fires in a cold, wet, and miserable bivouac. I never had a picquet out from the Brigade without visiting it so as to judge how it was posted, and how to withdraw it either at night or in case of abrupt necessity.

We had also a sharp skirmish at Vic Begorre, but the brunt of it fell on the 3rd Division, where one of the most able officers got himself killed where he had no business to be—Major Sturgeon, of the Staff. I hold nothing to be more unsoldierlike than for officers well mounted to come galloping in among our skirmishers. The officers of companies have always some little exertion to restrain impetuosity, and your galloping gentlemen set our men wild sometimes. We Light Division, while ever conspicuous for undaunted bravery, prided ourselves upon destroying the enemy and preserving ourselves; for good, light troops, like deer-stalkers, may effect feats of heroism by stratagem, ability, and cool daring.

At Tarbes [20 March] we fell in with the enemy, strongly posted, but evidently only a rear-guard in force. The Duke made immediate dispositions to attack them, and so mixed up did we appear, that we concluded a large number of the enemy must be cut off. The Light Division, however, alone succeeded in getting up with them. Our three Battalions of the 95th were most sharply engaged. Three successive times the enemy, with greatly superior force, endeavoured to drive them off a hill, but the loss of the enemy from the fire of our Rifles was so great that one could not believe one's eyes. I certainly had never seen the dead lie so thick, nor ever did, except subsequently at Waterloo. Barnard even asked the Duke to ride over the hill and see the sight, which he consented to do, saying, " Well, Barnard, to please you, I will go, but I require no novel proof of the destructive fire of your Rifles."

At this period we lived capitally. It was delightful to see one of our soldiers with a piece of cold bacon, slicing it over his bread like an English haymaker.

We had at this time exceedingly wet weather. Notwithstanding the fulness of the Garonne, however, after a feint or two and some skilful demonstrations to deceive the enemy, the Duke succeeded [4 April] in throwing over the 3rd, 4th, and 6th Divisions with as much ease as he had previously overcome what seemed to others insurmountable difficulties. These Divisions were strongly posted under Marshal Beresford as a *tête du pont*. They were barely established on the opposite side when such a torrent of rain fell, our bridge could not stem the flood. It was hauled to the shore, and, of course, our communication cut off. Marshal Beresford had every reason to apprehend an attack, for the enemy, being in his own country, possessed perfect information, and would know the moment the bridge was impassable. The Marshal wrote very strongly to the Duke, who was ferried over in a little boat with one or two of his Staff, while their horses swam across. His Grace quickly but narrowly examined the position, which was excellent, behind a very difficult ravine. " Beresford," said the Duke, "you are safe enough; two such armies as Soult's could make no impression on you. Be assured, he is too clever a General to attempt to drive you into the river." Our Division was immediately opposite the bridge, but on the left, or opposite bank, to the Marshal. The river soon subsided sufficiently to enable us to relay the bridge, and at daylight on the 10th of April the Light Division crossed, followed by the remainder of the army, except Lord Hill's corps, which was posted on the Pyrenees side of Toulouse. It was evidently the Duke's intention to attack Soult's position this day. Nor were we long on the march before each general officer had his point of rendezvous designated.

The battle of Toulouse [10 April] has been so often fought and refought, I shall only make two or three remarks. Sir Thomas Picton, as usual, attacked when he ought not, and lost men. The Spaniards made three attacks on a very important part of the enemy's position defended by a strong redoubt. The first was a very courageous though unsuccessful attack; the second, a most gallant, heavy, and persevering one, and had my dear old Light Division been pushed forward on the right of the Spaniards in place of remaining inactive, that attack of the Spaniards would have succeeded. I said so at the moment. The third attempt of the Spaniards was naturally, after two such repulses, a very poor one. At this period, about two o'clock in the afternoon, the Duke's Staff began to look grave, and all had some little disaster to report to His Grace, who says, " Ha, by God, this won't do ;

I must try something else." We then saw the heads of the 4th and 6th Divisions coming into action immediately on the right flank of the enemy, having been conducted to that particular and vulnerable spot by that gallant, able, and accomplished soldier, my dear friend, John Bell, A.Q.M.G., 4th Division.

I must record an anecdote of John. He was mounted on a noble English hunter, but the most violent and difficult horse to manage I ever rode to hounds, and would of course, in a fight, be equally so. This animal knew by the mode in which she was mounted whether her rider was an artist or not, and in a moment would throw her rider down by way of fun. Colonel Achmuty, a noble fellow, would ride John Bell's horse awkwardly, and she would then plunge like a devil, but if *ridden*, she was as quiet as possible. John Bell had on this horse a very large and high-peaked Hussar saddle, with his cloak strapped on the pique before, a favourite mode of General Robert Craufurd, who indeed gave Bell the identical saddle. Over this pique Craufurd's black muzzle could barely be discovered (he was a short man), so entrenched was he. In conducting their Divisions, the Staff officers moved on small roads through a country intersected by deep and broad ditches full of water. Many of them attempted to ride on the flanks, but no one succeeded but Bell on his fiery horse. At one ditch John Bell was fairly pitched over the pique on to the neck of his horse, a powerful mare six feet high. "Oh," says John, in telling this story, "Ah, to get there was extraordinary, but wait! The horse tossed up her head, and by some violent exertion pitched me over the pique back again to my saddle." "Oh, John!" I exclaimed, "how is that possible?" "With that, Harry, I have nothing to do."

But to the fight. The 4th and 6th Divisions were brought up in most gallant style, carrying redoubt after redoubt, which were ably defended by the enemy. It was the heaviest fighting I ever looked at, slow owing to the redoubts. The ground was gained step by step, and so was the battle of Toulouse. Our Cavalry lost a brilliant opportunity of distinguishing themselves and punishing the rearguard of the French.

This battle appeared to me then, and does the more I reflect on it, the only battle the Duke ever fought without a weight of attack and general support. It was no fault of the Duke's. There are fortunate days in war as in other things. Our attacks were commenced by that of the 3rd Division; then came those of the Spaniards, in which the Light Division did not support as the 4th Division supported us at the heights of Vera. Thus, until the afternoon, we literally had done rather worse than nothing. The success of this battle is to be attributed mainly to the 4th and 6th Divisions, but I will ever assert that the second attack was most heavy and energetic, and would have succeeded if my dear old Division had been shoved up. As a whole, the French lost a great number of men and were thoroughly defeated. The French have now agitated a claim to the victory, which they are as much borne out in as they would be in claiming the victory at Waterloo.

The next day [11 March] various were the reports flying about camp as to peace, etc. In the afternoon I was posting a picquet, and in riding forward no nearer than usual to a French sentry, the fellow most deliberately fired at me. I took off my cocked hat and made him a low bow. The fellow, in place of reloading his musket, presented arms to me, evidently ashamed of what he had done.

Peace was soon made known. The French moved out of Toulouse, and we occupied it. (The most slippery pavement to ride over in Europe is that of the streets of Toulouse.) My Division was most comfortably cantoned in the suburbs. I and my wife, and two or three of my dear old Rifle comrades—Jack Molloy and young Johnstone (not the Rifle hero of Badajos and Ciudad Rodrigo, old Willie)—had a delightfully furnished château. We got a French cook, and were as extravagant and wanton in our ideas as lawless sailors just landed from a long cruise. The feeling of no war, no picquets, no alerts, no apprehension of being turned out, was so novel after six years' perpetual and vigilant war, it is impossible to describe the sensation. Still, it was one of momentary anxiety, seeing around us the promptitude, the watchfulness, the readiness with which we could move and be in a state of defence or attack. It was so novel that at first it was positively painful—at least, I can answer for myself in this feeling. I frequently deemed the old Division in danger, who had never even lost a picquet, or, to my recollection, a sentry, after so many years' outpost duty.

We had one melancholy duty to wind up our period of war—the funeral of poor Colonel Coghlan, 61st Regiment. The officers of the army attended, the Duke himself as chief mourner. Many is the gallant fellow we had all seen left on the field or with some trifling ceremony consigned to his long home ; but this funeral, in the midst of a populous city, in a graveyard, after a ceremony in a Protestant chapel, where the corpse was placed, in the custom of our home and infancy, while the service was read by a clergyman, after death in the last battle, and nearly at the end of it, too—all so tended to excite our comrade-like feelings, it positively depressed us all, for the love a soldier bears another tried and gallant soldier is more than fraternal.

Toulouse, a royalist city, soon rushed into the extravagant and vivacious joy of France. We had theatres, balls, fêtes, etc., until the army moved into regular cantonments. There we had plenty of room and quarters, no squabbling about the shade of a tree in bivouac, or your stable being previously occupied by cavalry or artillery horses. Abundance of food, drink, and raiment, and the indolence of repose, succeeded the energetic and exciting occupation of relentless and cruel war. I had a safeguard in a lovely young wife; but most of our gallant fellows were really in love, or fancied themselves so, and such had been the drain by conscription of the male population, you never saw a young Frenchman. The rich and fertile fields in this part of France were cultivated by female exertion.

My Division went to Castel Sarrasin [towards the end of April]. This place is situated on the Tarne, which divides it from Marsac, where were a body of French troops; but, as they seldom came to visit us, we seldom encroached upon them, for the Napoleonist officers were brutally sulky and so uncivil, John Bull could not put up with it with impunity. This part of France is a garden, and the views, trees, beautiful rivers, etc., and the idleness rendered it a perfect Elysium. I say "idleness;"—because it was so totally novel, it was amusing. Fortunately—for we were *nine months* in arrear of pay—money was so scarce that a trifle of ready money produced a great deal. Among the rich inhabitants money was never seen, any more than young men. Rents were paid in produce, wages in kind, purchases made by barter. Oh, dear John Bull, grumbling, still liberal John Bull, had you witnessed, felt, and suffered all this, and then had the best rooms in your house occupied by soldiers (for, however orderly, there is much riot and fun ever going on amongst them), you would now wear the yoke of the national debt as a light burden!

CHAPTER XIX.

HARRY SMITH PARTS FROM HIS WIFE BEFORE START-
ING FOR THE WAR IN AMERICA.

My happiness of indolence and repose was doomed
to be of short duration, for on the 28th of
August I was in the Battle of Bladensburg, and at
the capture of the American capital, Washington,
some thousands of miles distant. Colborne, my
ever dear, considerate friend, then in command
of his gallant Corps, the 52nd, sent for me, and
said, "You have been so unlucky, after all your
gallant and important service, in not getting your
Majority, you must not be idle. There is a force,
a considerable one, going to America. You must
go. To-morrow we will ride to Toulouse to head-
quarters; send a horse on to-night—it is only thirty-
four miles—we will go there and breakfast, and ride
back to dinner." I said, very gratefully, "Thank
you, sir; I will be ready. This is a kind act of
yours;" but as I knew I must leave behind my
young, fond and devoted wife, my heart was ready
to burst, and all my visions for our mutual happiness were banished in search of the bubble reputa-
tion. I shall never forget her frenzied grief when,

with a sort of despair, I imparted the inevitable separation that we were doomed to suffer, after all our escapes, fatigue, and privation ; but a sense of duty surmounted all these domestic feelings, and daylight saw me and dear Colborne full gallop thirty-four miles to breakfast. We were back again at Castel Sarrasin by four in the afternoon, after a little canter of sixty-eight miles, not regarded as any act of prowess, but just a ride. In those days there were men.

On our arrival in Toulouse, we found my name rather high up—the third, I think—on the list of Majors of Brigade in the A.G.'s office desirous to serve in America. We asked kind old Darling who had put my name down. He said, "Colonel Elley," afterwards Sir John. He had known my family in early life, and was ever paternally kind to me. He had asked my ever dear friend, General Sir Edward Pakenham, to do so, which he readily did. Colborne then said, "My old friend Ross, who commanded the 20th Regiment while I was Captain of the Light Company, is going. I will go and ask him to take you as his Major of Brigade." Ross knew me on the retreat to Coruña, and the affair, in a military point of view, was satisfactorily settled. But oh ! the heaviness of my heart when I had to impart the separation now decided on to my affectionate young wife of seventeen years old ! She bore it, as she did everything, when the energies of her powerful mind were called forth, exclaiming, " It is for your advantage, and neither of us must repine. All your friends have been so kind in arranging the prospect before you so satisfactorily." At the word "friends" she burst into a flood of tears, which relieved her, exclaiming, "You have friends everywhere. I must be expatriated, separated from relations, go among strangers, while I lose the only thing on earth my life hangs on and clings to!"

Preparation was speedily made for our journey down the Garonne, which we performed in a small boat, accompanied by our kind friend Digby. My wife was to accompany me to Bordeaux, there to embark for England with my brother Tom, who had recently suffered excessively in the extraction of the ball he had received in his knee five years previously at the Coa. The great difficulty I had was to get my regimental pay (nine months being due to me), and I only did so through the kindness of our acting-paymaster, Captain Stewart, and every officer readily saying, "Oh, give us so much less the first issue, and let Smith have what would otherwise come to us." Such an act, I say, testifies to the mutual friendship and liberality we acquired amidst scenes of glory, hardship, and privation.

Before I left my old Brigade, the 52nd Regiment, the 95th Regiment (Rifle Brigade now), the 1st and 3rd Caçadores,* with whom I had been so many

---

* The 3rd Caçadores at this period were commanded by a fine gallant soldier and a good fellow, but as he rejoiced in a name of unusual length—Senhor Manuel Terçeira Caetano Pinto de Silvuica y Souza—we gave him the much shorter appellation of "Jack Nasty Face," for he was an ugly dog, though a very good officer.—H.G.S.

eventful years associated—and I may say, most happily—all gave me a parting dinner, including the good fellows, the Portuguese, whom I never had any chance of seeing again.   Our farewell dinner partook of every feeling of excitement.   The private soldiers, too, were most affectionate, and I separated from all as from my home.   The Portuguese are a brave, kind-hearted people, and most susceptible of kindness.   We had also ten men a Company in our British Regiments, Spaniards, many of them the most daring of sharpshooters in our corps, who nobly regained the distinction attached to the name of the Spanish infantry in Charles V.'s time.   I never saw better, more orderly, perfectly sober soldiers in my life, and as vedettes the old German Hussar did not exceed them.   The 52nd Regiment I was as much attached to as my own corps, with every reason.

My old 1st Battalion embarked at Dover just before Talavera, 1050 rank and file.   During the war only 100 men joined us.   We were now reduced to about 500.   There was scarcely a man who had not been wounded.   There was scarcely one whose knowledge of his duty as an outpost soldier was not brought to a state of perfection, and when they were told they must not drink, a drunken man was a rare occurrence indeed, as rare as a sober one when we dare give a little latitude.   My old Brigade was equal to turn the tide of victory (as it did at Orthez) any day.

It was early in May when we left Castel Sarrasin, where we had been happy (oh, most happy!) for

a month—an *age* in the erratic life we had been
leading.   We were quartered in the house of a
Madame La Rivière, an excellent and motherly
woman, a widow with a large family and only one
son spared to her—the rest had perished as soldiers.
Never was there a more happy and cheerful family,
and never did mother endeavour to soothe the acute
feelings of a daughter more than did this good lady
those of my poor wife.   We often afterwards heard
of her in Paris in 1815.

Our voyage down the Garonne in our little skiff
was delightful.   We anchored every night.   In
youth everything is novel and exciting, and our
voyage was such a change after marching!   The
beauties of the scenery, and the drooping foliage
on the banks of the river, added to our enjoyment.
We landed each night at some town or village, and
ever found a comfortable inn which could give us
a dinner.   After such privations as ours, the delight
of being able to order dinner at an inn is not to be
believed.   On reaching Bordeaux, the most beautiful city I was ever in, I found I had only three
or four days to prepare to reach the fleet and the
troops embarked in the Gironde (a continuation of
the Garonne), and that I was to embark on board
his Majesty's ship the *Royal Oak*, 74, Rear-Admiral
Malcolm, for the troops under General Ross were
destined for a peculiar and separate service in
America.   I did, of course, all I could to draw the
attention of my poor wife from the approaching
separation.   There was a theatre, various spectacles,

sights, etc., but all endeavour was vain to relieve
the mind one instant from the awful thought of that
one word "separation." Digby was most kind to
her. He had an excellent private servant, who was
to embark with her for London. My brother Tom
was to her all a brother could be, and in the transport she was to proceed in were several old and
dear Rifle friends going to England from wounds.
I wished her to go to London for some time before
going down to my father's, for the benefit of masters
to learn English, etc.—for not a word could she
speak but her own language, French, and Portuguese,—and to every wish she readily assented.

Time rolls rapidly on to the goal of grief, and
the afternoon arrived when I must ride twenty
miles on my road for embarcation. Many a year
has now gone by, still the recollection of that
afternoon is as fresh in my memory as it was
painful at the moment—oh, how painful! To see
that being whose devotedness in the field of three
years' eventful war, in a life of such hardship at the
tender age of fourteen, had been the subject of
wonder to the whole community, in a state bordering on despair, possessing, as she did, the strong
and enthusiastic feelings of her country-women—
who love with a force cooler latitudes cannot boast
of—*this* was to me an awful trial, and although she
had every prospect of care and kindness, to be
separated conveyed to the sensitive mind of youth
(for I was only twenty-four *) every anguish and

* He was nearly twenty-seven. See p. 1 *n.*

horror that is to be imagined. I left her insensible and in a faint. God only knows the number of staggering and appalling dangers I had faced; but, thank the Almighty, I never was unmanned until now, and I leaped on my horse by that impulse which guides the soldier to do his duty.

I had a long ride before me on the noble mare destined to embark with me. On my way I reached a village where I received the attention of a kind old lady, who from her age had been exempt from having any troops quartered on her; but, the village being full of Rifle Brigade, Artillery, and Light Division fellows, the poor old lady was saddled with me. The Artillery readily took charge of my horse. The kind old grandmamma showed me into a neat little bedroom and left me. I threw myself on the bed as one *alone* in all the wide world, a feeling never before experienced, when my eye caught some prints on the wall. What should they be but pictures in representation of the *Sorrows of Werther*, and, strange though it be, they had the contrary effect upon me to that which at the first glance I anticipated. They roused me from my sort of lethargy of grief and inspired a hope which never after abandoned me. The good lady had a nice little supper of *côtelettes de mouton*, and the most beautiful strawberries I ever saw, and she opened a bottle of excellent wine. To gratify her I swallowed by force all I could, for her kindness was maternal.

We soon parted for ever, for I was on horseback

before daylight, *en route* to Pouillac, a village on the Garonne, where we were to embark. On my ride, just at grey daylight, I saw something walking in the air. "It is like a man," I said, "certainly, only that men do not walk in the air." It advanced towards me with apparently rapid strides, and in the excited state of mind I was in, I really believed I was deluded, and ought not to believe *what I saw*. Suspense was intolerable, and I galloped up to it. As I neared my aeronaut, I found it a man walking on stilts about twenty-five feet high. In the imperfect light and the distance, of course the stilts were invisible. The phenomenon was accounted for, and my momentary credulity in I did not know what called to mind stories I had heard recounted, evidently the results of heated imaginations. This walking on stilts is very general in the deep sands of this country.

On reaching Pouillac, I found my trusty old groom West waiting for me. He led me to a comfortable billet, where my portmanteau, all my worldly property, and my second horse, which was to embark with me, were reported "All right, sir." Old West did not ask after "Mrs.," but he looked at me a thousand inquiries, to which I shook my head. I found a note for me at our military post-office from dear little Digby, as consolatory as I could expect.

I was detained two days at Pouillac, in the house of another widow, an elderly lady (all women in France of moderate or certain age were widows at this period). One morning I heard a most extraordinary shout of joyful exclamation, so much so I ran into the room adjoining the one I was sitting in. The poor old woman says, "Oh, come in and witness my happiness!" She was locked in the arms of a big, stout-looking, well-whiskered Frenchman. "Here is my son, oh! my long-lost son, who has been a [prisoner] in England from the beginning of the war." The poor fellow was a *sous-officier* in a man-of-war, and, having been taken early in the war off Boulogne, for years he had been in those accursed monsters of inhuman invention, "the hulks," a prisoner. He made no complaint. He said England had no other place to keep their prisoners, that they were well fed when fed by the English, but when, by an arrangement with France at her own request, that Government fed them, they were half starved. The widow gave a great dinner-party at two o'clock, to which I was of course invited. The poor old lady said, "Now let us drink some of this wine: it was made the year my poor son was taken prisoner. I vowed it should never be opened until he was restored to me, and this day I have broached the cask." The wine was excellent. If all the wine-growers had sons taken prisoners, and kept it thus until their release, the world would be well supplied with good wine in place of bad. Poor family! it was delightful to witness their happiness, while I could but meditate on the contrast between it and my wretchedness. But I lived in hope.

CHAPTER XX.

VOYAGE TO BERMUDA—RENDEZVOUS IN THE CHESA-
PEAKE—BATTLE OF BLADENSBURG AND CAPTURE
OF WASHINGTON — HARRY SMITH SENT HOME
WITH DISPATCHES.

THAT afternoon, after seeing my horses off, I
embarked in a boat, and I and all my personal
property, my one portmanteau, reached the *Royal
Oak*, at her anchorage a few miles below, about
eight o'clock. I found General Ross had not
arrived, but was hourly expected. We soldiers had
heard such accounts of the etiquette required in a
man-of-war, the rigidity with which it was exacted,
etc., that I was half afraid of doing wrong in anything I said or did. When I reached the quarters,
the officer of the watch asked my name, and then, in
the most gentlemanlike and unaffected manner, the
lieutenant of the watch, Holmes (with whom I afterwards became very intimate), showed me aft into
the Admiral's cabin. Here I saw wine, water,
spirits, etc., and at the end of the table sat the finest-
looking specimen of an English sailor I ever saw.
This was Admiral Malcolm, and near him sat
Captain Dick, an exceedingly stout man, a regular

representation of John Bull. They both rose immediately, and welcomed me on board in such an honest and hospitable manner, that I soon discovered the etiquette consisted in nothing but a marked endeavour to make us all happy. The fact is that Army and Navy had recently changed places. When I joined the Army, it was just at a time when our Navy, after a series of brilliant victories, had destroyed at Trafalgar the navy of the world. Nine years had elapsed, and the glories of the Army were so fully appreciated by our gallant brothers of the sea service, we were now by them regarded as the heroes whom I well recollect I thought them to be in 1805.

The Admiral says, "Come, sit down and have a glass of grog." I was so absorbed in the thought that this large floating ship was to bear me away from all I held so dear, that down I sat, and seized a bottle (gin, I believe), filled a tumbler half full, and then added some water. "Well done!" says the Admiral. "I have been at sea, man and boy, these forty years, but d—— me, if I ever saw a stiffer glass of grog than that in my life." He afterwards showed me my cabin, telling me he was punctual in his hours. "I breakfast at eight, dine at three, have tea in the evening, and grog at night, as you see; and if you are thirsty or want anything, my steward's name is Stewart, a Scotchman like myself—tell the Marine at the cabin door to call him and desire him to bring you everything you want." I shall never forget the kindness I received on board the *Royal Oak,* and subsequently on board the *Menelaus* (commanded by poor Sir Peter Parker), and from every ship and every sailor with whom I became associated. Our Navy are noble fellows, and their discipline and the respect on board for rank are a bright example to the more familiar habits of our Army.

General Ross arrived next morning, with his A.D.C., Tom Falls, a Captain in the 20th, and Lieut. De Lacy Evans (subsequently of great notoriety), both as good-hearted fellows as ever wore a sword. The fleet sailed in the afternoon. The troops all embarked in men-of-war, with the lower-deck guns out. We had on board a Company of Artillery; otherwise the force consisted of the 4th Regiment, the 44th, and the 85th. We had a very slow but beautiful passage to St. Michael's, one of the Western Islands, where, as Admiral Malcolm said, " that d——d fellow Clavering, the Duke of York's enemy, had the impudence to call on me," and we embarked live bullocks, fruit, and vegetables.

The parts capable of cultivation in this island are most fertile, and the inhabitants (all Portuguese) looked cheerful and happy. I could then speak Portuguese like a native. One day on shore I walked into a large draper's shop, where I was quite struck by the resemblance of the man behind the counter to my old clerk, Sergeant Manuel. After some little conversation, I discovered he actually was his brother. At first I doubted it, but he fetched me a bundle of letters in which my name frequently appeared. It was an extraordinary rencontre, and my friend Señor Manuel's attention to me was very "gostozo" indeed.

We sailed for Bermuda in a few days. It was a long passage, but we had fine weather until we neared Bermuda, when we fell in with a violent thunderstorm, which carried away the mizen top-mast of the *Royal Oak*.

Much of my time was spent with my friend Holmes, and many is the time I have walked the quarter-deck with him. In any state of grief or excitement, some one who participates and sympathizes in your feeling is always sought for, and this warm-hearted fellow fully entered into all I must feel at the fate of my wife—a foreigner in a foreign land, to whom, though surrounded by many kind friends, everything was strange, every-thing brought home the absence of that being on whom her life depended.

On reaching Bermuda we found the 21st Regi-ment awaiting us, and a communication from the Admiral, Cochrane, Commander-in-chief of the Navy (who commanded on the coast of America 170 Pennons of all descriptions), that a Battalion of Marines was organized under Colonel Malcolm, the Admiral's brother, upwards of 800 strong, so that General Ross's force became respectable. The Admiral proposed to *rendezvous* in Chesapeake Bay so soon as possible.

Ross organized his force into three Brigades,

one commanded by Colonel Thornton, the second
by Colonel Brooke, the third, which comprised all
Naval auxiliaries, by Colonel Malcolm.   A Brigade-
Major was appointed to each.   I was put in orders
Deputy Adjutant-General ; Evan , Deputy Quartermaster-General.   The price of things on this spot
in the ocean was enormous; I, Evans, Macdougall,
of the 85th, Holmes of the Navy, etc., dined on
shore at the inn one day, and were charged fifteen
Spanish dollars for a miserable turkey; but the
excellent fish called a " groper " made up for the
price of the turkey.

General Ross left the troops here, and proceeded
to join the Naval Commander-in-chief in a frigate.
I was the only Staff officer left with Admiral Malcolm,
who was quite as much a soldier in heart as a
sailor ; he prided himself very much on having
brought home the Duke of Wellington (when
Sir A. Wellesley) from India, and he landed his
army at Mondego Bay, before Vimiera.   I never
saw a man sleep so little : four hours a night was
plenty, and half that time he would talk aloud in
his sleep, and if you talked with him would answer
correctly, although next morning he recollected
nothing.

To get from the anchorage at Bermuda is
difficult, and the wind was contrary, and appeared
so likely to continue so, that the Admiral resolved
on the boldest thing that was ever attempted, viz.
to take the whole fleet through the North-east
Passage—a thing never done but by one single

frigate. There was only one man in the island who would undertake to pilot the 74 *Royal Oak* through. The passage is most intricate, and the pilot directs the helmsman by ocular demonstration, that is, by looking into the water at the rocks. It was the most extraordinary thing ever seen, the rocks visible under water all round the ship. Our pilot, a gentleman, said there was only one part of the passage which gave him any apprehension. There was a turn in it, and he was afraid the *Royal Oak* was so long her bows would touch. When her rudder was clear, on my honour, there appeared not a foot to spare. The breeze was very light ; at one period, for half an hour, it almost died away. The only expression the Admiral was heard to make use of was, " Well, if the breeze fails us, it will be a good turn I have done the Yankees." He certainly was a man of iron nerves. The fleet all got through without one ship touching. The Admiral's tender, a small sloop, ran on a rock, but was got off without injury.

At night, after the fleet was well clear (and the bold attempt was of every importance to the success of our expedition, which, as we now began to observe, evidently meditated the capture of Washington), we had rather a good passage to the mouth of the Chesapeake, where we met the Admiral Chief in Command and General Ross. We did not anchor, having a leading wind to take us up the bay. We were going ten knots when the frigate struck on the tail of a bank, with a crash like an earthquake ; she got over, however, without injury. We anchored off the mouth of the Patuxen, the river which leads to Washington.

Next day all the Staff were assembled on board the *Tonnant*, and all the Admirals came on board. We had present—Sir A. Cochrane, Admiral Cockburn (of great renown on the American coast), Admiral Malcolm, Admiral Codrington, Captain of the Fleet, and, if I recollect right, Sir T. Hardy, but he left us next day. After much discussion and poring over bad maps, it was resolved the force should sail up the serpentine and wooded Patuxen in the frigates and smaller vessels. This we did, and it was one of the most beautiful sights the eye could behold. The course of the large river was very tortuous, the country covered with immense forest trees ; thus, to look back, the appearance was that of a large fleet stalking through a wood. We went up as far as we could, and the Navy having very dexterously and gallantly burned and destroyed Commodore Barney's flotilla, which was drawn up to oppose our passage [19, 20 Aug.], the army was landed about thirty-six miles from Washington. I cannot say my dear friend General Ross inspired me with the opinion he was the officer Colborne regarded him as being. He was very cautious in responsibility—awfully so, and lacked that dashing enterprise so essential to carry a place by a *coup de main*. He died the death of a gallant soldier, as he was, and friendship for the man must honour the manes of the brave.

We fell in with the enemy on our second day's march, well posted on the eastern bank. We were told that the only approach to their position was by a bridge through the village of Bladensburg. The day we landed, a most awful spectacle of a man named Calder came in to give us information. He was given in my charge, the secret service department having been confided to me. The poor wretch was covered with leprosy, and I really believe was induced to turn traitor to his country in the hope of receiving medical [aid] from our surgeons, in the miserable state of disease he was in. If such was his object, he is partly to be pardoned. He was a very shrewd, intelligent fellow, and of the utmost use to us. He was afterwards joined by a young man of the name of Brown, as healthy a looking fellow as he was the reverse, who was very useful to us as a guide and as a scout.

When the head of the Light Brigade reached the rising ground, above the bridge, Colonel Thornton immediately proposed to attack, which astonished me [Battle of Bladensburg, 24 Aug.]. We old Light Division always took a good look before we struck, that we might find a vulnerable part. I was saying to General Ross we should make a feint at least on the enemy's left flank, which rested on the river higher up, and I was in the act of pointing out the position, guns, etc., when Colonel Thornton again proposed to move on. I positively laughed at him. He got furiously angry with me ; when, to my horror and astonishment, General Ross consented to this isolated and premature attack. "Heavens!" says I, "if Colborne was to see this!" and I could not refrain from saying, "General Ross, neither of the other Brigades can be up in time to support this mad attack, and if the enemy fight, Thornton's Brigade must be repulsed." It happened just as I said. Thornton advanced, under no cloud of sharpshooters, such as we Light Division should have had, to make the enemy unsteady and render their fire ill-directed. They were strongly posted behind redoubts and in houses, and reserved their fire until Thornton was within fifty yards. Thornton was knocked over, and Brown, commanding the 85th Light Infantry, and Captain Hamilton, a noble fellow from the 52nd, were killed, and the attack repulsed. "There," says I, "there is the art of war and all we have learned under the Duke given in full to the enemy!" Thornton's Brigade was ordered to hold its own until the arrival of the Brigade consisting of the 4th and 44th under Brooke, many men having dropped down dead on the march from the heat, being fat and in bad wind from having been so long on board. As the Brigades closed up, General Ross says, "Now, Smith, do you stop and bring into action the other two Brigades as fast as possible." "Upon what points, sir?" He galloped to the head of Thornton's people, and said, "Come on, my boys," and was the foremost man until the victory was complete. He had two horses shot under him, and was shot in the clothes in two or three places. I fed the fight for him with every possible vigour. Suffice it to say we licked the Yankees and took all their guns, with a loss of upwards of 300 men, whereas Colborne would have done the same thing with probably a loss of 40 or 50, and we entered Washington for the barbarous purpose of destroying the city. Admiral Cockburn would have burnt the whole, but Ross would only consent to the burning of the public buildings. I had no objection to burn arsenals, dockyards, frigates building, stores, barracks, etc., but well do I recollect that, fresh from the Duke's humane warfare in the South of France, we were horrified at the order to burn the elegant Houses of Parliament and the President's house. In the latter, however, we found a supper all ready, which was sufficiently cooked without more fire, and which many of us speedily consumed, unaided by the fiery elements, and drank some very good wine also.* I shall never forget the destructive majesty of the flames as the torches were applied to beds, curtains, etc. Our sailors were artists at the work. Thus was fought the Battle of Bladensburg, which wrested from the Americans their capital Washington, and burnt its Capitol and other buildings with the

---

* Ross wrote, " So unexpected was our entry and capture of Washington, and so confident was Madison of the defeat of our troops, that he had prepared a supper for the expected conquerors ; and when our advanced party entered the President's house, they found a table laid with forty covers " (*Dictionary of National Biography*, " Ross*!*").

ruthless firebrand of the Red Savages of the woods. Neither our Admirals nor the Government at home were satisfied that we had not allowed the work of destruction to progress, as it was considered the total annihilation of Washington would have removed the seat of government to New York, and the Northern and Federal States were adverse to the war with England.

We remained two days, or rather nights, at Washington, and retired on the third night in a most injudicious manner. I had been out in the camp, and when I returned after dark, General Ross says, " I have ordered the army to march at night." " To-night ? " I said. " I hope not, sir. The road you well know, for four miles to Bladensburg, is excellent, and wide enough to march with a front of subdivisions. After that we have to move through woods by a track, not a road. Let us move so as to reach Bladensburg by daylight. Our men will have a night's rest, and be refreshed after the battle. I have also to load all the wounded, and to issue flour, which I have also caused to be collected." (I had seized in Washington everything in the shape of transport, and Baxter, the Staff Surgeon, brought away every wounded man who could travel.) General Ross said, " I have made the arrangement with Evans, and we must march." I muttered to myself, " Oh, for dear John Colborne ! "

We started at nine, and marched rapidly and in good order to Bladensburg, where we halted for about an hour to load the wounded. The barrels of flour were arranged in the streets, the heads knocked in, and every soldier told to take some. Soldiers are greedy fellows, and many filled their haversacks. During a tedious night's march through woods as dark as chaos, they found the flour far from agreeable to carry and threw it away by degrees. If it had not been for the flour thus marking the track, the whole column would have lost its road. Such a scene of intolerable and unnecessary confusion I never witnessed. At daylight we were still not three miles from Bladensburg. Our soldiers were dead done, and so fatigued, there was nothing for it but to halt and bring into play the flour, which was soon set about, while we Staff were looking out like a Lieutenant of the Navy in chase, to see the Yankees come down upon us with showers of sharpshooters. Thanks to their kind consideration they abstained from doing so, but we were very much in their power.

I now began to see how it was that our Light Division gentlemen received so much credit in the army of the dear Duke. I recommend every officer in command to avoid a night march as he would the devil, unless on a good road, and even thus every precaution must be taken by all staff officers to keep up the communications, or regularity cannot be ensured. I have seen many night marches, but I never yet saw time gained, or anything, beyond the evil of fatiguing your men and defeating your own object. You may move before daylight, *i.e.* an hour or two, if the nights are light. By this means, about the time the column requires collection, daylight enables you to do it. You have got a start of your enemy, your men are in full vigour either to march rapidly or, in case of difficulty, to fight. But avoid night marches. However, owing to their want of knowledge of the art of war, the enemy on this occasion allowed us to get to our boats perfectly unmolested.

On one of the days we were near Washington a storm came on, a regular hurricane. It did not last more than twenty minutes, but it was accompanied by a deluge of rain and such a gale that it blew down all our piles of arms and blew the drums out of camp. I never witnessed such a scene as I saw for a few minutes. It resembled the storm in Belshazzar's feast,* and we learnt that even in the river, sheltered by the woods, several of our ships at anchor had been cast on their beam ends.

We gave out we were going to Annapolis, and thence to Baltimore to re-act the conflagration of Washington, and the bait took. Some American gentlemen came in under a flag of truce, evidently to have a look at us, but avowedly to ask how private property had been respected. Their observations were frustrated by our vigilance. I was sent out to receive them, and nothing could

---

* The biblical account of Belshazzar's feast (Daniel v.) does not mention a storm. Sir H. Smith's mental picture was no doubt derived from engravings of Martin's representation of the scene.

exceed their gentlemanlike deportment. I loaded them with questions about roads, resources, force, etc., etc., at Annapolis and Baltimore. It was evident they took the bait, for that night we heard their army was off in full force to Annapolis, leaving us quietly to get down to our ships. We made arrangements for the care and provisioning of the wounded we had left at Bladensburg, and the attention and care they received from the Americans became the character of a civilized nation.

We reached our landing-place unmolested, and at our leisure embarked our army, which began to suffer very much from dysentery. A long sea voyage is the worst possible preparation for long and fatiguing marches. The men are fat, in no exercise, have lost the habit of wearing their accoutrements, packs, etc.—in short, they are not the same army they were on embarcation. Before our men left the Gironde, thirty miles a day would have been nothing to them.

General Ross, just before we went on board, sent for me (there never was a more kind or gallant soldier), and said, "Smith, the sooner I get my dispatch home the better. As you know, it is nearly ready, and as poor Falls, my A.D.C., is too unwell, it is my intention you should be the bearer of my dispatches, and that Falls should go home for the benefit of his health." This most unexpected arrangement set me on the *qui vive* indeed. I had not been in England for seven years. Wife, home, country, all rushed in my mind at once. The

General said, " A frigate is already ordered by the Admiral."

This day my information man, Calder the Leper, came to me, and told me that Brown had been taken and would be hung. I was much distressed. Although one cannot admire a traitor to his country, yet I was some degree of gratitude in his debt, and I said, " Well, Calder, but can we do nothing to save him ? " " Well, now I calculate that's not to be denied, and if I hear General Ross say, ' If I catch that rascal Brown, I will hang him like carrion,' he may be saved, for I would go at once among our people (they will not injure me), and I will swear I heard General Ross say so." I immediately went to the General. On the first view of the thing, his noble nature revolted at making an assertion he never intended to abide by. At length, however, to save the poor wretch's life, he consented, and in course of a desultory conversation with Calder, dovetailed the words required into it. I saw Calder catch at it. When he left the General's tent, he said to me, " Well, now, I calculate Brown may yet live many years." He left us that night with a purse of money and a long string of medical instructions for the benefit of his health from one of our surgeons. " Ah," says he, " this will save *me* " (meaning the medical advice) ; " I can save Brown." I had an hiero-glyphical note from him brought by a slave, just before I sailed [30 ? Aug. 1814], to say " All's right, you may reckon." I told this story afterwards to the Prince Regent. He was exceedingly amused.

The *Iphigenia* frigate, Captain King, was to take me home, and Captain Wainwright of the *Tonnant* was to be the bearer of the naval dispatches. Sir Alexander Cochrane, Admiral Cockburn, and Evans, burning with ambition, had urged General Ross to move on Baltimore. The General was against it, and kindly asked my opinion. I opposed it, not by opinions or argument, but by a simple statement of facts.

"1. We have, by a ruse, induced the enemy to concentrate all his means at Baltimore.

"2. A *coup de main* like the conflagration of Washington may be effected once during a war, but can rarely be repeated.

"3. The approach to Baltimore Harbour will be effectually obstructed." "Oh," says the General, "so the Admirals say; but they say that in one hour they would open the passage." I laughed. "It is easier said than done, you will see, General." (The passage defied their exertions when tested.)

"4. Your whole army is a handful of men, and the half of them are sick from dysentery.

"5. Your success in the attack on Washington is extraordinary, and will have a general effect. Your success on Baltimore would add little to that effect, admitting you were successful, which I again repeat I doubt, while a reverse before Baltimore would restore the Americans' confidence in their own power, and wipe away the stain of their previous discomfiture."

General Ross says, "I agree with you. Such is my decided opinion." "Then, sir, may I tell Lord Bathurst you will not go to Baltimore?" He said, "Yes." I was delighted, for I had a presentiment of disaster, founded on what I have stated.

The day we were to sail in the *Iphigenia*, as I left the *Tonnant*, kind-hearted General Ross, whom I loved as a brother, accompanied me to the gangway. His most sensible and amiable wife was at Bath. I promised to go there the moment I had delivered my dispatches, and of course I was charged with a variety of messages. In the warmth of a generous heart he shook my hand, and said, "A pleasant voyage, dear Smith, and thank you heartily for all your exertions and the assistance you have afforded me. I can ill spare you." My answer was, "Dear friend, I will soon be back to you, and may I assure Lord Bathurst you will not attempt Baltimore?" "*You may*." These were the last words I ever heard that gallant soul utter. He was over-ruled: attempted Baltimore [12 Sept. 1814], failed, and lost his noble life. A more gallant and amiable man never existed, and one who, in the continuance of command, would have become a General of great ability. But few men, who from a Regiment to a Brigade are suddenly pushed into supreme authority and have a variety of conflicting considerations to cope with—Navy,

Army, country, resources, etc., are at the outset perfectly at home.

The *Iphigenia* had a most extraordinary passage from the Chesapeake to our anchorage at Spithead. We were only twenty-one days. The kindness I received from Captain King I shall never forget. The rapidity of our voyage was consonant to my feelings and in perfect accordance with my character.

CHAPTER XXI.

HARRY SMITH ONCE MORE IN ENGLAND—REUNION
WITH HIS WIFE IN LONDON—INTERVIEW WITH THE
PRINCE REGENT—DINNER AT LORD BATHURST'S—
A JOURNEY TO BATH—HARRY SMITH INTRODUCES
HIS WIFE TO HIS FATHER—VISIT TO WHITTLESEY
—HE RECEIVES ORDERS TO RETURN TO AMERICA
UNDER SIR EDWARD PAKENHAM.

WAINWRIGHT and I started from the George Inn,
Portsmouth, which I well knew, with four horses at
five o'clock. I do not know what he considered
himself, but I was of opinion that, as the bearer of
dispatches to Government, I was one of the greatest
men in England. Just before we started, our outfit
merchant and general agent, tailor, etc., by name
Meyers, who had been very civil to me going out
to South America, begged to speak to me. He
said, "I find the *Iphigenia* is from America, from
the Chesapeake: that little box under your arm
contains, I see, dispatches." "Well," I said, "what
of that?" "If you will tell me their general
purport, whether *good news* or *bad*, I will make
it worth your while, and you may secure some
pounds for a refit." At first I felt inclined to

P

knock him down. On a moment's reflexion I thought, "every one to his trade," so I compromised my feelings of indignation in rather a high tone of voice, and with "I'd see you d—— first; but of what use would such general information be to you?" He, a knowing fellow, began to think *the pounds* were in my thoughts, so he readily said, "I could get a man on horseback in London two hours before you, and good news or bad on 'Change' is my object. Now do you understand?" I said, "Perfectly, and when I return to America I shall expect a capital outfit from you for all the valuable information I have afforded you. Good-bye, Meyers."

Oh! the delight of that journey. I made the boys drive a furiously good pace. D—— me, if I had rather be beating off a leeshore in a gale, tide against me! The very hedgerows, the houses, the farms, the cattle, the healthy population all neatly clothed, all in occupation; no naked slaves, no burned villages, no starving, wretched inhabitants, no trace of damnable and accursed war! For seven years, an immense period in early life, I had viewed nothing beyond the seat of a war, a *glorious* war, I admit, but in that glory, death in its most various shapes, misery of nations, hardships, privations, wounds, and sickness, and their concomitants. The wild excitement bears a soldier happily through. My career had been a most fortunate one. Still the contrast around me was as striking as the first appearance of a white and clothed man

to a naked savage. The happy feeling of being in
my native land once more, in health and in possession of every limb, excited a maddening sensation
of doubt, anxiety, hope, and dread, all summed up
in this—"Does your young wife live? Is she
well?" Oh! the pain, the hope, the fear, and the
faith in Almighty God, who had so wonderfully
protected me, must have turned the brain if endur-
ance had continued, for I had never heard of her
since we parted.

At twelve o'clock we were in London, and
drove to Downing Street, where I lodged my dispatches; then we sought out a bivouac, I and poor
Falls. The navy man was off to the Admiralty.
Every inn was full near Downing Street, at least
where I desired to be. At last we got to the
Salopian Coffee-house in Parliament Street. The
waiter said, "One spare bedroom, sir; nothing
more." "Oh, plenty!" we said. We had been
feasting on the road on that indigenous-to-England
luxury of bread, butter, cream, and tea. All we
wanted was an hour or two's sleep, for, at that time
of night, as to finding any one, we might as well
have been back in America! The chambermaid
said, "Only one room, sir." "Plenty," we said.
"But only one bed, gentlemen!" "Plenty," we
said. "Bring up the portmanteau, West." When
we got to the room and proceeded (West and I) to
divide this copious bed into two by hauling half
the clothes on the floor, according to our custom
of seven years, the astonishment of the poor

chambermaid is not to be described. We bundled her out and were asleep before a minute.

By daylight I was in a hackney coach, and drove to the British (the Scotch) barracks of my old Rifle comrades. There I asked the porter the name of any officer he knew. At last he stammered out some. "Colonel Ross? What regiment?" says I. "He had a green jacket when he came up." I knew it was my dear friend John Ross. "Where is the room?" I said. "Oh, don't disturb the gentleman, sir; he is only just gone to bed." Says I, "My friend, I have often turned him out, and he shall quickly be broad awake now." He showed the room. In I bolted. "Halloa, Ross, stand to your arms." "Who the devil are you?" "Harry Smith," I said; "fall in." Our joy was mutual. "Well, but quiet, John; is my wife alive and well?" "All right, thank God, Harry, in every respect as you would wish. I was with her yesterday." "Where, John? where?" "In Panton Square, No. 11." It is difficult to decide whether excess of joy or of grief is the most difficult to bear; but seven years' fields of blood had not seared my heart or blunted my naturally very acute feelings, and I burst into a flood of tears. "Oh, thank Almighty God." Soon I was in Panton Square, with my hand on the window of the coach, looking for the number, when I heard a shriek, "Oh Dios, la mano de mi Enrique!" Never shall I forget that shriek; never shall I forget the effusion of our gratitude to God, as we held each other in an embrace of love few can ever have known, cemented by every peculiarity of our union and the eventful scenes of our lives. Oh! you who enter into holy wedlock for the sake of connexions—tame, cool, amiable, good, I admit—you cannot feel what we did. That moment of our lives was worth the whole of your apathetic ones for years. We were unbounded in love for each other, and in gratitude to God for all His mercies. Poor little Pug was, in her way, as delighted to see me as her more happy mistress, and many an anecdote was told me of her assisting by moaning pitifully when my wife grieved aloud, as she was sometimes induced to do.

This happy reunion effected, I was off to Downing Street, where my Lord Bathurst received me in the kindest manner, and said, "The intelligence you bring is of such importance, the Prince Regent desires to see you. We will go immediately." I said, "My Lord, be so good as to allow me to take the map I brought you." "It is here." And off we started to Carlton House. We were shown into a large room where Lord Bathurst fortunately left me for half an hour, which enabled me somewhat to allay my excited imagination and return to the battlefields. I was soon deep in thought, when a sort of modesty came over me at the idea of approaching England's (*actual*) king. I gave my head a toss, saying, "I never quailed before the dear Duke of Wellington, with his piercing eye, not will I now, and General Ross begged of me to talk;" for His Royal Highness, the story went, complained that "the bearer of dispatches will never talk." Johnny Kincaid says I was an "impudent fellow." At any rate, I determined, if I saw His Royal Highness really desired me to be communicative, I would not be unready. While I was forming all sorts of plans for both attack and defence, in came Lord Bathurst: "The Prince will see you." So I said, "My Lord, if we were in camp, I could take your Lordship all about, but I know nothing of the etiquette of a court." So he says, "Oh, just behave as you would to any gentleman; His Highness's manner will soon put you at ease. Call him 'Sir,' and do not turn your back on him." "No," says I, "my Lord, I know that; and my profession is one of 'show a good front.'" In we went to the Prince's dressing-room, full of every sort of article of dress, perfumes, snuff-boxes, wigs, every variety of article, I do believe, that London could produce. His Highness rose in the most gracious manner, and welcomed me to his presence by saying, "General Ross strongly recommended you to my notice * as an officer who can afford me every information of the service you come to report, the importance of which is marked by the firing of the Parliament and Tower guns you now hear." I

---

* "From Major-General Ross to Earl Bathurst.

"*Tonnant* in the Patuxent, Aug. 30, 1814.

"Captain Smith, assistant adjutant-general to the troops, who will have the honor to deliver this dispatch, I beg leave to recommend to your lordship's protection, as an officer of much merit and great promise, and capable of affording any further information that may be requisite" (Given in W. James's *Military Occurrences of the Late War* (1818), ii. p. 498).

could not refrain from smiling within myself at Harry Smith of the Light Division sitting with the Prince Regent, and all London in an uproar at the news he brought. I was perfectly thunderstruck at the military questions the Prince asked me. He opened a map of America, and then referred to the plan of Washington I had brought home, with the public buildings burnt marked in red. He asked the name of each, and in his heart I fancied I saw he thought it a barbarian act. On all other topics he spoke out. I said it was to be regretted a sufficient force had not been sent to hold Washington. His Highness said, "What do you call a sufficient force?" I said, "14,000 men." He very shrewdly asked on what I based such an opinion. I talked of Navy, of population, etc., and perfectly satisfied His Highness I did not give an opinion at random. He asked a variety of questions, and laughed exceedingly when I told him the anecdote of Calder's promising to save Brown. When I got up to leave the room, and was backing out, His Highness rather followed me, and asked if I were any relation of his friend, Sir —— Smith, in Shropshire. I said, "No." He then said, "I and the country are obliged to you all. Ross's recommendations will not be forgotten, and, Bathurst, don't forget this officer's promotion." It was the most gentlemanlike and affable interview I could possibly imagine.

That evening I was to dine at Lord Bathurst's, at Putney. I never met a more amiable-mannered

man than Lord Bathurst ; and his secretary, Punch
Greville,* volunteered to drive me out in his
tilbury.   When I got into the drawing-room, who
should be there but my dear friend Lord Fitzroy
Somerset ? He had been recently married.   At
dinner I sat between Lady Fitzroy and an elderly
gentleman whose name I did not know, and, as the
party was small, and I the lion, every one induced
me to talk.   Lord Fitzroy and I across the table
got back into Spain ; and, of course, as I regarded
the Duke of Wellington as something elevated
beyond any human being, and I was in high spirits,
I did not hesitate to launch forth our opinion of
him.   The elderly gentleman who sat next me said,
" I am very glad to hear you speak in such raptures
of the Duke.   He is my brother."   I laughed, and
said, " I have not exceeded in anything, to the best
of my judgment."   After dinner Lord Fitzroy
Somerset and I had a long talk.   He had travelled
after Toulouse, in a little carriage from Bordeaux
to Cadiz with the Duke, and their conversation
frequently turned on the Army.   Fresh are the
words on my mind at this moment.   " The Duke
often said to me, ' The Light, 3rd and 4th Divisions
were the *élite* of my army, but the Light had this
peculiar perfection.   No matter what was the arduous
service they were employed on, when I rode up next
day, I still found a *Division*.   They never lost one
half the men other Divisions did.' "   I was delighted,

* Charles Cavendish Fulke Greville (1794–1865), Clerk to the
Privy Council from 1821 ; author of the *Greville Memoirs ;* known to
his friends as Punch, or the Gruncher (*Dict. Nat. Biog.*).

for this was what we so prided ourselves on. I have often heard our soldiers bullying one another about the number such a Company had lost, always attaching discredit to the loss. It was a peculiar feeling, and one which actuated them throughout the war, combined with the most undaunted bravery and stratagem as sharpshooters.

But I must revert to domestic matters. My wife had refused all the entreaties of my family to leave London before my return. She availed herself of masters, and saw so many friends daily. She had a forcible impression that I should not be long away. We started for Bath, and I wrote to my father to come to London in a few days, and we would return with him to Whittlesea. We found poor Mrs. Ross in the highest spirits at the achievement of our arms under her husband. Poor thing! at that very moment of her excessive happiness he was in a soldier's bloody grave. The delight of our journey to and from Bath is not to be described. Everything was modern, novel, and amusing to my wife: every trifle called forth a comparison with Spain, although she admitted that there was no comparison between our inns and the Spanish *posadas*, so accurately described in *Gil Blas*. No brutal railroads in those days, where all are flying prisoners. We dined where we liked; we did as we liked. At the last stage back into London, my wife, in looking at a newspaper (for she began to read English far better than she spoke), saw my promotion to the rank of Major—"The reward," she said, "of our separation."

On arrival in London we found my father had arrived from the country. I had not seen him for seven years. In this period *he* had been deprived of his devoted wife, leaving him eleven children, *I*, of a mother; for everything that word comprises in its most comprehensive sense I had lost. Our pleasure at meeting, as may be supposed, was excessive, while we mingled our tears for the departed. As my wife had just come off a journey, and it was late in the afternoon, I would not show her to my father until she was dressed for dinner: a little bit of vanity and deception on my part, for I led him to believe she was of the stiff Spanish school, as stately as a swan and about as proud as a peacock. She liked the fun of the deception, and promised to dress in full Spanish costume, and act up to the supposition. In she came, looking—oh! if I could but describe her! but in place of acting either the swan or the peacock, she bounded into my father's arms, who cried like a child, between joy, admiration, astonishment and delight at seeing so young and beautiful a creature who had gone through so much, and showed a heart evidently framed for love. She was now nearly eighteen, but a woman—not a girl, and certainly a person of most distinguished appearance, especially in her Spanish costume; not handsome, if beauty depends on regularity of features, for she had the dark complexion of the fairer part of her countrywomen, but with a colour beneath the clearest skin of olive which gave a lustre to her countenance—a countenance

Walker & Cockerell. ph. sc.

Juana Maria (Lady) Smith.

illumined by a pair of dark eyes possessing all
the fire of a vivid imagination, and an expression
which required not the use of speech.   Her figure
was beautiful, and never was any costume so
calculated to exhibit it in perfection and in all its
graces as that of her native land.   She had a profusion of the darkest brown hair; teeth, though not
regular, as white as pearls; with a voice most silvery
and sweet in conversation, and she would sing the
melancholy airs and songs of constancy of her
country (so celebrated for them) with a power and
depth of voice and feeling peculiar to Spain.   Her
foot and ankle were truly Spanish.   She danced
beautifully.   Thus it was that the natural grace of
her figure and carriage was developed, while the
incomparable elegance and simplicity of her manner
was a thing not to be forgotten, rarely to be met
with.   Her pronunciation of English at this period
was most fascinating, and when she wanted a word,
the brilliancy and expression of the eye would supply
it.   It flashed perpetually as she spoke, and filled up
the intervals her slight knowledge of our language
could not supply.   She was animated and intelligent,
with a touching tone of confidence and gentleness
which made the hearer a willing listener to her
words, but still her meaning was supplied by her
vivid countenance.   Such was the being my affectionate and kind-hearted father held locked in his
paternal embrace, the faithful wife of his son.   They
were ever afterwards friends in every sense of the
word, and, as he was the best and boldest horseman

I ever saw in my life, and she could ride beautifully and any horse, they were inseparable. Poor "Old Chap," my war horse, which, together with her Andalusian "Tiny," I had sent to him, was dead, but, the morning after our arrival at Whittlesea, we were taken to the stall. There was Tiny in *such* condition! The meeting between my wife and the horse was, as she said, that of compatriots in a foreign land. It was rendered still more amusing by the little pug and horse equally recognizing each other, for many a day had Tiny carried Pug. (My dear little thorough-bred horse I had so cried over * was still alive and fresh, but alas! I had grown out of his memory. He was standing in the next stall, and had acquired the name of "Old Jack.") My wife let Tiny loose, to the alarm of my father, who expected to see him fly off full speed into his garden, which he prided himself on considerably. To his astonishment, and to mine too (for my father told me the groom could barely lead him), she says, "Now don't make a noise, and he will follow me like a dog," which he did into the drawing-room, occasionally licking her hand or face when she allowed him. The saddle, however, was soon on him, and, as if proud to show off that he was broken in like a Mameluke's, she figured him so that few Mamelukes, jerreed † in hand, could have touched her with effect.

* See p. 158.
† Byron, *The Giaour :*

"Swift as the hurled on high jerreed,
    Springs to the touch his startled steed."

In the midst of [happiness] I had the most melancholy visit to pay to my mother's tomb. If ever souls on earth could commune, I was so fascinated by the hallowed spot, which contained all which I so adored from my infancy, my consoler, my counsellor, my guide to the holy hill of God, I really believed I heard her speak when I prayed over her head and again vowed my promises at parting. Oh! that she could have lived to know my elevation, my being the bearer of dispatches to our King, that she could have seen my wife, that she could have shared, Heaven bless her, in the happiness of her children around! This one blank was for the moment all I lacked. I consoled myself that while we were revelling on earth with every uncertainty before us, she, my mother, was in heaven, where I dare firmly believe she is, for God is gracious and bountiful.

On my return from that hallowed and sacred spot, I found letters from the Horse Guards. The first was to order me to London immediately, the next was to tell me what I little anticipated. General Ross, contrary to his own opinion and his promise, had attempted Baltimore [12 Sept.], failed, as I anticipated, and lost his gallant life from not following the dictates of his own good sense and ability. My dear friend Sir Edward Pakenham was appointed to succeed him. I was appointed A.A.G. to the increased force going out! I had been nearly three weeks under the paternal and hospitable roof—my only holiday for years—when that blighting word

" separation " was again to be imparted to my faithful and adoring wife; and, cut off from all social ties of happiness and endearment, I was again immediately, in the very middle of winter, to encounter the stormy Atlantic and all the horrors of war in the distance. It is only a repetition of the former tale to talk of my poor wife's distress. It was agreed she was to accompany me to London, and my father was to bring her back; and twenty-four hours later, while brothers and sisters re-echoed each others' promises, and indeed feelings, of affection, we started back to London, with hearts as heavy as they were light coming down. I little thought then of what I had to go through, witness, and endure, but, if I had, my task would still have been to affect a cheerfulness in the prospect of more promotion which, I avow candidly, I did not feel. However, I was a soldier, and as much wedded to my profession and a sense of duty as any man, so I lit up my torch of hope and did all in my power to cheer and comfort her I so loved.

On our arrival in London I immediately went to poor dear Sir Edward Pakenham, who was delighted to see me, and said that we must be in Portsmouth in a few days, and that the *Statira* frigate was waiting for us. I then sought out Macdougall of the 85th, who before I left the Army had been acting, in place of sick Falls, as A.D.C. to poor Ross, and I readily learned all that occurred before the service lost that gallant soldier. My firm and faithful friend John Robb, surgeon of the 95th when I joined, was appointed Inspector-General of Hospitals, and he and I agreed to send our baggage by coach, and go down together to Portsmouth in a post chaise on Sunday afternoon, for the *Statira* was to sail on Monday. Old West was started off per coach, and at three o'clock on Sunday, the — November, the horrible scene of parting was again to be endured. It was less painful to me than the first, I admit, for my dear wife was now known and beloved by all my family; but to her the dread of separation, and separation for the exploits of war, was as painful as before, and, when I tore myself from her, which I was literally obliged to do, that heart must be hard indeed that was not, as mine was, ready to break. I can see her now, with her head resting on the chimney-piece (as I left the room, and took a farewell glance) in a state bordering on despair. My father, too, was awfully overcome.

In a few minutes I was rolling on my road to Portsmouth, deeply absorbed, I admit, but my companion Robb was a man of strong mind, of whom I had a high opinion, and not to appear desponding before him, I exerted all my energy and began to talk of my plans on my return. Robb said—the only thing I ever heard him say that I thought would have been as well unsaid—"Oh, that's capital! a fellow going out to be killed by an American Rifleman, talking of what he will do when he comes back!" Now, such is the perversity of human nature, this so put up my blood, that grief and anguish were mitigated in a determined spirit of opposition.

We arrived at the George at twelve at night, and found West, who reported all right. We found an order directing us to be on board by ten o'clock, as the ship would get under weigh at twelve, and we knew that our men of war are punctual fellows.

The next morning, at breakfast, we directed old West to parade our portmanteaus. My kit had increased just double, viz. I had now *two* portmanteaus. " Here they are, sir," says West. " Why, that is not mine, West ! " He overhauled it, and soon agreed with me. We went to the coach ; there was no other. So I opened it, and, to my horror, in place of my things, it contained the dirty linen of a Frenchman and his silk stockings and evening pantaloons, etc., etc. Upon a little inquiry from poor old West, we learned that two coaches were loading at the same time, one for Dover, the other for Portsmouth. It was evident, therefore, my red coats were in company with my French friend. In my portmanteau were all my boots, my uniform, and my flannel waistcoats. We were to embark immediately, and I had nothing for it but to go to my *friend,** and tell him, " Now's the time for the outfit: I have lost my portmanteau." He very kindly undertook to write to Charing Cross and send back the Frenchman's, and in three weeks after the failure at New Orleans my portmanteau

* See p. 209.

was sent out to me by my dear friend John Bell. It is a very odd coincidence that, on my first going abroad to South America, I lost my kit and all my large stock of silver given me by my poor mother —some teaspoons, etc. On that occasion I never recovered anything.

CHAPTER XXII.

SAILS WITH SIR EDWARD PAKENHAM ON THE EXPE-
DITION AGAINST NEW ORLEANS—REVERSE OF
8 JANUARY, 1815, AND DEATH OF PAKENHAM—
SIR JOHN LAMBERT SUCCEEDS TO THE COMMAND,
APPOINTS HARRY SMITH HIS MILITARY SECRETARY
AND WITHDRAWS THE FORCE.

WE soon reached our frigate, and oh, so crowded
as she was!—Sir Edward Pakenham and all his
Staff, the Commanders of the Engineers and Artillerymen with their Staff, and about thirty pas-
sengers! The most of us slept in cots in the
steerage. Young D'Este, the real Duke of Sussex,*
was a fund of great amusement, the most gentlemanlike, kind-hearted young fellow possible, affable
to a degree, and most unpretending; but he had a
thirst for obtaining information, I never beheld
before. Consequently he laid himself open to some
very peculiar replies to his queries. He proved
himself on shore, like all the royal family, a gallant

* Augustus Frederick (b. 1794), only son of Augustus Frederick
Duke of Sussex (son of George III.), by his marriage with Lady
Augusta Murray. The two children of this marriage, when disinherited
by the Royal Marriage Act, took the name D'Este.

and intrepid soldier, and the best shot with a rifle
for a youth that I have almost ever seen. He
attached himself passionately to me on board and on
shore, and if he ever became Elector of Hanover, I
was to have been his Secretary.

We had a very agreeable party of gallant old
Peninsular soldiers, and dear Sir Edward was one
of the most amusing persons imaginable—a high-
minded and chivalrous fellow in every idea, and,
to our astonishment, very devoutly inclined ; and
Major Gibbs, who was afterwards killed on the
same day as Sir Edward, was a noble fellow.

The *Statira* was a noble frigate ; she had a
full complement of men, and was in crack order,
having every individual on board but the individual
who had put her in—that Irish Captain Stackpoole,
of duelling celebrity, who had very shortly before
been shot in the West Indies by a Lieutenant of
another ship on whom he saddled a quarrel origi-
nating in an occurrence when both were middies.
The Lieutenant denied all recollection of it to no
purpose. Stackpoole insisted on his going out.
The Lieutenant, it was said, had never fired a pistol
in his life, but at the first shot Stackpoole fell dead.
I never saw a body of officers and men more
attached than these were to their last Captain.
Every one had some anecdote of his kindness and
ability as a seaman. The propensity which cost
him his life can be attributed, I am firmly of opinion,
to nothing but a strain of insanity upon that particular subject alone. His prowess as a shot with a

pistol, it was asserted, was inconceivable, but "the battle is not always to the strong."

On this voyage I had two opportunities of writing to my wife, or, rather, sending her the sheets of a sort of journal which she made me promise to keep. Our Captain, Swaine, a neighbour of mine in Cambridgeshire, was of the old school, and made everything snug at night by shortening sail, to the great amusement of poor Stackpoole's crew, accustomed to carry on night and day. But for this, we should have been off the mouth of the Mississippi at the time when Sir Edward was informed a fleet and his army would rendezvous for an assault on New Orleans. As it was, we did [not] reach the fleet until [25 Dec.] three days after the landing had been effected, and our army under Major-General Sir J. Keane, now Lord Keane (as noble a soldier as our country ever produced) had sustained a sharp night-attack. Stovin, the A.G., had been shot through the neck, and I was at the head of the department.

I never served under a man whose good opinion I was so desirous of having as Sir Edward Pakenham, and proud was I to find I daily succeeded. I was always with him, and usually lay in my cloak in his room. The second day after we reached General Keane [28 Dec.], the army was moved up to reconnoitre the enemy's position, or to attack, if we saw it practicable. I was that day delighted with Sir Edward: he evinced an animation, a knowledge of ground, of his own resources and the strength of the enemy's position, which reminded us of his brother-in-law, *our Duke.* The Staff were very near the enemy's line, when I saw some rifle-men evidently creeping down and not farther off than a hundred yards, and so I very abruptly said, " Ride away, Sir Edward, behind this bank, or you will be shot in a second. By your action you will be recognized as the Commander-in-Chief, and some riflemen are now going to fire." The American riflemen are very slow, though the most excellent shots. My manner was so impressive he came away. As we were returning that evening he called me to him, and said, "You gentlemen of the Craufurd school" (he was very fond of our old Light Division) "are very abrupt and peremptory in your manner to your Generals. Would you have spoken to Craufurd as you did to me to-day?" I said, ' Most certainly, for if I had not, and one of us had been killed or wounded, and he became aware I observed what I did when I spoke to you, he would have blown me up as I deserved. He taught us to do so." How my dear friend Sir Edward laughed !

We soon found that, with our present force, the enemy's position was impregnable. A Brigade was, however, daily expected, under Sir J. Lambert. While we were looking out with our telescopes, Sir Edward turned very abruptly to me, and said, " Now for a Light Division [opinion]. What do you say, Smith, as to the practicability of an attack on the enemy's line ?" I replied, "His position is strong—his left being on an impracticable morass, his right on the Mississippi; the ground is a dead flat, intersected with ditches which will impede our troops. The enemy has, literally, a breastwork, and plenty of men upon it, and their fire will sweep the plain with unerring precision, causing us great loss; for we can produce no fire, flank or otherwise, to render them uneasy or unsteady. As yet, the enemy has not occupied the opposite bank of the river. He has two armed vessels in the river. We must destroy these as soon as possible, possess the right bank of the Mississippi, enfilade the enemy's position with our fire (the width of the river being only from seven to eight hundred yards), and, so soon as we open a fire from the right bank, we should storm the work in two, three, or more columns." "You Rifle gentlemen have learnt something, I do believe." I did not know at the time whether he said this in jest or not, for he was a most light-hearted fellow; but, when we got back to the house we put up in, he sent for me. He had a plan of the works and position of the enemy before him, and said, "Smith, I entirely [concur] in all you said in the field to-day. In the meanwhile, we must facilitate our communications by roads in our rear, etc. I will erect batteries and destroy the ships, and, when the batteries are complete, they shall open on the enemy. If they can destroy the enemy's defence in any part, or silence the fire of his batteries, the army shall storm at once. Lambert's arrival is very uncertain." I remarked, if Lambert's arrival was so uncertain, we had no alternative, and under any circumstances the ships must be destroyed and batteries erected, whether Lambert's force arrived or not.

We succeeded in destroying one ship—we *might have* destroyed both. We erected several batteries, their defences principally sugar-casks,—for here on the plain, on the banks of the Mississippi, if you dug eight inches, water followed : hence to erect batteries with earth was impracticable, and we had not sufficient sand-bags. The defences of our batteries, therefore, were reported complete on the night of the 31st December. The army was formed into two columns of attack—one threatening the right flank, the other the left, and a party was hid in the reeds in the morass on the enemy's left flank with orders to penetrate, if possible, and disturb the enemy's left.

At daybreak on the 1st of January, 1815, our troops were formed, and our batteries opened. They had not the slightest effect on the enemy. On the contrary, his shot went through the imperfect defence, caused our noble artillerymen great loss, and silenced our batteries. Hence there was no attack, and Sir Edward still more strenuously adhered to the necessity of occupying the right bank of the river. The troops were withdrawn, except such strong picquets as were left to protect the guns in the [batteries].

Poor Sir Edward was much mortified at being obliged to retire the army from a second demonstration and disposition to attack, but there was nothing for it. It came on to rain in the evening, and was both wet and cold. Sir Edward slept in a little house in advance of his usual quarters. He told me to stay with him, and all his Staff to return to the usual house. He said, "Smith, those guns must be brought back; go and do it." I said, "It will require a great many men." "Well," he says, "take 600 from Gibbs's Brigade." Off I started. The soldiers were sulky, and neither the 21st nor the 44th were distinguished for discipline—certainly not of the sort I had been accustomed to. After every exertion I could induce them to make, I saw I had no chance of success—to my mortification, for to return and say to Sir Edward I could not effect it, was as bad as the loss of a leg. However, the night was wearing, and my alternative decided; so I told him as quietly as I could. He saw I was mortified, and said nothing, but jumped up in his cloak, and says, "Be so good as to order my horse, and go on and turn out Gibbs's whole Brigade quietly." They were under arms by the time he arrived, and by dint of exertion and his saying, "I am Sir Edward Pakenham, etc., and Commander-in-Chief," as well as using every expression to induce officers and soldiers to exertion, just as daylight appeared he had completed the task, and the Brigade returned to its ground. As we were riding back Sir Edward said, "You see, Smith, exertion and determination will effect anything." I was cruelly mortified, and said, "Your excitement, your name, your energy, as Commander-in-Chief with a whole Brigade, most certainly has done that which I failed in with 600 men, but I assure you, Sir Edward, I did all I could." His noble heart at once observed my misery. He said, " I admire your mortification ; it shows your zeal. Why *I* barely effected, with all the exertion of the Commander-in-Chief, and, as you say, a Brigade, what I expected you to do with one-fourth of the men ! " He might have added, " and I did with some of the guns what you dare not even recommend to me." Oh, how I was comforted ! To fall in his estimation would have been worse than death by far.

In a day or two we had information that Lambert's Brigade, the 7th Fusiliers and the 43rd Foot, [had arrived]. Two such Corps would turn the tide of a general action. We were rejoiced ! Sir Edward then made preparations to cross the river, and so to widen a little stream as to get the boats into the Mississippi. The story has been too often told to repeat. Lambert's Brigade landed, and, upon a representation made to Sir Edward by Major Sir G. Tylden, who was an Assistant Adjutant-General like myself, but a senior officer (as kind a fellow as ever lived), that, in Stovin's incapacity from his wound, he must be at the head of the Adjutant-General's Department, Sir Edward sent for me. "Smith," he said, " it was my intention you should have remained with me, Tylden with Lambert ; but he claims his right as senior officer. You would not wish me to do an unjust thing when the claim is preferred?" I said, with my heart in my mouth, " Certainly not, sir." (I do believe I was more attached to Sir Edward, as a soldier, than I was to John Colborne, *if possible.*) "You must, therefore, go to Lambert. I will [enter] this arrangement in Orders; but, rely on it, I shall find enough for you and him to do too."

The night of the 7th January, the rivulet (or bayou, as then called) was reported dammed, and the boats above the dam ready for the banks of the Mississippi to be cut. The water within the banks was higher than the level of the water in the bayou, consequently so much water must be let into the bayou as to provide for the level. In the meanwhile, the enemy had not been asleep. They had been apprised of our operations to establish ourselves on the right bank; they had landed the guns from the second ship (which we ought to have destroyed), and were respectably in possession of that which we must turn them out of. Sir Edward Pakenham went to inspect the bayou, the boats, etc. I heard him say to the engineer, " Are you satisfied the dam will bear the weight of water which will be upon it when the banks of the river are cut?" He said, " Perfectly." " I should be far more so if a second dam was constructed." The engineer was positive. After dark the banks were cut, the dam went as Sir Edward seemed to anticipate, and the delay in repairing it prevented the boats being got into the river in time for the troops under Colonel Thornton of the 85th to reach their ground and

make a simultaneous attack with the main body,
according to the plan arranged. Sir John Lambert's
Brigade, the *élite* 7th Fusiliers and 43rd, were in
reserve. Sir Edward said, " Those fellows would
storm anything, but, indeed, so will the others, and
when we are in New Orleans, I can depend upon
Lambert's Reserve." We were all formed in three
columns [8 Jan.], about 6000 British soldiers and
some sailors : a column under Colonel Renny of
the 21st were destined to proceed on the banks of
the river and right of the enemy, and carry a
powerful battery which enfiladed the whole position :
General Keane's Brigade was to assail the enemy's
right-central position : General Gibbs's Brigade
to attack well upon the enemy's left : General
Lambert's Brigade to be in reserve nearer Gibbs's
Brigade than Keane's.

About half an hour before daylight, while I was
with General Lambert's column, standing ready, Sir
Edward Pakenham sent for me. I was soon with
him. He was greatly agitated. " Smith, most
Commanders-in-Chief have many difficulties to contend with, but surely none like mine. The dam,
as you heard me say it would, gave way, and
Thornton's people will be of no use whatever to
the general attack." I said, " So impressed have
you ever been, so obvious is it in every military
point of view, we should possess the right bank of
the river, and thus enfilade and divert the attention
of the enemy ; there is still time before daylight to
retire the columns now. We are under the enemy's

fire so soon as discovered." He says, "This may
be, but I have twice deferred the attack. We are
strong in numbers now comparatively. It will cost
more men, and the assault must be made." I again
urged delay. While we were talking, the streaks of
daylight began to appear, although the morning
was dull, close, and heavy, the clouds almost touching
the ground. He said, "Smith, order the rocket to be
fired." I again ventured to plead the cause of
delay. He said, and very justly, "It is now too
late : the columns would be visible to the enemy
before they could move out of fire, and would lose
more men than it is to be hoped they will in the
attack. Fire the rocket, I say, and go to Lambert."
This was done. I had reached Lambert just as the
stillness of death and anticipation (for I really
believe the enemy was aware of our proximity to
their position) [was broken by the firing of the
rocket]. The rocket was hardly in the air before
a rush of our troops was met by the most murderous
and destructive fire of all arms ever poured upon
column. Sir Edward Pakenham galloped past me
with all his Staff, saying, "That's a terrific fire,
Lambert." I knew nothing of my General then,
except that he was a most gentlemanlike, amiable
fellow, and I had seen him lead his Brigade at
Toulouse in the order of a review of his Household
Troops in Hyde Park.* I said, "In twenty-five

* Sir J. Lambert was always in the Guards, and prided himself on
being Adjutant of the Grenadier Guards, as his eldest son now is.—
H.G.S. (1844).

minutes, General, you will command the Army. Sir Edward Pakenham will be wounded and incapable, or killed. The troops do not get on a step. He will be at the head of the first Brigade he comes to, and what I say will occur." A few seconds verified my words. Tylden came wildly up to tell the melancholy truth, saying, " Sir Edward Pakenham is killed. You command the Army, and your Brigade must move on immediately." I said, " If Sir Edward Pakenham is killed, Sir John Lambert commands, and will judge of what is to be done." I saw the attack had irretrievably failed. The troops were beat back, and going at a tolerable pace too ; so much so, I thought the enemy had made a sortie in pursuit, as so overpowering a superiority of numbers would have induced the French to do. " May I order your Brigade, sir, to form line to cover a most irregular retreat, to apply no other term to it, until you see what has actually occurred to the attacking columns ? " He assented, and sent me and other Staff Officers in different directions to ascertain our condition. It was (summed up in few words) that every attack had failed ; the Commander-in-Chief and General Gibbs and Colonel Renny killed ; General Keane, most severely wounded ; and the columns literally destroyed. The column for the right bank were seen to be still in their boats, and not the slightest impression had been made on the enemy.

Never since Buenos Ayres had I witnessed a reverse, and the sight to our eyes, which had looked on victory so often, was appalling indeed. Lambert desired me, and every Staff Officer he could get hold of, to go and reform the troops, no very easy matter in some cases. However, far to the rear, they (or, rather, what were left) were formed up, Sir John meanwhile wondering whether, under all the circumstances, he ought to attack. He very judiciously saw that was impossible, and he withdrew the troops from under a most murderous fire of round shot. Soon after this we heard the attack on the right bank, which succeeded easily enough. The extent of our loss was ascertained : one-third.

The Admirals came to the outlying picquet-house with faces as long as a flying jib : a sort of Council of War was held. I had been among the troops to find out how the pluck of our soldiers [stood]. Those who had received such an awful beating and been so destroyed were far from desirous to storm again. The 7th and 43rd, whose loss had been trifling, were ready for anything, but their veteran and experienced eyes told them affairs were desperate. One Admiral, Coddrington, whose duty as Captain of the Field was to have seen it supplied with provisions, said, " The troops must attack or the whole will be starved." I rather saucily said, " Kill plenty more, Admiral ; fewer rations will be required." A variety of opinions were agitated. I could observe what was passing in Sir J. Lambert's mind by the two or three remarks he made. So up I jumped, and said,

" General, the army are in no state to renew the attack.   If success now attended so desperate an attempt, we should have no troops to occupy New Orleans ; our success even would defeat our object, and, to take an extreme view, which every soldier is bound to do, our whole army might be the sacrifice of so injudicious an assault."   A thick fog was coming on.   I said, " We know the enemy are three times our number.   They will endeavour immediately to cut off our troops on the right bank, and we may expect an attack in our front.   The fog favours us, and Thornton's people ought to be brought back and brought into our line.   The army is secure, and no farther disaster is to be apprehended."   The General was fully of my opinion, as was every officer of experience.   I think my noble friend, " fighting MacDougall," was the only one for a new fight.   That able officer, Sir A. Dickson, was sent to retire Thornton, and, thanks to the fog, he succeeded in doing so unmolested, though, at the very time our people were crossing the river, a powerful body of the enemy (as I had supposed they would) were crossing to dislodge Thornton ; and the woods on the right bank so favoured their species of warfare, that Thornton would have met the fate he did at Bladensburg but for Lambert's cool judgment. This was my view of the position then, and it is now.

The number of wounded was three times what the Inspector-General Robb was told to calculate on, but never did officer meet the difficulties of his position with greater energy, or display greater resources within himself. He was ably assisted in the arrangements of boats, etc., by that able sailor, Admiral Malcolm, and I firmly assert not a wounded soldier was neglected.

Late in the afternoon I was sent to the enemy with a flag of truce, and a letter to General Jackson, with a request to be allowed to bury the dead and bring in the wounded lying between our respective positions. The Americans were not accustomed to the civility of war, like our old *associates* the French, and I was a long time before I could induce them to receive me. They fired on me with cannon and musketry, which excited my choler somewhat, for a round shot tore away the ground under my right foot, which it would have been a bore indeed to have lost under such circumstances. However, they did receive me at last, and the reply from General Jackson was a very courteous one.

After the delivery of the reply to General Lambert, I was again sent out with a fatigue party —a pretty large one too—with entrenching tools to bury the dead, and some surgeons to examine and bring off the wounded. I was received by a rough fellow—a Colonel Butler, Jackson's Adjutant-General. He had a drawn sword, and no scabbard. I soon saw the man I had to deal with. I outrode the surgeon, and I apologized for keeping him waiting; so he said, " Why now, I calculate as your doctors are tired; they have plenty to do to-day."

There was an awful spectacle of dead, dying, and wounded around us. "*Do?*" says I, "why this is nothing to us Wellington fellows! The next brush we have with you, you shall see how a Brigade of the Peninsular army (arrived yesterday) will serve you fellows out with the bayonet. They will lie piled on one another like round shot, if they will only stand." "Well, I calculate you must get at 'em first." "But," says I, "what do you carry a drawn sword for?" "Because I reckon a scabbard of no use so long as one of you Britishers is on our soil. We don't wish to shoot you, but we must, if you molest our property; we have thrown away the scabbard."

By this time our surgeon had arrived. There were some awful wounds from cannon shot, and I dug an immense hole, and threw nearly two hundred bodies into it. To the credit of the Americans not an article of clothing had been taken from our dead except the shoes. Every body was straightened, and the great toes tied together with a piece of string. A more appalling spectacle cannot well be conceived than this common grave, the bodies hurled in as fast as we could bring them. The Colonel, Butler, was very sulky if I tried to get near the works. This scene was not more than about eighty yards away from them, and, had our fellows rushed on, they would not have lost one half, and victory would have been ours. I may safely say there was not a vital part of man in which I did not observe a mortal wound, in many bodies there were three or four such ; some were without heads ; there were others, poor fellows, whom I recognized. In this part of America there were many Spaniards and Frenchmen. Several soldiers and officers gathered round me, and I addressed them in their own language. Colonel Butler became furious, but I would not desist for the moment, and said, " The next time we meet, Colonel, I hope to receive you to bury your dead." "Well, I calculate you have been on that duty to-day," he said. God only knows I had, with a heavy heart. It was apparently light enough before him, but the effort was a violent one.

At night it was General Lambert's intention to withdraw his line more out of cannon shot, for we were on a perfect plain, not a mound as cover, and I and D'Este (His Royal Highness, as I used to call him) were sent to bring back Blakeney's Brigade. Blakeney was as anxious a soldier in the dark as he was noble and gallant when he saw his enemy. He would fain induce me to believe I did not know my road. I got all right, though, with the aid of D'Este, who, if the war had lasted, would have made as able a soldier as his ancestor George the Second. I did not regard myself, though, as Marlborough, who was little employed on any retiring duty.

That night I lay down in my cloak, in General Lambert's room, at twelve o'clock, so done that all care or thought was banished in sleep. Before daylight [9 Jan.] I awoke to the horror of the loss of the man I so loved, admired, and esteemed, and to the feelings of a soldier under such melancholy circumstances. Those feelings could be but momentary. It was my duty to jump on my horse and see what was going on at our post, which I did, after returning Almighty God thanks. Thence to the hospital to render the Inspector whatever aid he required in orderlies, etc. Robb deserved and received the highest encomiums for the arrangements, which secured every care to our wounded.

In returning from the outposts, I met General Lambert. Upon my assuring him everything was perfectly quiet, he said, " I will now ride to the hospital." " I was just going there, sir, and will ride with you." The General said, " You must have been pretty well done last night, for I did not see you when I lay down." " Yes, I had a long day, but we Light Division fellows are used to it." " Smith, that most amiable man and cool and collected soldier, Secretary Wylly, will take home the dispatches of the melancholy disaster, and of the loss of his General and patron, and I offer for your acceptance my Military Secretaryship." I laughed, and said, " Me, sir! I write the most illegible and detestable scrawl in the world." " You can, therefore," he mildly said, "the more readily decipher mine. Poor Pakenham was much attached to you, and strongly recommended you to me." I had borne up well on my loss before, but I now burst into a flood of tears, with—" God rest his gallant soul." From that moment to the present, dear General Lambert has ever treated me as one of his own family. Our lamented General's remains were put in a cask of spirits and taken home by his Military Secretary, Wylly, who sailed in a few days with dispatches of no ordinary character—a record of lamentable disaster, and anything but honour to our military fame.

It was resolved to re-embark the army, and abandon the idea of further operations against the city of New Orleans, for the enemy had greatly added to his strength in men and works on both banks of the river. This decision was come to although we were expecting reinforcements, the 40th and 27th Regiments, and that noble soldier, Sir Manley Power. The enemy continually cannonaded our position, and caused us some loss. We were obliged, however, to maintain an advance position to cover effectually the embarcation of all the impedimenta, etc., invariably giving out as a ruse that we were only disencumbering ourselves of wounded, sick, etc.

I was sent in, also, with a flag of truce to propose an exchange of prisoners. Two Companies of the 21st Regiment and many of our Riflemen had crowned the works, and, not being supported by the rush of the column, of course were taken prisoners. (It was all very well to victimize * old Mullins † ; the fascines, ladders, etc., could have been supplied by one word which I will not name,‡ or

* *I.e.* make a scapegoat of.
† Colonel Mullins was blamed for not having the ladders and fascines ready.
‡ Pluck?

how could these two Companies have mounted the works ?) Similarly we had several men of theirs taken the night the enemy attacked General Keane.*

In the negotiations for this exchange I was always met by a Mr. Lushington, General Jackson's Military Secretary, a perfect gentleman, and a very able man. He was well known in London, having been Under Secretary of the Legation. I never had to deal with a more liberal and clear-headed man. His education had not been military, however, and in conversation, by questions, etc., I always induced him to believe we had no intention of abandoning our attempts. On the afternoon when our prisoners were mutually delivered, I said, "We shall soon meet in New Orleans, and after that in London." He was evidently impressed with the idea that we meant to attack again, and I led him to the supposition that a night attack would succeed best. We parted excellent friends, and shook hands, and many notes of courtesy passed between us afterwards.

So soon as it was dark [18 Jan.] our troops began to move off, and about twelve o'clock all were well off the ground, and the picquets were

---

* After that attack I have always been of opinion that General Keane should have occupied the narrow neck of land behind the deep ditch which ran across from the river to the morass, and was afterwards (but then not at all) so strongly fortified by the enemy. I admit there were many, very many objections, but I still maintain there were more important reasons for its occupation, since our Army had been shoved into such a position, for, to begin from the beginning, it ought never to have gone there.—H.G.S.

retired. As we were so engaged, the enemy heard us, and in a moment opened a fire along their line, evidently under the belief that our night attack was actually about to be made. We retired, up to our necks in mud, through a swamp to our boats, and the troops and stores, etc. were all embarked in three days without interruption, or any attempt whatever, on the part of the enemy.

Thus ended the second awful disaster in America it had been my lot to be associated with—Buenos Ayres and New Orleans. In the circumstances of both, many military errors may be traced. But in the case of Buenos Ayres, Whitelock is more abused than he merits. General Leveson-Gower was the great culprit; an overbearing, disobedient man, whose first disobedience, like Adam's, entailed the misfortune. He was ordered, when advancing on Buenos Ayres, not to engage the enemy before it was invested. He did engage, beat them, and might, in the *melée*, have possessed the city. That he neglected, and he ought to have been dismissed our service, probably with greater justice than Whitelock, whose orders were wantonly disobeyed, and the Church of San Domingo shamefully surrendered. Had it been held, as it might, it would have enabled Whitelock, from the base of his other success, to have made an attempt either to rescue the force in San Domingo, or again to have moved against the city. Whitelock's plan of attack was injudicious, too many columns, no weight and ensemble, and when he knew the city was fortified at every street, he should have effected regular lodgments and pushed forward from their base. The troops behaved most gallantly.

Poor dear Sir Edward Pakenham, a hero, a soldier, a man of ability in every sense of the word, had to contend with every imaginable difficulty, starting with the most unwise and difficult position in which he found the Army. By perseverance, determination, and that gallant bearing which so insures confidence, he overcame all but one, which he never anticipated, a check to the advance of British soldiers when they ought to have rushed forward. There was no want of example on the part of officers. The fire, I admit, was the most murderous I ever beheld before or since; still two Companies were successful in the assault, and had our heaviest column rushed forward in place of halting to fire under a fire fifty times superior, our national honour would not have been tarnished, but have gained fresh lustre, and one of the ablest generals England ever produced saved to his country and his friends.

In General Lambert's dispatches he was good enough to mention me.*

* " From MAJOR-GENERAL LAMBERT to EARL BATHURST.

" His Majesty's Ship *Tonnant*, off Chandeleur's Island,
" January 28, 1815.

" Major Smith, of the 95th Regiment, now acting as Military Secretary, is so well known for his zeal and talents, that I can with great truth say that I think he possesses every qualification to render him hereafter one of the brightest ornaments of his profession."

CHAPTER XXIII.

CAPTURE OF FORT BOWYER—DISEMBARCATION ON
ILE DAUPHINE—END OF THE AMERICAN WAR—
VISIT TO HAVANA AND RETURN-VOYAGE TO
ENGLAND—NEWS OF NAPOLEON'S RETURN TO
POWER — HARRY SMITH AT HIS HOME AT
WHITTLESEY.

AFTER the Army was somewhat refreshed, an
attempt on Mobile was resolved on, for which
purpose the fleet went down to the mouth of
Mobile Bay. Here there was a wooden fort of
some strength, Fort Bowyer, which some time
previously had sunk one of two small craft of our
men-of-war which were attempting to silence it.
It was necessary that this fort should be reduced
in order to open the passage of the bay. It was
erected on a narrow neck of land easily invested,
and required only a part of the army to besiege it.
It was regularly approached, and when our breach-
ing batteries were prepared to burn or blow it to
the devil, I was sent to summon it to surrender.
The Americans have no particular respect for flags
of truce, and all my Rifle education was required to
protect myself from being rifled and to procure a

reception of my flag. After some little time I was received, and, upon my particular request, admitted into the fort, to the presence of Major Lawrence, who commanded, with five Companies, I think, of the 2nd Regiment. I kept a sharp look-out on the defences, etc., which would not have resisted our fire an hour. The Major was as civil as a vulgar fellow can be. I gave him my version of his position, and cheered him on the ability he had displayed. He said, " Well, now, I calculate you are not far out in your reckoning. What do you advise me to do? You, I suppose, are one of Wellington's men, and understand the rules in these cases." " This," I said, " belongs to the rule that the weakest goes to the wall, and if you do not surrender at discretion in one hour, we, being the stronger, will blow up the fort and burn your wooden walls about your ears. All I can say is, you have done your duty to your country, and no soldier can do more, or resist the overpowering force of circumstances." " Well, if you were in my situation, you would surrender, would you? " " Yes, to be sure." " Well, go and tell your General I will surrender to-morrow at this hour, provided I am allowed to march out with my arms and ground them outside the fort." " No," I said, " I will take no such message back. My General, in humanity, offers you terms such as he can alone accept, and the blood of your soldiers be on your own head." He said, " Well, now, don't be hasty." I could see the Major had some hidden object in view. I said, therefore, "Now, I tell you what message I will carry to my General. You open the gates, and one of our Companies will take possession of it immediately, and a body of troops shall move up close to its support; then you may remain inside the fort until to-morrow at this hour, and ground your arms on the glacis." I took out pen and ink, wrote down my proposition, and said, "There, now, sign directly and I go." He was very obstinate, and I rose to go, when he said, "Well, now, you are hard upon me in distress." "The devil I am," I said. "We might have blown you into the water, as you did our craft, without a summons. Good-bye." "Well, then, give me the pen. If I must, so be it;" and he signed. His terms were accepted, and the 4th Light Company took possession of the gate, with orders to rush in in case of alarm. A supporting column of four hundred men were bivouacked close at hand with the same orders, while every precaution was taken, so that, if any descent were made from Mobile, we should be prepared, for, by the Major's manner and look under his eyebrows, I could see there was no little cunning in his composition. We afterwards learned that a force was embarked at Mobile, and was to have made a descent *that very night*, but the wind prevented them. We were, however, perfectly prepared, and Fort Bowyer was ours.

The next day [12 Feb.] the Major marched out and grounded his arms. He was himself received very kindly on board the *Tonnant*, and his officers

were disposed of in the Fleet.   The fellows looked
very like French soldiers, for their uniforms were
the same, and much of the same cut as to buttons,
belts, and pipe-clay.

In a few days after the capture of this fort
the *Brazen* sloop-of-war arrived with dispatches
[14 Feb.].   The preliminaries of peace were signed,
and only awaited the ratification of the President,
and until this was or was not effected, hostilities
were to cease.   We were all happy enough, for
we Peninsular soldiers saw that neither fame nor
any military distinction could be acquired in this
species of milito-nautico-guerilla-plundering-warfare.
I got a letter from my dear wife, who was in health
and composure, with my family all in love with her,
and praying of course for my safe return, which she
anticipated would not be delayed, as peace was
certain.   I for my part was very ready to return,
and I thanked Almighty God from my heart that
such fair prospects were again before me, after such
another series of wonderful escapes.

Pending the ratification, it was resolved to
disembark the whole army on a large island
at the entrance of Mobile Bay, called Isle Dauphine.*   This was done.   At first we had great

---

* Cope's order of events (p. 192) is as follows : Disembarcation of
troops on Ile Dauphine, Feb. 8 ; surrender of Fort Bowyer, Feb. 11 ;
arrival of news of the preliminaries of peace, Feb. 14.   According to
the text, the disembarcation on Ile Dauphine would appear to have
followed the peace-news.   Cope, however, tells us that after the
surrender of Fort Bowyer, "preparations were made for re-embarking
the troops, and attacking Mobile."   Perhaps the troops had been
re-embarked by Feb. 14, and they were then disembarked again on
the island they had already occupied.

difficulty in getting anything like fresh provisions ;
but, as the sea abounded with fish, each regiment rigged out a net, and obtained a plentiful
supply.   Then our biscuit ran short.   We had
abundance of flour, but this began to act on
the men and produce dysentery.   The want of
ovens alone prevented our making bread.   This
subject engrossed my attention for a whole day, but
on awakening one morning a sort of vision dictated
to me, " There are plenty of oyster-shells, and there
is sand.   Burn the former and make mortar, and
construct ovens."   So I sent on board to Admiral
Malcolm to send me a lot of hoops of barrels by
way of a framework for my arch.   There was
plenty of wood, the shells were burning, the mortar
soon made, my arch constructed, and by three
o'clock there was a slow fire in a very good oven
on the ground.   The baker was summoned, and the
paste was made, ready to bake at daylight.   The
Admiral, dear Malcolm, and our Generals were
invited to breakfast, but I did not tell even Sir
John Lambert why I had asked a breakfast-party.
He only laughed and said, " I wish I could give
them a good one ! "   Oh, the anxiety with which I
and my baker watched the progress of our exertions !   We heard the men-of-war's bells strike
eight o'clock.   My breakfast-party was assembled.
I had an unusual quantity of salt beef and biscuit
on the table, the party was ready to fall to, when in
I marched at the head of a column of loaves and
rolls, all piping hot and as light as bread should be.

The astonishment of the Admiral was beyond all belief, and he uttered a volley of monosyllables at the idea of a soldier inventing anything. Oh, how we laughed and ate new bread, which we hadn't seen for some time! At first the Admiral thought I must have induced his steward to bake me the bread as a joke, when I turned to Sir John and said, "Now, sir, by this time to-morrow every Company shall have three ovens, and every man his pound and a half of bread." I had sent for the Quartermasters of Corps; some started difficulties, but I soon removed them. One said, "Where are we to get all the hoops?" This was, I admit, a puzzle. I proposed to make the arch for the mortar of wood, when a very quick fellow, Hogan, Quartermaster of the Fusiliers, said, "I have it: make a bank of sand, plaster over it; make your oven; when complete, scratch the sand out." In a camp everything gets wind, and Harry Smith's ovens were soon in operation all over the island. There were plenty of workmen, and the morrow produced the bread.

The officers erected a theatre, and we had great fun in various demi-savage ways. Bell, the Quartermaster-General, dear noble fellow, arrived, and a Major Cooper, and, of some importance to me, my stray portmanteau. I was half asleep one morning, rather later than usual, having been writing the greater part of the night, when I heard old West say, " Sir, sir." " What's the matter?" " Thank the Lord, you're alive."

"What do you mean, you old ass?" "Why, a navigator has been going round and round your tent all night; here's a regular road about the tent." He meant an alligator, of which there were a great many on the island. The young ones our soldiers used to eat. I tasted a bit once; the meat was white, and the flavour like coarsely-fed pork.

In this very tent I was writing some very important documents for my General; the sandflies had now begun to be very troublesome, and that day they were positively painful. I ever hated tobacco, but a thought struck me, a good volume of smoke would keep the little devils off me. I called my orderly, a soldier of the 43rd, and told old West, who chawed a pound a day at least, to give him plenty of tobacco, and he was to make what smoke he could, for of two evils this was by far the least. The old Peninsular soldiers off parade were all perfectly at home with their officers, and he puffed away for a long time while I was writing, he being under my table. After a time he put his head out with a knowing look, and said, " If you please, sir, this is drier work than in front of Salamanca, where water was not to be had, and what's more, no grog neither." I desired West to bring him both rum and water. " Now, your honour, if you can write as long as I can smoke, you'll write the history of the world, and I will kill all the midges."

The ratification at length arrived [5 March], and the army was prepared to embark. Sir John Lambert, Baynes his Aide-de-camp, and I were to go home in the *Brazen* sloop-of-war, with a Captain Stirling, now Sir James, who was ultimately the founder of the Swan River Settlement. A more perfect gentleman or active sailor never existed: we have been faithful friends ever since. As many wounded as the *Brazen* could carry were embarked, and we weighed with one of our noble men-of-war.

As soon as the word was given, we sailed to the Havannah for fresh provisions. We spent a merry week there, when Stirling and I were inseparable. We were all *fêted* at the house of a Mr. Drake, nominally a wealthy merchant, but actually in every respect a prince. I never saw a man live so superbly. He put carriages at our disposal; one for Sir John Lambert, and one for me and Stirling. He was married to a Spanish woman, a very ladylike person, who played and sang beautifully. I could speak Spanish perfectly, and the compatriot connexion I told her and her maiden sisters of made us friends at once. My spare time, however, was spent in the house of the Governor, Assuduco, who had a daughter so like my wife in age, figure, etc., and speaking English about as much as she could, I was never so much amused as in her society; and my wife and she corresponded afterwards. We stayed in the Havannah a week, and the Publidrenis * brought us all back again to the Prado of Madrid. Although the beauty of the ladies of the capital was wanting, the costumes were equally elegant.

* The public gardens.

The celebrated Woodville, the cigar manufacturer, asked us to a public breakfast at his house, four or five miles out of the city. He was about six feet two, as powerful a man as I ever saw ; his hair in profusion, but as white as snow ; the picture of health, with a voice like thunder. He was rough, but hospitable, and after breakfast showed us the various processes of his manufactory, and the number of hands each went through. "Now," says he, "Sir John, I have another sight to show you, which few men can boast of." With his fingers in his mouth, he gave a whistle as loud as a bugle, when out ran from every direction a lot of children, of a variety of shades of colour, all looking happy and healthy. Not one appeared above twelve or thirteen. "Ah," he said, "report says, and I believe it, they are every one of them my children." "Count them," he said to me. I did ; there were forty-one. I thought Stirling and I would have died of laughing. Sir John Lambert, one of the most amiable and moral men in the world, said so mildly, "A very large family indeed, Mr. Woodville," that it set Stirling and me off again, and the old patriarch joined in the laugh, with, "Ah, the seed of Abraham would people the earth indeed, if every one of his descendants could show *my* family."

After a week of great amusement we sailed from Havana. The harbour and entrance are perfectly beautiful : the works most formidable, but the Spaniards would not let us inside. Sailing into the harbour is like entering a large gateway ; the sails are almost within reach of the Moro rock, and there is a swell setting into the harbour, which gives the ship a motion, as if every wave would dash her on the Moro.

In the Gulf of Florida we encountered a most terrific gale, wind and current at variance, and oh, such a sea! We lay to for forty-eight hours; we could not cook, and the main deck was flooded. Sir John and I never got out of our cots: he perfectly good-humoured on all occasions, and always convincing himself, and endeavouring to convince us, that the gale was abating. The third morning Stirling came to my cot. "Come, turn out; you will see how I manage my craft. I am going to make sail, and our lubberly cut may set us on our beam-ends, or sink us altogether." A delightful prospect, indeed. He was and is a noble seaman, all anima-tion, and he was so clear and decided in his orders! Sail was made amid waves mountains high, and the *Brazen*, as impudent a craft as ever spurned the mighty billows, so beautifully was she managed and steered, rode over or evaded seas apparently over-whelming; and Stirling, in the pride of his sailor's heart, says, "There, now, what would you give to be a sailor?" It really was a sight worth looking at—a little bit of human construction stemming and resisting the power of the mighty deep.

As we neared the mouth of the British Channel, we had, of course, the usual thick weather, when a strange sail was reported. It was now blowing a fresh breeze; in a few minutes we spoke her, but did not make her haul her main-topsail, being a bit of a merchantman. Stirling hailed as we shot past. "Where are you from?" "Portsmouth." "Any news?" "No, none." The ship was almost out of sight, when we heard, "Ho! Bonapart*er*'s back again on the throne of France." Such a hurrah as I set up, tossing my hat over my head! "I will be a Lieutenant-Colonel yet before the year's out!" Sir John Lambert said, "Really, Smith, you are so vivacious! How is it possible? It cannot be." He had such faith in the arrangements of our government, he wouldn't believe it. I said, "Depend upon it, it's truth; a beast like that skipper never could have invented it, when he did not even regard it as news: 'No, no news; only Bonaparte's back again on the throne of France.' Depend on it, it's true." "No, Smith, no." Stirling believed it, and oh, how he carried on! We were soon at Spithead, when all the men-of-war, the bustle, the general appearance, told us, before we could either see telegraphic communication or speak any one, where "Bonaparter" was.

We anchored about three o'clock, went on shore immediately, and shortly after were at dinner in the George. Old West had brought from the Havannah two pups of little white curly dogs, a dog and bitch, which he said were "a present for missus." They are very much esteemed in England, these Havana lapdogs; not much in *my* way.

The charm of novelty which I experienced on my former visit to England after seven years' absence, was much worn off, and I thought of nothing but home. Sir John and I started for London in a chaise at night, and got only as far as Guildford. I soon found our rate of progression would not do, and I asked his leave to set off home. At that time he was not aware of all my tale. I never saw his affectionate heart angry before; he positively scolded me, and said, "I will report our arrival; write to me, that I may know your address, for I shall most probably very soon want you again." My wife and Sir John were afterwards the greatest friends.

So Mr. West and I got a chaise, and off we started, and got to London on a Sunday, the most melancholy place on that day on earth. I drove to my old lodgings, where I had last parted from my wife. They could assure me she was well, as she had very lately ordered a new riding-habit. So I ordered a post-chaise, and ran from Panton Square to Weeks' in the Haymarket, and bought a superb dressing-case and a heavy gold chain; I had brought a lot of Spanish books from the Havannah. So on this occasion I did not return to my home naked and penniless, as from Coruña.

I got to Waltham Cross about twelve o'clock. I soon found a pair of horses was far too slow for my galloping ideas; so I got four, and we galloped along then as fast as I could wish. I rattled away to the Falcon Inn in my native place, Whittlesea; for I dare not drive to my father's house. I sent quietly for him, and he was with me in a moment.

The people were in church as I drove past. My wife was there, so as yet she was safe from any sudden alarm. She and my sisters took a walk after church, when servants were sent in every direction in search of them, with orders quietly to say that my father wanted my sisters. A fool of a fellow being the first to find them, and delighted with his prowess, ran up, shouting, "Come home directly; a gentleman has come in a chaise-and-four"—who, he did not know. My poor wife, as he named no one, immediately believed some one had arrived to say I was killed, and down she fell senseless. My sisters soon restored her, and they ran home, to their delight, into my arms. My wife and I were never again separated,* though many an eventful scene was in store and at hand for us.

We were now all happiness. During my few months' absence nothing had occurred to damp their contentment; so we all blessed God Almighty that I had again been protected in such awful situations both by land and sea, while so many families had to grieve for the loss of their dearest relatives. Pug and Tiny recognized me. I heard from Sir John Lambert that he was to be employed with the army assembling at Brussels under the Duke, that I had better be prepared to join him at a few hours' notice, that my position near him would require horses. I knew that "Major of Brigade" was the berth intended for me. My wife was to accompany

---

* They were separated for a great part of a year during the Kafir War, 1835. Perhaps he is thinking especially of separation by sea.

ST. MARY'S, WHITTLESEY.

From a photograph by A. Gray, Whittlesey, 1900.

[*Opposite Vol. i. p.* 260.

me again to the war, but nothing affected us
when united; the word "separation" away, all was
smooth. All was now excitement, joy, hope and
animation, and preparation of riding-habits, tents,
canteens, etc., my sisters thinking of all sorts of
things for my wife's comfort, which we could as well
have carried as our parish church. My youngest
brother but one, Charles, was to go with me to join
the 1st Battalion Rifle Brigade, as a Volunteer,*
and his departure added to the excitement. I
never was more happy in all my life; not a thought
of the future (though God knows we had enough
before us), for my wife was going and all the agony
of parting was spared.

I immediately set to work to buy a real good
stud. Two horses I bought at Newmarket, and two
in my native place; and as Tiny the faithful was
voted too old, as was the mare I had with me in
Spain and Washington, I bought for my wife, from
a brother, a mare of great celebrity, bred by my
father, a perfect horse for a lady who was an
equestrian artist.

In a few days I had a kind letter from Sir John

* "During the Peninsular War, and how long before I know not,
it was very occasionally permitted to young men who had difficulty
in getting a commission, with the consent of the commanding officer,
to join some regiment on service before the enemy. In action the
Volunteer acted as a private soldier, carrying his musket and wearing
his cross-belts like any other man. After a campaign or two, or after
having distinguished himself at the storming of some town or fortress,
he would probably obtain a commission. He messed with the officers
of the company to which he was attached. His dress was the same
as that of an officer, except that, instead of wings or epaulettes, he
wore shoulder-straps of silver or gold, to confine the cross-belts."—
W. Leeke, *Lord Seaton's Regiment at Waterloo* (1866), vol. i. p. 6.

Lambert, saying I was appointed his Major of Brigade; and as he was to proceed to Ghent in Flanders, recommending me, being in Cambridgeshire, to proceed *viâ* Harwich for Ostend, as I must find my own passage unless I went on a transport. West was therefore despatched with my four horses *viâ* Newmarket for Harwich, and I intended so to start as to be there the day my horses would arrive.

The evening before we started, my father, wife, sisters, myself, and brothers had a long ride. On returning, at the end of the town, there was a new stiff rail, with a ditch on each side. I was riding my dear old mare, that had been at Washington, etc., and off whose back poor Lindsay had been killed;* she was an elegant fencer, and as bold as in battle. I said to my sisters, " I will have one more leap on my war-horse." I rode her at it. Whether she had grown old, or did not measure her leap, I don't know, but over she rolled. One of my legs was across the new and narrow ditch, her shoulder right upon it; I could not pull it from under her. I expected every moment, if she struggled, to feel my leg broken, and there was an end to my Brigade Majorship! I passed a hand down, until I got short hold of the curb, and gave her a snatch with all my force. She made an effort, and I drew my leg out, more faint than subsequently in the most sanguinary conflict of the whole war. I never felt more grateful for an escape.

* See p. 151.

CHAPTER XXIV.

HARRY SMITH AND HIS WIFE START TOGETHER FOR
THE WATERLOO CAMPAIGN—GHENT—BATTLE OF
WATERLOO.

MY wife and I and my brother Charles were to
start in a chaise at three o'clock the next morning.
I never saw my poor father suffer so much as at
thus parting from three of us at once, and feeling
that his companion, my wife, was lost to him. He
said, " Napoleon and Wellington will meet, a battle
will ensue of a kind never before heard of, and I
cannot expect to see you all again."

We reached Harwich in the afternoon, found
West, his horses, and all our things right, and went
to the Black Bull, from whence I had embarked
years before for Gottenburgh. There we found my
old acquaintance, the landlord, Mr. Briton, a man
as civil as full of information. He said I had no
chance of embarking at Harwich, unless I freighted
a small craft that he would look out, and fitted it up
for my horses.

Next day I came to terms with the skipper of a
sloop of a few tons' burden, himself and a boy the
crew. I couldn't help thinking of the 74's and

frigates in which I had been flying over the ocean. We measured it, and found there was just room for the horses, and a hole aft, called a cabin, for my wife and self and brother. I did not intend to embark the horses till the wind was fair—a fortunate plan, for I was detained in the Black Bull by foul winds for a fortnight. The wind becoming fair, in the afternoon we embarked all our traps. Mr. Briton amply provided us with provisions and forage, and brought his bill for myself, wife, brother, two grooms, five horses, lady's maid, sea stock, etc. I expected it to be fifty or sixty pounds; it was twenty-four and some shillings, and we had lived on the fat of the land, for having been half-starved so many years, when once in the flesh-pots of England, we revelled in a plenty which we could scarcely fancy would last.

A gentle breeze carried us over to Ostend in twenty-four hours, where we landed our horses by slinging them and dropping them into the sea to swim ashore. My wife's noble mare, which we called the " Brass Mare " after her son of that ilk, when in the slings and in sight of the shore, neighed most gallantly, and my wife declared it an omen of brilliant success. We went to the great inn of Ostend. The difference between it and our late bivouac, the Black Bull, is not to be described. I found an English horse-dealer there. I bought two mules of him and a stout Flanders pony for our baggage, and in three days we were *en route* for Ghent, stopping one night at Bruges, where was an excellent inn, and the best Burgundy I had drunk up to that hour. My wife was delighted to be once more in campaigning trim.

When we reached Ghent we found Sir John Lambert had reached it the day before. Louis XVIII. was there, his Court and idlers, and Ghent was in as great a state of excitement as if the Duke of Marlborough was again approaching. I found our Brigade were all New Orleans Regiments—three of the best regiments of the old Army of the Peninsula, the 4th, 27th, and 40th, and the 81st in garrison at Brussels. We were ordered to be in perfect readiness to take the field with the warning * we had been so many years accustomed to.

Louis held a Court while we were there. I was near the door he entered by. He was very in-active, but impressive in manner. He laid his hand on my shoulder to support himself. His great topic of conversation was how delighted he was to see us, and how much he was indebted to our nation. A more benign countenance I never beheld, nor did his subsequent reign belie the benignity of his expression.

While at Ghent I waited on Sir John Lambert every morning just after breakfast for orders. On one occasion we heard a voice thundering in the passage to him, "Hallo there, where the devil's the door ?" I went out, and to my astonishment saw our noble friend Admiral Malcolm. "Why, where the devil has Lambert stowed himself ? The

* See p. 80.

house is as dark as a sheer hulk." He was delighted to see us, and sang out, "Come, bear a hand and get me some breakfast; no regular hours on shore as in the *Royal Oak*." He had been appointed to the command of the coast. He was very much attached to the Duke. During our stay at Ghent we had Brigade parades almost every day, and my General, an ex-Adjutant of the Guards, was most particular in all guard mountings, sentries, and all the correct minutiæ of garrison. The three regiments were in beautiful fighting trim, although the headquarters ship with the Grenadiers, the 27th, had not arrived from America. Poor 27th! in a few days they had not two hundred men in the ranks.

As we anticipated, our march from Ghent was very sudden. In an hour after the order arrived we moved *en route* for Brussels. We reached Asche on the afternoon of the 16th June. The rapid and continuous firing at Quatre Bras, as audible as if we were in the fight, put us in mind of old times, as well as on the *qui vive*. We expected an order every moment to move on. We believed the firing to be at Fleurus. As we approached Brussels the next day [17 June], we met an orderly with a letter from that gallant fellow De Lancey, Q.M.G., to direct us to move on Quatre Bras.

In the afternoon, after we passed Brussels, the scene of confusion, the flying of army, baggage, etc., was an awful novelty to us. We were directed by a subsequent order to halt at the village of Epinay, on the Brussels side of the forest of Soignies, a

report having reached his Grace that the enemy's
cavalry were threatening our communication with
Brussels (as we understood, at least).   The whole
afternoon we were in a continued state of excitement.   Once some rascals of the Cumberland
Hussars, a new Corps of Hanoverians (not of the
style of our noble and gallant old comrades, the 1st
Hussars), came galloping in, declaring they were
pursued by Frenchmen.   Our bugles were blowing
in all directions, and our troops running to their
alarm-posts in front of the village.   I went to report
to Sir John Lambert, who was just sitting quietly
down to dinner with my wife and his A.D.C.   He
says very coolly, " Let the troops—— ; this is all
nonsense ; there is not a French soldier in the rear
of his Grace, depend on it, and sit down to dinner."
I set off, though, and galloped to the front, where a
long line of baggage was leisurely retiring.   This
was a sufficient indication that the alarm was false,
and I dismissed the troops and started for the
débris of a magnificent turbot which the General's
butler had brought out of Brussels.   This was in
the afternoon.

Such a thunderstorm and deluge of rain now
came on, it drenched all that was exposed to it, and
in a few minutes rendered the country deep in mud
and the roads very bad.   All night our baggage
kept retiring through the village.

In the course of the night, Lambert's Brigade
were ordered to move up to the position the Duke
had taken up in front of the forest of Soignies,

and our march was very much impeded by waggons
upset, baggage thrown down, etc. [18 June]. We
met Sir George Scovell, an A.Q.M.G. at head-
quarters, who said he was sent by the Duke to
see the rear was clear, that it was choked between
this and the Army, and the Duke expected to be
attacked immediately; our Brigade must clear the
road before we moved on. Our men were on fire
at the idea of having to remain and clear a road
when an attack was momentarily expected, and an
hour would bring us to the position. The wand
of a magician, with all his spells and incantations,
could not have effected a clear course sooner than
our 3000 soldiers of the old school.

This effected, General Lambert sent me on to
the Duke for orders. I was to find the Duke himself, and receive orders from no other person.
About 11 o'clock I found his Grace and all his staff
near Hougoumont. The day was beautiful after
the storm, although the country was very heavy.
When I rode up, he said, "Hallo, Smith, where
are you from last?" "From General Lambert's
Brigade, and they from America." "What have
you got?" "The 4th, the 27th, and the 40th; the
81st remain in Brussels." "Ah, I know, I know
but the others, are they in good order?" "Excellent, my lord, and very strong." "That's all
right, for I shall soon want every man." One of
his staff said, "I do not think they will attack
to-day." "Nonsense," said the Duke. "The
columns are already forming, and I think I have

discerned where the weight of the attack will be
made. I shall be attacked before an hour. Do
you know anything of my position, Smith?"
"Nothing, my lord, beyond what I see—the general
line, and right and left." "Go back and halt
Lambert's Brigade at the junction of the two great
roads from Genappe and Nivelles. Did you
observe their junction as you rode up?" "Particularly, my lord." "Having halted the head of the
Brigade and told Lambert what I desire, ride to
the left of the position. On the extreme left is
the Nassau Brigade *—those fellows who came over
to us at Arbonne, you recollect.† Between them
and Picton's Division (now the 5th) I shall most
probably require Lambert. There is already
there a Brigade of newly-raised Hanoverians,
which Lambert will give orders to, as they and
your Brigade form the 6th Division. You are the
only British Staff Officer with it. Find out, therefore, the best and shortest road from where
Lambert is now halted to the left of Picton and
the right of the Nassau troops. Do you understand?" "Perfectly, my lord." I had barely
turned from his Grace when he called me back.
"Now, clearly understand that when Lambert is
ordered to move from the fork of the two roads
where he is now halted, you are prepared to conduct him to Picton's left." It was delightful to
see his Grace that morning on his noble horse

* Under Vivian on the extreme left were the 1st German Hussars,
but the Nassau Regiment was under Cooke on the right.

† See p. 155.

Copenhagen—in high spirits and very animated, but so cool and so clear in the issue of his orders, it was impossible not fully to comprehend what he said; delightful also to observe what his wonderful eye anticipated, while some of his staff were of opinion the attack was not in progress.

I had hardly got back to Lambert, after reconnoitring the country and preparing myself to conduct the troops, when the Battle of Waterloo commenced. We soon saw that where we should be moved to, the weight of the attack on Picton would be resisted by none but British soldiers. For a few seconds, while every regiment was forming square, and the charge of Ponsonby's Brigade going on (which the rising ground in our front prevented us seeing), it looked as if the formation was preparatory to a retreat. Many of the rabble of Dutch troops were flying towards us, and, to add to the confusion, soon after came a party of dragoons, bringing with them three eagles and some prisoners. I said to General Lambert, "We shall have a proper brush immediately, for it looks as if our left will be immediately turned, and the brunt of the charge will fall on us." At this moment we were ordered to move to the very spot where the Duke, *early in the morning*, had expected we should be required. Picton had been killed, Sir James Kempt commanded on the left of the road to Genappe, near La Haye Sainte ; his Division had been already severely handled,

and we took their position, my old Battalion of
Riflemen remaining with us.

The Battle of Waterloo has been too often
described, and nonsense enough written about the
Crisis,* for me to add to it.   Every moment was a
crisis, and the controversialists had better have left
the discussion on the battle-field.   Every Staff officer
had two or three (and one four) horses shot under
him.   I had one wounded in six, another in seven
places, but not seriously injured.   The fire was
terrific, especially of cannon.

Late in the day, when the enemy had made his
last great effort on our centre, the field was so
enveloped in smoke that nothing was discernible.
The firing ceased on both sides, and we on the left
knew that one party or the other was beaten.   This
was the most anxious moment of my life.   In a few
seconds we saw the red-coats in the centre, as stiff
as rocks, and the French columns retiring rapidly,
and there was such a British shout as rent the air.
We all felt then to whom the day belonged.   It was
time the " Crisis " should arrive, for we had been at
work some hours, and the hand of death had been
most unsparing.   One Regiment, the 27th, had
only two officers left—Major Hume, who commanded from the beginning of the battle, and

---

* In 1833, Major G. Gawler, of the 52nd, published *The Crisis of
Waterloo*, in which he claimed for his regiment the honour of having by
their flank-attack defeated the Imperial Guards in their last charge,
an honour generally given to the Guards. His contention was supported by Rev. W. Leeke in *Lord Seaton's Regiment at Waterloo*
(1866).

another—and they were both wounded, and only a hundred and twenty soldiers were left with them.

At this moment I saw the Duke, with only one Staff officer remaining, galloping furiously to the left. I rode on to meet him. "Who commands here?" "Generals Kempt and Lambert, my lord." "Desire them to get into a column of companies of Battalions, and move on immediately." I said, "In which direction, my lord?" "Right ahead, to be sure." I never saw his Grace so animated. The *Crisis* was general, from one end of the line to the other.

That evening at dark we halted, literally on the ground we stood on; not a picquet was required, and our whole cavalry in pursuit. Then came the dreadful tale of killed and wounded; it was enormous, and every moment the loss of a dear friend was announced. To my wonder, my astonishment, and to my gratitude to Almighty God, I and my two brothers—Tom, the Adjutant of the 2nd Battalion Rifle Brigade, who had, during the day, attracted the Duke's attention by his gallantry, and Charles, in the 1st Battalion, who had been fighting for two days—were all safe and unhurt, except that Charles had a slight wound in the neck. In the thunderstorm the previous evening he had tied a large silk handkerchief over his stock; he forgot to take it off, and probably owed his life to so trifling a circumstance. There was not an instance throughout the Army of *two* brothers in the field escaping. We were three, and I could hardly credit my own eyes. We had nothing to eat or drink. I had some tea in my writing-case, but no sugar. It had been carried by an orderly, although in the ranks. He found me out after the battle, and I made some tea in a soldier's tin for Sir James Kempt, Sir John Lambert, and myself; and while we were thus regaling, up came my brother, of whose safety I was not aware.

Captain McCulloch of the 95th Regiment wished to see me. He was a dear friend whom I had not seen since he was awfully wounded at Foz d'Aruz [Foz d'Aronce] on Massena's retreat, after having had seven sabre-wounds at the Coa, in Massena's advance, and been taken prisoner. He was in a cottage near, awfully wounded. I found him lying in great agony, but very composed. "Oh, Harry, so long since we have met, and now again under such painful circumstances; but, thank God, you and Tom are all right." I had brought all my remaining tea, which he ravenously swallowed. The ball had dreadfully broken the elbow of the sound arm, and had passed right through the fleshy part of his back, while the broken bone of the arm previously shattered at Foz d'Aruz was still exfoliating, and very painful even after a lapse of years. I got hold of a surgeon, and his arm was immediately amputated. When dressed, he lay upon the stump, as this was less painful than the old exfoliating wound, and on his back he could not lie. He recovered, but was never afterwards able to feed himself or put on his hat, and died, Heaven help him, suddenly of dysentery.

No one, but those who have witnessed the awful scene, knows the horrors of a field of battle—the piles of the dead, the groans of the dying, the agony of those dreadfully wounded, to whom frequently no assistance can be rendered at the moment ; some still in perfect possession of their intellect, game to the last, regarding their recovery as more than probable, while the clammy perspiration of death has already pounced upon its victim; others, again, perfectly sensible of their dissolution, breathing into your keeping the feelings and expressions of their last moments—messages to father, mother, wife, or dearest relatives.   Well might Walter Scott say—

> " Thou canst not name one tender tie
> But here dissolved its relics lie."

Often have I myself, tired and exhausted in such scenes, almost regretted the life I have adopted, in which one never knows at any moment how near or distant one's own turn may be. In such dejection you sink into a profound sleep, and you stand up next morning in fresh spirits. Your country's calls, your excitement, honour and glory, again impel, and undauntedly and cheerfully you expose that life which the night before you fancied was of value. A soldier's life is one continued scene of excitement, hope, anticipation; fear for himself he never knows, though the loss of his comrade pierces his heart.

Before daylight next morning [19 June] a Staff officer whose name I now forget, rode up to where we were all lying, and told us of the complete *déroute* of the French, and the vigorous pursuit of the Prussians, and that it was probable that our Division would not move for some hours. At daylight I was on horseback, with a heart of gratitude as became me, and anxious to let my wife know I was all right. I took a party of each Regiment of my Division with me, and went back to the field; for I was now established as Assistant-Quartermaster-General.

I had been over many a field of battle, but with the exception of one spot at New Orleans, and the breach of Badajos, I had never seen anything to be compared with what I saw. At Waterloo the *whole* field from right to left was a mass of dead bodies. In one spot, to the right of La Haye Sainte, the French Cuirassiers were literally piled on each other; many soldiers not wounded lying under their horses; others, fearfully wounded, occasionally with their horses struggling upon their wounded bodies. The sight was sickening, and I had no means or power to assist them. Imperative duty compelled me to the field of my comrades, where I had plenty to do to assist many who had been left out all night; some had been believed to be dead, but the spark of life had returned. All over the field you saw officers, and as many soldiers as were permitted to leave the ranks, leaning and weeping over some dead or dying brother or comrade. The battle was fought on a Sunday, the 18th June, and I repeated to myself a verse from the Psalms of that day—91st Psalm, 7th verse: "A thousand shall fall beside thee, and ten thousand at thy right hand, but it shall not come nigh thee." I blessed Almighty God our Duke was spared, and galloped to my General, whom I found with some breakfast awaiting my arrival.

So many accounts and descriptions have been given of the Battle of Waterloo, I shall only make one or two observations. To those who say the ultimate success of the day was achieved by the arrival of the Prussians, I observe that the Prussians were part of the whole on which his Grace calculated, as much as on the co-operation of one of his own Divisions; that they ought to have been in the field much sooner, and by their late arrival seriously endangered his Grace's left flank; and had Napoleon pushed the weight of his attack and precipitated irresistible numbers on our left, he would have forced the Duke to throw back his left and break our communication with the Prussians. The Duke's army was a heterogeneous mass, not the old Peninsular veterans; young 2nd Battalions most of them, others intermixed with the rabble of our allied army. Thus the Duke could not have counter-manœuvred on his left, as he would have been able with his old army; and we had one Division under Colville far away to our right.

Napoleon fought the battle badly; his attacks were not simultaneous, but partial and isolated, and enabled the Duke to repel each by a concentration. His cavalry was sacrificed early in the day. If

Napoleon did not desire to turn our left flank, and the battle is to be regarded as a fight hand to hand, he fought it badly.

By a general attack upon our line with his overpowering force of artillery, followed up by his infantry, he might have put *hors-de-combat* far more of our army than he did. His cavalry would have been fresh, and had he employed this devoted and gallant auxiliary late in the day as he did early, his attempts to defeat us would have been far more formidable.

His artillery and cavalry behaved most nobly, but I maintain his infantry did not. In proof, I will record one example. On the left, in front of the 5th Division, 25,000 of the Young Guard attacked in column. Picton was just killed, and Kempt commanded. It is true this column advanced under a galling fire, but it succeeded in reaching the spot where it intended to deploy. Kempt ordered the Battalion immediately opposite the head of the column to charge. It was a poor miserable Battalion compared with some of ours, yet did it dash like British soldiers at the column, which went about. Then it was that Ponsonby's Brigade got in among them, and took eagles and prisoners.

As a battle of science, it was demonstrative of no manœuvre. It was no Salamanca or Vittoria, where science was so beautifully exemplified : it was as a stand-up fight between two pugilists, "mill away" till one is beaten. The Battle of Waterloo, with all its political glory, has destroyed the field movement of the British Army, so scientifically laid down by Dundas, so improved on by that hero of war and of drill, Sir John Moore. All that light-troop duty which he taught, by which the world through the medium of the Spanish War was saved, is now replaced by the most heavy of manœuvres, by squares, centre formations, and moving in masses, which require time to collect and equal time to extend; and all because the Prussians and Russians did not know how to move quicker, we, forsooth, must adopt their ways, although Picton's Division at Quatre Bras nobly showed that British infantry can resist cavalry in any shape. It is true the Buffs were awfully mauled at Albuera, but what did my kind patron, Sir William Stewart, order them to do? They were in open column of companies right in front, and it was necessary at once to deploy into line, which Sir William with his light 95th had been accustomed to do on any company: he orders them, therefore, to deploy on the Grenadiers; by this the right would become the left, what in common parlance is termed "clubbed;" and while he was doing this, he kept advancing the Grenadiers. It is impossible to imagine a battalion in a more helpless position, and it never can be cited as any criterion that a battalion must be in squares to resist cavalry. At the Battle of Fuentes d'Oñoro, the overwhelming French cavalry, having rapidly put back our very inferior force, were upon a regiment of infantry of the 7th Division, to the right of the Light

Division, before either were aware. The French advance of the Chasseurs Britanniques, I think (it was *one* of the mongrels, as we called those corps, anyhow), was imposing, heavy, and rapid (I was close to the left of our infantry at the time), but it made not the slightest impression on the regiment in line; on the contrary, the Chasseurs were repulsed with facility and loss.

But to return to our narrative. A party was sent to bury the dead of each regiment as far as possible. For the Rifle Brigade, my brother Charles was for the duty. In gathering the dead bodies, he saw among the dead of our soldiers the body of a French officer of delicate mould and appearance. On examining it, he found it was that of a delicate, young, and handsome female. My story ends here, but such is the fact. What were the circumstances of devotion, passion, or patriotism which led to such heroism, is, and ever will be, to me a mystery. Love, depend upon it.

That afternoon we moved forward by the Nivelles road. I had to go into my General's room. I was not aware he was there, and entered abruptly. He was changing his shirt, when I saw he had received a most violent contusion on his right arm. It was fearfully swelled (in those days our coat-sleeves were made very large), and as black as ebony from the shoulder to the wrist. " My dear General," I said, " what an arm! I did not know you had been wounded." " No, nor you never would, if accident had not shown you." He made me promise to say nothing, about which I compromised by saying, " To no one but to a surgeon, whom you must see. An arm in that state, if inflammation succeed, might slough, and you would lose it." The General would not see a surgeon, and thank God he got well.

But turn we now to the poor wife. I left her at daylight on the 18th, prepared to get on her horse and go to Brussels, to await the result of the storm of war which I had prepared her for. Her tale of wonder must form a separate and distinct narrative.

CHAPTER XXV.

JUANA'S STORY.*

WHEN the troops had moved forward on the morning of the 18th June, I, as you directed, got on my horse and went to Brussels, intending to await the result of the pending battle. On arrival I found my baggage and servant in the great square, and an order had just arrived for the whole of the baggage of the army to move on the road towards Antwerp, and afterwards to cross the canal about five miles from Brussels, at a village on the Antwerp side. On reaching the village I dismounted, the baggage was unloaded, and West was endeavouring to get something for me to eat in the inn. It was about five o'clock. Suddenly an alarm was given that the enemy was upon us. West brought my mare to the door as quickly as I could run downstairs, but from the noise, confusion, and everything, my horse was perfectly frantic. West succeeded in tossing me up, but my little pug, Vitty, was still below. I said, "Now, West, give me my dog;" when, as he put her into my lap,

---

* The MS. is in Harry Smith's hand, and the wording is probably his.

I dropped my reins. West, knowing I always gathered up my reins before I jumped up, let go, and off flew the mare with such speed that, with the dog in my lap, it was all I could do for some time to keep my seat. I had the snaffle rein in my hand, but I could not restrain her; the curb rein was flying loose, and I couldn't stoop to get hold of it. She flew with me through the streets of Malines, across a bridge over the river, the road full of horses and baggage, still flying away, away, until I was perfectly out of breath. I saw a waggon upset lying immediately before me across the road, and I knew that if I could not turn her on one side, I must inevitably be knocked to pieces. The mare would not answer my snaffle rein, and I felt her charge the waggon as at a fence to leap it. The height was beyond the spring of my horse. As the animal endeavoured to leap, the loose curb rein caught. This brought her at once to a halt, and I was precipitated on her head, pug and all. I had come at this rate eight miles, over a road covered with mud and dirt. The mare was as much out of breath as I was. I managed to get back into the saddle, and felt that now was my only chance to get hold of the curb. I succeeded in doing so, and we were then on terms of equality.

Having righted my habit, I looked back and saw some five or six men on horseback, whom of course I construed into French Dragoons, although, if I had considered a moment, I should have known that no Dragoon could have come the pace *I* did;

but I was so exhausted, I exclaimed, "Well, if I am to be taken, I had better at once surrender." The first horseman proved to be one of my servants, riding one of the Newmarket horses, having taken the animal from West against his orders. The others were a Commissary, an officer of the Hanoverian Rifles, and an officer, I regret to say, of our own Hussars. I addressed myself to the Hussar, who appeared the oldest of the party. " Pray, sir, is there any danger ? " (I had forgotten almost all the little English I knew in my excitement.) "Danger, mum ! When I left Brussels the French were in pursuit down the hill." "Oh, sir, what shall I do ?" "Come on to Antwerp with me." He never pulled up. During the whole conversation we were full gallop. One of the party says, "You deserve no pity. You may well be fatigued carrying that dog. Throw it down." I was very angry, and said I should deserve no pity if I did.

Our pace soon brought us to Antwerp, where the Hussar was very civil, and tried to get me a room in one of the hotels. This he soon found was impossible, as all the English visitors at Brussels had fled there. We must now go to the Hôtel de Ville and try for a billet. Whilst standing there, the officer having gone inside, I was an object of curious attention. I was wet from head to foot with the black mud of the high-road. On my face the mud had dried, and a flood of tears chasing each other through it down my cheeks must have

given me an odd appearance indeed. While standing on horseback there, an officer of the English
garrison, whom I did not know (he must have
learnt my name from my servant) addressed me by
name. "Mrs. Smith, you are in such a terrible
plight, and such is the difficulty of your getting
in anywhere, if you will come with me, I will conduct you to Colonel Craufurd, the Commandant of
the Citadel; his wife and daughters are most kind
and amiable people, and readily, I know, would they
contribute with happiness anything to your comfort." My situation was not one to stand on
delicacy. I therefore promptly accepted this offer,
leaving my kind Hussar in the Hôtel de Ville.
When I arrived, nothing could exceed the kindness
of all, which was as striking at the moment as it
seems to me now. I was stripped from a weight
of mud which, with my long riding-habit, I could
hardly move under. A shower of hot water again
showed my features, and I was put in the clothes
of good Mrs. Craufurd, a very tall woman; and in
these comfortable dry clothes I was nearly as
much lost as in the case of mud I had been washed
out of.

The hospitality of this night ought to have
soothed me, but the agony of hope, doubt, and fear
I was in absorbed every other feeling, although
I was so sensible of kindness.

The next day [19 June] the officer who had
so kindly brought me to Colonel Craufurd came to
tell me a great quantity of baggage was momentarily

arriving: could I give him any directions or clue to find mine? In about an hour he returned with my spare horses, old trusty West, who had never left anything behind, my baggage, and my maid.

In the afternoon we heard of the battle having been fought and won, but no news of my husband. So, contrary to the wishes of my kind host and hostess, I ordered my horse to be ready at three o'clock in the morning to rejoin my husband, whatever shape fate had reduced him to. It was all I could do to resist the importunity of those kind people who wished me to remain. But at three o'clock [20 June] West and I were on horseback, desiring baggage, servants, and horses to follow. In conversation with West, I ascertained that at the village we fled from, my mattrass, and in it my dressing-case (bought on a Sunday at Weeks' *) with all my fortune, two Napoleons, had been left in the inn. When I arrived, I asked the landlord of the little wretched inn about it. He pretended he knew nothing, but old cunning West got information in the stable-yard, and gave a boy five francs to conduct him to the hayloft where my treasure was. West soon transported what he called *ours* to me, and upon opening it, I found my important dressing-case there untouched. I had something in the shape of breakfast. In the mean time my servants had arrived, the lost mattrass was restored to the baggage, and West and I, in light

* See p. 259.

marching order, started for Brussels. We were only five miles away, and arrived by seven in the morning.

Seeing some of our Rifle soldiers, with an eagerness which may be imagined, I asked after my husband, when to my horror they told me that Brigade-Major Smith of the 95th was killed. It was now my turn to ask the "Brass Mare" to gallop, and in a state approaching desperation I urged her to the utmost speed for the field of battle to seek my husband's corpse. The road from Brussels to the field almost maddened me, with wounded men and horses, and corpses borne forward to Brussels for interment, expecting as I was every moment to see that of my husband, knowing how he was beloved by officers and soldiers. The road was nearly choked which was to lead me to the completion, as I hoped, of my life; to die on the body of the only thing I had on earth to love, and which I loved with a faithfulness which few can or ever did feel, and none ever exceeded. In my agony of woe, which of course increased as my expectations were not realized (it was now Tuesday), I approached the awful field of Sunday's carnage, in mad search of Enrique. I saw signs of newly dug graves, and then I imagined to myself, "O God, he has been buried, and I shall never again behold him!" How can I describe my suspense, the horror of my sensations, my growing despair, the scene of carnage around me? From a distance I saw a figure lying; I shrieked,

"Oh, there he is!" I galloped on. "No, it is not he! Find him I will, but whither shall I turn?" O ye in peaceful homes, with every comfort around you, you wonder how I did not sink under my afflictions, a foreigner in a strange land, thus at once bereft of my all! I will tell you. Educated in a convent, I was taught to appeal to God through Jesus Christ. In this my trouble I did so. At this moment, as a guardian angel, a dear and mutual friend, Charlie Gore, A.D.C. to Sir James Kempt, appeared to me. In my agony and hope, hope alone of finding the body, I exclaimed, "Oh, where is he? Where is my Enrique?" "Why, near Bavay by this time, as well as ever he was in his life; not wounded even, nor either of his brothers." "Oh, dear Charlie Gore, why thus deceive me? The soldiers tell me Brigade-Major Smith is killed. Oh, my Enrique!" "Dearest Juana, believe me; it is poor Charles Smyth, Pack's Brigade-Major. I swear to you, on my honour, I left Harry riding Lochinvar in perfect health, but very anxious about you." "Oh, may I believe you, Charlie! my heart will burst." "Why should you doubt me?" "Then God has heard my prayer!" This sudden transition from my depth of grief and maddening despair was enough to turn my brain, but Almighty God sustained me. Gore told me he had returned to Brussels to see poor Charlie Beckwith, who had lost, or must lose, his leg; and that he was then in the act of looking for the grave of our mutual friend, poor Charlie Eeles. Gore said,

" I am now going to Mons : can you muster strength
to ride with me there ? "   I said, "Strength ? yes,
for anything now ! " and we reached Mons at twelve
o'clock at night.   I had been on the same horse
since three in the morning, and had ridden a distance from point to point of sixty miles ; and after
all the agony, despair, relief, and happiness I had
gone through in one day, I ate something, and lay
down until daylight next morning [21 June], when I
rapidly pushed on to Bavay, on my really wonderful
thoroughbred mare.

I first met Sir John Lambert, who showed me
where Enrique was to be found.   Until I saw him,
I could not persuade myself he was well, such a
hold had my previous horror taken of my every
thought and feeling.   Soon, O gracious God, I
sank into his embrace, exhausted, fatigued, happy,
and grateful—oh, how grateful !—to God who had
protected him, and sustained my reason through
such scenes of carnage, horror, dread, and belief in
my bereavement.

[Narrative resumed.]

I was afterwards told all this, and I could not
but reflect on what we had all gone through since
the morning we had parted with my father, and
how his prediction of a terrific struggle had been
verified.   Our adventures formed the subject of a
long letter, and from him came one soon after.

" Never did I receive two letters with such

pleasure as your two last after the glorious Battle of Waterloo. For three of you, my sons, to have been so hotly engaged, and to have come off unhurt, must not have been chance or fate ; but Providence seems to have watched over you all and protected you. How grateful ought we all to be to the Almighty God! I assure you my prayers have ever been offered up to the Throne of Grace for the protection of you all, and a safe return to England."

This letter is now on my table before me, fresh as when written,* while the author, God bless him, has mixed with the earth to which all must return. He lived to the age of 87, and died in Sept. 1844, a strong and healthy man until within a few months of his dissolution. It is difficult to say whether he was the more proud of having three sons at Waterloo, or grateful to Almighty God for their preservation.

* See Appendix II., pp. 376, 380.

CHAPTER XXVI.

OUR march to Paris was unaccompanied by anything to relate except that I had a gallop round Mons and a good look on Malplaquet, but could picture to myself no position, while I felt as a soldier standing on the classic ground of the gallant achievements of my country and our former army of heroes (for I regard Marlborough and Wellington as the greatest men England or the world ever produced). But the latter days of Wellington are as conspicuous for ability and energy as the days of his youth. Poor Marlborough dwindled into imbecility, and became a miser. To Wellington his country has ever been enthusiastically grateful while Marlborough, by ill-treatment, was driven into voluntary banishment. Although I love

Wellington with a fervour which cannot be exceeded, I pray my God he may never outlive his mental faculties, but leave this world and the country and cause he has so eminently served while that world and country are still in admiration and wonder.   Alava, the Spanish General, so attached and devoted to the Duke (by-the-bye, he was a Captain of a Spanish battleship or frigate, I forget which), told me and Juana two years after the Battle of Waterloo that the night after that eventful day, the Duke got back to his quarters at Waterloo about nine or ten at night.   The table was laid for the usual number, while none appeared of the many of his staff but Alava and Fremantle. The Duke said very little, ate hastily and heartily, but every time the door opened he gave a searching look, evidently in the hope of some of his valuable staff approaching.   When he had finished eating, he held up both hands in an imploring attitude and said, " The hand of Almighty God has been upon me this day," jumped up, went to his couch, and was asleep in a moment.   At this period he was not aware of the extent of his wonderful victory.

When we approached the capital, we found the French army strongly posted in a position near St. Denis and the previously shamefully abandoned post of Mont Martre. From this position we expected to have to drive them, but a day or two's suspense relieved us.   In a day or two we went to see the *entrée* of Louis into Paris—a humble spectacle indeed compared to the magnitude of the struggle that brought it about.

Lieut.-General Sir Lowry Cole had now arrived to take the command of the 6th Division, previously under Lambert. The 5th, 6th, and Brunswickers composed the Reserve, about 17,000, Sir James Kempt, the senior General, commanding; whose Quartermaster-General, Sir William Gomm, gave all orders for marching, bivouac, etc. Now it became my province to do so, and I never felt more proud than in having the movement and arrangement of march of 17,000 soldiers.

Our army was in the environs of Paris, the 5th Division at Clichy, the 6th at Neuilly, the Brunswickers near Clichy. The house I and my wife occupied in the town of Neuilly we found was a sort of country residence belonging to a nice old lady in Paris. There was a beautiful and most productive garden, and an establishment of regular gardeners. When I sent for the head man and desired him to take to his mistress the vegetables he was accustomed to send her, and to obey her orders, whatever they were, he was thunderstruck. I said, " If the garden is not kept in real good order, then I will show you what an Englishman is." The poor old lady, hearing this, came out to thank us, and we often dined with her in Paris. She lived in great style, and was of use to my wife in showing her milliners, etc., for a refit _à la mode_ was necessary.

Our life was now one of continued pleasure and excitement—nothing but parties at night and races by day. At these I was steward. The crowd of foreign officers being very unruly in riding in after the race-horses, I put some proper fellows of soldiers at the distance-post (who, having resisted many a charge of French cavalry, cared little for an unarmed galloping man), with orders to run the rope across to stop this disorder. My orders were obeyed, as I expected, and that gallant hero, Marshal Blucher, not seeing the rope, rode his horse full speed against it and fell, and in the crash the noble old fellow broke his collar-bone, to my annoyance and distress.

While one day walking in my garden at Neuilly, my old friend Tom Fane, who had come to Paris as one of the sight-seers, came full gallop up to me and Juana, "Hurrah, Harry, the *Gazette* has arrived! You are Lieutenant-Colonel, and here is a case for you; it has some order in it, I think. I found it at the Military Secretary's office, and, being to your address, brought it. Let me open it." It was the Order of Companion of the Bath, which pleased poor Tom more than it did me. Thus again had I and Juana cause to be grateful to Almighty God, not only for perfect safety, but for worldly distinction and promotion. It was barely fourteen months since the Battle of Toulouse. I had crossed the Atlantic to and from America four times; fought a gallant action, and captured the metropolis of that world; brought home dispatches, and received £500; was in communication with ministers, and honoured by a long audience of His Royal Highness the Prince Regent; again went out; again was under fire for three weeks, and in the sanguinary disaster at New Orleans; was in the Battle of Waterloo, and had been promoted from Captain to Lieut.-Colonel and Companion of the Bath; without a wound; restored to my wife in health and contentment, and nothing to distress or annoy me beyond the loss and wounds of so many gallant and dear friends. Cold must that heart be which could not feel to its inmost core God Almighty's providence.

While in our cantonments around Paris we had frequent reviews with Emperors, Kings, etc., as spectators, and nothing could exceed the style and bearing of our army. The conduct, too, was exemplary. The taking down of the horses from Venice, from the Place du Carrousel; the execution of poor Ney, that hero of reality, not romance; the desire of Blucher to destroy the bridge of Jena, which the Duke of Wellington prevented; the escape of La Vallette, etc., kept us all in a state of excitement, while the lions of Paris, then the *entrepôt* of every article of value in the arts, afforded daily occupation. Not a valuable picture in Europe but was in the Place du Carrousel. It was my delight to stand, often an hour at a time, looking at Paul Potter's small painting of the bull and the peasant behind the tree, and I have been so fascinated I have expected the bull to charge.

In the autumn [1815] it became necessary to move the army into more permanent quarters, and my Division, the 6th, was sent to St. Germain, that magnificent and ancient resort of former kings. The woods were in perfect order, and cut into beautiful *foci* and avenues like radii of circles, for hunting in the French style. The Duke de Berri had hounds, and was passionately fond of the sport. The stag was turned out, there were relays of hounds in couples, and huntsmen of various denominations with large French horns, all in a *costume de chasse*, with large cocked hats and a *couteau de chasse* by their sides. The carriages, full of ladies of the court and others, assembled in one of the *foci*, or centres, from which the avenues radiated. When the stag crossed into another part of the wood, the carriages galloped to the "*focus*" of that part of the forest where the hunt was now going on, and such a crash of horns as there was to denote that the stag had changed his direction! The Duke went galloping up and down the avenues, changing very frequently from one fat brute of a horse to another. My wife and I, who went out every day and galloped after the Duke, an ill-tempered fellow, up and down the avenues, were barely able to keep our real good hunters warm. It was, however, capital fun, although foreign to our ideas of hunting. I always fancied myself a figure in a tapestry, hunting being a favourite subject for that kind of delineation.

At the *mort* (or death), or when the stag was at bay, there was always a great row of horns and shouting, but *no dog-language*. On one occasion the stag, a noble animal, was at bay, and fiercely contending with the hounds. The Duke de Berri jumped off his horse and drew his *couteau de chasse*, making great demonstration of going up to the stag, while his courtiers were screeching, "Oh, monsieur, monsieur, prenez garde, pour l'amour de Dieu." He reminded me of the Irish hero, "Hold me, Jim; you know my *temper*," for the Duke had no real idea of doing anything of the sort, although, when the poor noble animal had been shot by some of the *piqueurs*, the Duke then ran in *valorously* and dipped his *couteau* in the beautiful animal's chest. For this feat a lot of us were determined to play the Duke a trick, and the next hunting-day we contrived to break down the paling of the forest and to induce the stag to bolt. We succeeded to our hearts' content, and away into the open went stag safe enough, the hounds in no wind after him. The Duke and all his equipage were soon planted, and he was in a furious passion. The *couteau de chasse* was not required that day.

The most ridiculous thing is that they do not let the hounds "tear him and eat him" while their blood is up. The stag is taken to the kennel and skinned, and all the meat cut into small pieces and put again into the hide, and the hounds then, in this cold-blooded way, rush at a *mess*, instead of the whole pack, in a state of excitement, falling on the hunted animal reeking with fatigue.

We were all amused one day at observing a

man elegantly mounted on an English horse in the full costume of the French *chasse* (*couteau*, etc.), when who should this be but our own dear Duke! He looked so neat and smart, and we had such a laugh. He himself had a beautiful pack of hounds and some boxed stags, which gave runs sometimes, but he was not of the age for a sportsman.

About this time I and Will Havelock set on foot a pack of foxhounds. We sent to England for hounds. The numbers of our pack being thirteen couple, we sent to Brussels for [five couple more] from the Prince of Orange's establishment. This pack afterwards became a capital one.

On the conclusion of the treaty between the Allied Powers and France, by which an Army of Occupation was designated to remain on the northern boundary of France for three or five years, the large armies (except their quota of the contingent) marched back to their respective countries. Of the British Army four Divisions alone were to remain. Mine was reduced, and being no longer on the staff, I joined my regiment. Some of my old comrades said to Charlie Beckwith, who had also joined, "Now, how will Harry Smith, after a career of such extended authority, like to come back to the command of a Company?" Charlie says (for he loved me), "In the execution of his duty and care of his Company he will be an example to us all."

My corps was moved again into the environs of Paris preparatory to its march to the north. I was now visited by the deepest distress and grief, for three days expecting the death of all I loved and cherished—my dear wife. Nothing but vigour of mind and a good constitution saved her. I had encountered many previous difficulties, dangers, and disasters, but never aught like this. God in His continued mercy spared her to me. Praised be His Name.

She was scarcely fit to move when we marched from Paris to Louvres [16 Jan. 1816] and an adjacent village. My Company went to Vernais. We were again under Sir John Lambert, who had been moved from one Brigade to another. My wife drove herself in my tilbury; I marched with my men. We had a large cold château as a quarter, with a very civil landlord. I had with me the hounds—eighteen couple. He put them up most kindly, and appeared delighted—so much so that I had no delicacy in asking him to get me a dead horse or to buy a dying brute for a few shillings. To my astonishment, he regarded the request as a direct insult. It was all I could do to make him understand I had no idea of offending. He was with difficulty appeased, but I saw he never forgot the dead horse, any more than the Antiquary's nephew the "*phoca* or seal."

From hence we marched to Cambray, around which place and Valenciennes the greater part of the army was to be cantoned. Three fortresses were to be garrisoned by us. The Duke's head-quarters were to be at Cambray. One day Major Balvaird came to me. He was my commanding officer (I being only a *Brevet* Lieut.-Colonel and *Captain* under his command). He was an excellent fellow, and as gallant a soldier as ever lived, a bosom friend, and a Scotchman with a beautiful accent. "Weel, Harry, mi mon, the deevil is in it. I have an order to send a Captain to the depôt at Shorncliffe. You are the first for my duty, my lad. You canna be more hurt at being ordered than I am to order you. So be prepared. There is a just ane chance for you, but you must be prepared." My mortification was excessive, for with my habits, hounds, horses, and wife, etc., the income I should get in England was not at all to my desire. However, I said nothing to my wife, always hoping something might turn up.

On the march one night my Company was in a wretched little village, my quarters a miserable dirty little farmhouse. On any other occasion I should have cared more than my wife herself, but she was still very delicate, and I was awfully afraid of a relapse. It was February, and the cold very severe. In watching her, I did not go to sleep until just before it was time to jump up and march, when I had a curious dream that the Duke of Wellington sent for me and said, "Smith, I have two staff-appointments to give away, you shall have one," and that as I went out, poor Felton Hervey, the Military Secretary, said, "You are a lucky fellow,

Harry, for the one you are to have is the most preferable by far." I told my wife this dream, and said, " Mark my words if it does not turn out to be true."

On reaching our cantonment at Bourlon, a little beyond Cambray, I had just put up my Company when General Lambert sent for me. " Smith," he says, " I am ordered to send a field officer to Cambray, who, in conjunction with an officer of Engineers, is to take over Cambray, its guns, stores, etc., from the French Commander and Engineers. It may lead to something further. I therefore wish you to start at daylight; the duty is important." *His* wish was *my* law. Off I started. I had scarcely completed the transfer when the General Orders were put into my hand in which I saw I was appointed Major de Place, or Town-Major of Cambray, and Charlie Beckwith Major de Place of Valenciennes, each with the pay or allowance of Assistant Quartermaster-General, to which department we were to report. Thus my dream was verified, for, as Cambray was headquarters, and I had none of that horrid duty, billeting on the inhabitants, which was attached to Valenciennes (the headquarters A.Q.M.G. being desired to do it), I was given the better place of the two, as Hervey said in my dream.

CHAPTER XXVII.

SOON after our establishment at Cambray, I received a note from one of His Grace's Aides-de-Camp. "The Duke desires you will come to him immediately, and bring with you the sheet of Cassini's map of the environs of Cambray." Fortunately I had this map. I asked myself what in the name of wonder the Duke could want. Off I cut. "Well, Smith, got the map?" I opened it. "Now, where is my château?" "Here, my lord." "Ah, the coverts are very well shown here. Are there foxes in all these?" "Yes, my lord, too many in every one." "Well, then, hounds must always know their own country"—he drew his finger as a line across the map. "Now, your hounds hunt that side, mine this."

On one occasion, when Lord Castlereagh was staying with His Grace, the former wanted to see some coursing in France, and about 2 o'clock in the afternoon the Duke sent for me to bring some greyhounds. We went out, and were lucky in finding, and killed a brace. I never saw a man in such spirits as the Duke. He rode like a whipper-in.

I once trained some greyhounds for the Duke, almost puppies, against some of the same age which that noble fellow, Sir Edward Barnes had bred. We were to meet near the Duke's château, where there were plenty of hares. We had great sport to beat Sir Edward every match. My wife rode her " Brass" seventeen miles before we looked for a hare. The Duke made her one of his umpires. She rode every course, and back again at night.

Poor Felton Hervey was prejudiced against Spanish greyhounds, and he and the present Duke of Richmond got out some English hounds to the Peninsula to beat my celebrated " Moro," which Harry Mellish, a gallant hero alike as soldier and sportsman, declared the best dog he ever saw in his life. Of course the English dogs had no chance.

While at Cambray I had two dogs, sons of the " Moro," and we had a great coursing party—the Duke of Wellington, Lord Hill (who had beautiful English greyhounds), Sir Hussey Vivian, etc. We were near the Duke's château, where there were plenty of right good hares. Hervey objected to my Spaniards running. We had been coursing all day and not a hare was killed, so I rode up to the Duke and said, " My lord, this won't do. A hare must be killed to go to the château." The Duke said, " Ah! but how?" " My Spaniards should kill you a hare, my lord." The sun was

almost down. Felton Hervey says, " Lord Hill's
' Laura ' and ' Rattler ' shall get a hare. We will put
them in slips ; Smith shall call ' Loo,' and if they
don't kill their hare, then let the Moro blood try,
and I will halloo them out of their slips." At it we
went. A hare jumped up under the nose of Lord
Hill's dogs. I hallooed. The hare hadn't twenty
yards' law. " Ah," says the Duke, " you gave the
hare no chance." " Plenty, my lord. They won't
kill her." After a terrific course she fairly beat
them. Hervey was very angry. It was nearly
dark, when hares run like devils. My dogs, two
brothers, were in the slips. So late in the evening
hares are sly. One jumped up sixty yards off,
and Hervey hallooed. The honesty of the field
went with me, and all sung out, " Shame, Hervey !
your dogs were close to their hare." " Never mind,"
I said. " My lord, you shall have the hare." I was
on that wonderful horse Lochinvar, and never did
I so ask him to go along. My dogs soon closed
with their hare, when I knew, if they once turned
her with such a law, she was ours. We had a
terrific course, and killed her in a bank, within three
yards of a covert where she would have been safe.
I galloped back in triumph with my hare, for not
a horse could live with Lochinvar, and I threw the
hare down at his Grace's feet. Hervey was furious,
and insisted that I and Lochinvar acted third greyhound. I did not, and I gained accordingly. The
Duke laughed, and turned round to go home, saying,
" Thank you for the hare, Smith. We should have

gone home without one but for your Spanish greyhounds."

Coming home from riding one afternoon, I overtook the Duke on the bank of the canal, all alone. When I rode up I must either pass him, or saddle myself on him as companion, neither of which etiquette or delicacy tolerated. After my usual salutation, the Duke, with his brilliant imagination in trifles as well as things of moment, said, "If not in a hurry, ride home with me." After a little talk about hounds, greyhounds, etc., he said, "What! no dogs with you?" I said, "On Sundays, my lord, I never take them out." "Very proper," he said, "although I fear in our late struggle we respected Sunday but little. All our great battles were fought on that holy day which ought to be." "Yes," said I, "my lord, so was Trafalgar, and so was that dire disaster, New Orleans." "Was it?" he said. "You were there, were you not?" "Indeed was I, my lord." His Grace never mentioned dear Sir Edward Pakenham, and of course I never did, although my heart was full of him. "Tell me all about it." I did so. "What! the troops stood and fired in column, did they? What corps?" I named them. "Ah," he said, "they had not been accustomed to victory, but it was quite right to keep two such corps as the 7th Fusiliers and the 43rd in reserve." "We ought not to have landed where we did, my lord." "Certainly not," he said. "I was consulted about those lakes, and I immediately asked, 'Is there navigation there for

purposes of trade?' When I was answered 'No,'
I said, ' Then it is injudicious to use them to land
an army, and craft of any size will never get up
to land the troops.'"

I had received and carried many orders from
his Grace, but of course never held a military conversation with him before. I was never so struck
as by the pointed questions he asked and the more
rapid questions my answers elicited. In half an
hour's ride he was perfectly acquainted with all
I could tell him, and said, " I am glad I have had
this conversation with you. It agrees as nearly
as may be with the opinion I had previously formed.
If you are not engaged, you and Juana come and
dine with me to-day. Her friend Alava will be
there." I was as proud as may be, because I knew
by this his Grace was satisfied with my explanation.
How I longed to tell him how I loved and admired
his brother-in-law, Sir Edward Pakenham! But
although I talked of " the General," I never made
use of the magic word (to me at least) " Pakenham."

One night, at a great ball at the Duke's, the
Prince and Princess Narinska were present, and a
lot of Russian and Cossack officers. The Princess
was the only Russian lady, a very beautiful and
accomplished woman. The Duke wished that the
mazurka should be danced in compliment to her,
but none of our ladies would stand up with the
Princess. So the Duke came up to my wife, and
took her hand: " Come, Juana, now for the Russian
fandango ; you will soon catch the step." A young

Russian came forward as her partner. The Princess danced elegantly, and the Duke was as anxious as I was that Juana should acquit herself well. She did, and he was as pleased as possible.

The Duke was in great spirits in those days, and whenever he was surrounded by Emperors and Kings he showed himself the great man that he was. His attention to them was most marked, but we ever observed that his Grace felt he was the representative of our King and country, and we could see the majesty and still the delicacy with which he conducted himself.

On one occasion the King of Prussia begged to see as many of the British Army by themselves as could be collected, and the majority were assembled not far from the pillar erected by the French in honour of the victory of [Denain*], and which was equally in honour of the Duke of Marlborough. (The French never gained a battle until [Marlborough] was so madly taken away by the intrigues of the British Government.) The King arrived much before his time, and our troops were not formed

---

* Battle of Denain, 24 July, 1712. Denain is only about five miles from Cambray. Marlborough was removed from the command of the armies of the Grand Alliance by the intrigues of Oxford and St. John in order to force the allies into the peace of Utrecht. The withdrawal of the British troops in the field a little later was immediately followed by the first really serious defeat sustained by the allies in the central field of the war since Marlborough had assumed the command ; Villars cutting up and annihilating an isolated force of 8000 men under the Earl of Albemarle, who were holding a bridge across the Scheldt at Denain to cover Eugene's force besieging Landrécy. For the clearing up of this passage (left incomplete in the MS.) I am indebted to my colleague, Mr. H. W. Appleton, M.A.

to receive him.   The Duke's quick eye detected his approach in the distance, and he says, "Hallo, Fremantle, there he is!   He will be upon us before we are ready, and we can't keep him back with picquets.   Ride up and make him take a long détour until you see we are ready, although a few minutes will suffice us."   Our troops were in position like lightning, and it was beautiful to see the Duke so animated, so cool, so proud of his Army and the rapidity with which we all moved to act up to his wishes.   He was altogether very popular with his Army, but not so much so as after Toulouse.   He felt that everything that occurred at his head-quarters must be a precedent for the guidance of all the Armies he was in command of, and he was frequently rigid, as it seemed, to extremes, particularly in all cases of disputes between officers and the French inhabitants.   At Cambray it was part of my duty to receive all complaints, and, generally speaking, our own people were the aggressors.   When the French were, his Grace demanded that *their* authorities should make an equal example.   This correct principle of action was as highly extolled by all thinking men as it deserved, especially as the French had degraded themselves all over the world (except in dear old England which we protected) by acts of cruelty, oppression, and tyranny towards the inhabitants. The Duke said, "We are Englishmen and pride ourselves on our deportment, and that pride shall not be injured in my keeping."   On parting with his Army, he thanked the British contingent after all the others. " He begs them to accept his best acknowledgments for the example they have given to others by their own good conduct, and for the support and assistance they have invariably afforded him to maintain the discipline of the Army." This I thought at the time, and I do so more now, was the highest compliment his Grace could pay us We had saved Europe, and now we were thanked for our conduct in quarters, when in occupation of the country of our enemy, who had been the oppressors of the world ; although, as good does come out of evil, so has Europe been wonderfully improved owing to the liberal principles moderately derived from the madness of French democracy.

Our life in Cambray was one excess of gaiety My dear old friend and commander, Sir Andrew Barnard, had been appointed Commandant, so that surrounded by my old generals, friends, and comrades, I was at home at once. We were both young ; my wife was beautiful. We were fêted and petted by every one. I was the huntsman of a magnificent pack of hounds, steward of races, riding steeplechases, etc. My wife was taken the greatest notice of by every one, especially by the Duke who, having known her as a child, always called her his Spanish heroine, Juana. She rode beautifully hunting, was the best of waltzers, and sang melodiously. We were surrounded by the best society. All England's nobility poured forth to see the lion of the day, the Duke's headquarters

No wonder that in the midst of this gaiety and in his land of plenty, after the life of hardship and privation which we had led, we should have been somewhat intoxicated by the scene around us, and I spent a lot of money which, had I saved it prudently, would have now nearly accumulated to a fortune. I had prize-money for the Peninsula, for Washington, and for Waterloo paid at this period. I had money left me by my grandmother. All went as fast as I could get it.

In 1817, I and a friend went to look over the field of Waterloo. The wood of Hougoumont had been cut down, which very much altered the appearance of the ground, as did the want of troops, etc. To those unaccustomed to look at ground with and without troops, the difference cannot well be explained. I trod, however, upon this immortal field with a thrilling sensation of gratitude to Almighty God, first for personal safety and for the additional honour and glory my country's Army had acquired there, and next for the beneficial results to Europe ensured by the achievement of that wonderful battle. The left of the position as well as the centre was as during the battle, with the exception of the many tombs and monuments erected to mark the spots where lay interred so many gallant spirits, and many is the burning tear I shed over the mounds of some of my dearest friends, many of England's brightest sons and rising soldiers. No one can feel what a soldier does on such a spot, especially one who was in the midst of the strife. But nothing struck me so forcibly as the small extent of the field. It appeared impossible that so many thousands of troops could have contended on so constricted a space, the one spot on earth which decided the fate of Emperors and Kings, and the future destiny of nations.

Every year we had a grand review of the whole Army of the contingencies. One year the Duke of Kent was the Review-Marshal. The last year of occupation, viz. the third, we had an immense sham-fight, which ended on the heights of Fimare, where the Army passed in review [23 Oct.] the Emperor of Russia, King of Prussia, the Grand Duke Constantine, the Grand Duke Michael, etc. In the course of the day the Duke, riding with their Majesties, saw Juana. He called her up and presented her to the Emperor of Russia, "Voilà, Sire, ma petite guerrière espagnole qui a fait la guerre avec son mari comme la héroine de Saragosse." The Emperor shook her hands, and asked her to ride for some time with him as she spoke French fluently, when he put a variety of questions to her about the war in Spain, all of which she could answer as intelligently as most officers. At night she danced with the Grand Duke Michael, an excellent waltzer. When the Emperor's courtiers observed the attention paid by the Emperor to my wife, they sought out the husband. I was in my Rifle uniform. One fellow said, "Are you aware to whom Madame has had the honour to be presented?" "To be sure," I said, saucily, "and by *whom*—the greatest man in the world."

That night, riding into Valenciennes on the *pavé*, both sides of the road being covered with troops marching to their cantonments, it was very cold, and I was clapping my hands on my shoulders, *à l'anglaise*, when my wife says, "You have lost your Star of the Bath." I had felt something catch in the lace of my sleeve, so I turned back. A column of Russian Cuirassiers were marching over the ground I had traversed, and the sides of the road being excessively dusty, I said to myself, "What nonsense! I can never find it," and was in the act of turning back to my wife, when a flat-footed dickey dragoon horse, having set his hollow foot upon it, tossed it under my horse's nose out of the dust upon the *pavé*. It is a most ridiculous occurrence to record, but my astonishment at the time was excessive. The star was bruised by the horse's foot, in which shape I wore it twenty-nine years.

The period of occupation was now reduced to three years, and the Army was prepared to with-draw—to *our* mortification, for we should have been delighted with two years more. It was now, on winding up my private accounts which had been miserably neglected, I discovered my money was far exceeded by my debts. I therefore, as one of my auxiliaries, put up to raffle, for 250 napoleons, a celebrated thoroughbred horse, the

Young Lochinvar, by Grouse, out of Dab Chick,
Vandyke's dam. This horse I had bought for a
large sum in my native town, just before the Battle
of Waterloo, from a gentleman who had bought
him at Newmarket for an immense price and
whose circumstances compelled him to become a
bankrupt. My father was aware of his pending
situation, and just on the eve of it bought
Lochinvar. I had ridden him hunting three years ;
he was the only horse in the Army that was never
planted in the deep fields of France. As a horse
he was as celebrated as His Grace was as a
General, 16 hands high and equal to 14 stone.
It went to my heart to part with him. My wife
said, "Oh, I will have a ticket." "Oh, nonsense,
it is only throwing five napoleons away." However, she had her own way, as wives always have
(especially Spanish wives), and, by another piece
of my continued good luck, her ticket won the
horse, and I had Lochinvar in my stable, while the
245 napoleons readily found claimants. It was
a piece of fortune I was very grateful for. I
loved the horse, and he carried me in that stiff
county of Kent afterwards, as he had ever done
elsewhere.

From the day on which I presented my billet
to my landlord in Cambray, I was much struck
with his manly bearing and open conduct. He
was a man of a large family, a Monsieur Watin,
and his brother, also with a family, resided with
him. He showed me all his house and his stables

(he had built a kitchen and servants' rooms for any one who should be quartered on him). He said, "In this life, happiness is not to be attained, but it must not be impeded. I am aware of the way French officers behave in quarters. I hear you English are less *exigeant*. This part of the house I reserve for myself and my brother, the rest I give to you." And I certainly had the best, for he only reserved to himself one sitting-room. I said, "I have more than enough." "No, no," he said, "when you give a soirée you shall have this too." I was three years in his house, and I never had a word with either him or any member of his family. On the contrary, nothing could be more amicable. In the course of the second year my father came and paid me a visit for near three months. Never was man more happy and delighted. He was fond of field sports and of flowers. The Bishop of Cambray had a magnificent garden, and many an hour did my father spend there. When he arrived, of course I begged him to tell us what he liked best at table. "Oh, anything," he says, "only take care your French cook does not make the pastry with oil, which I know they do, but with butter." I had an excellent cook, and I told him to be careful about his pastry, which was, of course, made with oil. Every day my father praised the pastry. After some weeks I let him into the secret. "Ah," says he, "such through life is prejudice." He was far from disliking French wines. The day he left us—"Well, it is very true that you and the poor man of the house live very friendly, but you have the whole nearly. I shall go home now and pay my taxes with delight. Even were they double, readily would I pay rather than have such a fellow as you and your establishment quartered on me!" Poor dear father! I had been your pet son. Everything I practised that was manly, you taught me, and to my equestrian powers and activity, which first brought me into notice, did I owe my rapid rise in the service.

The day having at length arrived when we were to leave Cambray, [27 Oct. ?] Sir Andrew Barnard and I were asked to at least twenty breakfasts. My first was with the family on whom we were billeted, and if they had been our nearest relations no greater feeling could have been evinced. Monsieur Watin was a great carpenter. To him I gave a capital chest of tools, to his brother, who was a sportsman (in his way), I gave one of Manton's double-barrelled guns, and my wife made many presents to the female part of the family. Then came my nineteen breakfasts with Barnard. We positively sat down a few minutes with all our hosts and ate something; both of us laughing and saying, "We have been together in situations when the sight of such breakfasts would have been far from objectionable, but 'enough is as good as a feast.'" I never was so tired of the sight of food. I felt as though I never could feel the sensation of hunger again. All this attention, however, was very gratifying,

JOHN SMITH.

(Sir Harry Smith's father.)

From a picture painted by J. P. Hunter, Somersham, Hunts, May, 1837.

[*Opposite Vol. i. p.* 314.

and upon parting with our worthy family, as our carriage drove through the streets, there was nothing but waving of handkerchiefs and adieus. The garrison had marched two days before. The most complimentary letter I ever read was addressed to the Commandant Barnard by the Mayor, a Monsieur Bethune, a Bonapartist too, to the purport that, although every Frenchman must rejoice at the cessation of the foreign occupation of his country, as individuals he and all the city would and must ever remember the English with gratitude for their generosity and liberality, and for the impartial justice ever shown by Barnard during his three years' Commandantship. In a French fortress the Commandant has far more authority than the Prime Minister in England. Thus we parted from Cambray, where we had had three years' gaiety amidst the wealth and aristocracy of England, in the country of an enemy that had contended and struggled to subdue our own in a most sanguinary war by sea and land, lasting with but little intermission from 1798 to 1815. The garrison of Cambray was composed of a Brigade of Guards,—the 1st Battalion Grenadiers under Colonel the Hon. William Stewart, and the Coldstreams under Colonel Woodford. I never before or since served with such correct soldiers, and they had the very best non-commissioned officers. There were peculiarities in the mode in which the officers performed their duties, but, according to their own rules, it was a lesson of rectitude, zeal, honour, and manliness. I quite agree with Johnny Kincaid that the officers in our Army who come from our aristocracy are ever most zealous as officers, and certainly most agreeable as companions, and I have now served with most corps of the Army, Hussars, Guards, Infantry, etc.

CHAPTER XXVIII.

ON reaching Calais I could not avoid calling to
memory the British possession of that celebrated
fortress, for so many years the bone of contention
and strife. All was bustle and embarcation. We
embarked in a small vessel [31 Oct. ?], and the wind
obliged us to go to Ramsgate. The London
Custom House had provided for baggage to be
examined at Ramsgate as well as at Dover, and
nothing could be more liberal and gentlemanlike
than the Custom House officers (of course acting
under instructions). My wife had an immense
box of French dresses which, being all extended
on account of the large flounces then worn,
required great room. While I was passing my
baggage, one of the officers said, "And that large
box—what does it contain ? " I said, " My wife's
dresses." " I have not the least doubt of it, sir, as
you say so, sir ; but I declare I never saw such a
box of ladies' dresses in my life before." Then

came her guitar. "What is this?" "Oh, hand it along, it's naught but a fiddle."

The celebrated Cavalry officer, Sir John Elley, a very tall, bony, and manly figure of a man, with grim-visaged war depicted in his countenance, with whiskers, moustaches, etc. like a French Pioneer, came over to Dover during the time of our occupation of France. He was walking on the path, with his celebrated sword belted under his *surtout*. As the hooking up of the sword gave the coat-flap the appearance of having something large concealed under it, a lower order of Custom officer ran after him, rudely calling, "I say, you officer, you! stop, stop, I say! What's that under your coat?" Sir John turned round, and drawing his weapon of defence in many a bloody fight, to the astonishment of the John Bulls, roared out through his moustache in a voice of thunder, "That which I will run through your d——d guts, if you are impertinent to me!"

My Regiment was at Shorncliffe, and thither I and my wife proceeded, parting with many friends of the Guards, some of whom she has never seen since. I was given an entirely new Company, that is, one composed of recruits. I interceded with Colonel Norcott, however, to give me a few of my dear old comrades into each squad, and with their help and example I soon inspired the rest with the feelings of soldiers. There was a pack of hounds too in the neighbourhood, and though it is a stiff, bad country, fox-hunting is fox-hunting in any shape, and I had two noble hunters, Lochinvar and a celebrated mare, besides the " Brass Mare" for my wife.   My whole income at the moment was my pay, 12s. 6d. a day.   One day, after a capital run with the hounds, Mr. Deedes asked me to dine with him, and I had a post-chaise to go in to dinner, which cost me 17s.   Thus—

> " How happy's the soldier who lives on his pay,
>   And spends half-a-crown out of sixpence a day ! "

My Battalion was ordered to Gosport, and soon after at Shorncliffe, which had been the depôt of the Regiment during the whole war, not a Rifleman was left.   I marched [about Dec. 24–28] in command of the Headquarters Division, all our old soldiers.   Neither they nor I could help remarking the country as a difficult one to make war in.   You would hear the men, " I say, Bill, look at that wood on the hill there and those hedgerows before it. I think we could keep that ourselves against half Soult's Army.   Ah, I had rather keep it than attack it !   But, Lord, the war's all over now."

When I first joined at Shorncliffe we heard of nothing but "the French are coming over."   We have been in among *them*, I take it, since.   They never could have got to London through such a stiff country.   We would have destroyed the roads and cut down the trees to make those d——d things they used to do—*abattis* * ; besides, where

---

* " Few good riders haggle at a ditch, but an abattis of trees, with their trunks towards their friends, and their branches spread out towards the foe, is a less manageable obstacle."—H. Havelock, in his account of his brother W. H. (Buist's *Annals of India for* 1848).

would be the use of all their capering cavalry, etc. ?

During this march, when the men were billeted in the inns and scattered over the country, I could not divest myself of the feeling of insecurity I had acquired after so many years' precautionary habits ; and although I repeated to myself a hundred times daily, "You are in England," the thought would arise, "You are in the power of your enemy." Before dismissing the men, I always told them the hour I should march in the morning, and men who were billeted either ahead or on the sides of the road were to join their Companies as I arrived. During the whole march I never had a man absent or irregular. Such a band of practised and educated soldiers may never again traverse England.

My wife posted from Shorncliffe into Sussex— to Beauport, Sir John Lambert's temporary seat, where the kind family insisted on her staying until I came to fetch her to Gosport, which I did soon after. On arrival at Gosport we were led to believe we should be a year or two there, and we began to (what is called) make ourselves comfortable.

We had a great number of guards and sentries literally over nothing. One night, however, on visiting the different guards and counting them, I found every man present. I asked, "What! no man on sentry ? " " Oh no, sir ; the 86th, whom we relieved, say they always bring in all sentries at night." "Why, this is a new way—new to us." " Certainly," the sergeants said.

The following day I and two or three officers went to inspect every sentry's post. We found some with orders "to see that no one took that gun away" (a 32-pounder dismounted), one "to see as them goats did not leave the rampart." He was one of our soldiers, and I said, "Confound you, did you take such an order from a storekeeper?" He said, "Why, I hardly look on it as a *horder*, only civil-like of me; and you know, sir, goats were worth looking after at Dough Boy Hill" (near Almaraz, so called from our having nothing to eat for three weeks but dough and goats' flesh, and very little of either).* I represented all this to Lord Howard of Effingham, who very readily entertained the report, and sentries were all taken off, where not required. Colonel Norcott soon after joined.

While we were here 300 of our oldest and best soldiers were discharged. Every one came to say farewell to my wife; and there was a touching parting between officers and soldiers, now about to be dispersed through Great Britain, after so many years' association under such eventful circumstances. There was not one who could not relate some act of mutual kindness and reciprocity of feeling in connexion with the many memorable events in which they had taken part. I and many of the officers marched several miles on the road with these noble fellows. In the Barrack Square they had prayed me to give them the word of command

* See p. 19, bottom.

to march off. "Sure," says an Irishman, "it's the last after the thousand your honour has given us." I did so; but when the moment arrived to part every man's tears were chasing each other down his bronzed and veteran cheeks. They grasped their officers' hands,—"God bless your honour!" then such a shout and cheer. Such feelings in times of peace are not, cannot be acquired. My faithful old West was of the party; but he parted from me and his mistress in our house. Poor faithful, noble fellow, as gallant as a lion, he had been with me from Vimiera and Coruña until 1819.

The 18th June, the first anniversary of the Battle of Waterloo which we had spent in England, was such a day throughout the Regiment, with dinners for the soldiers, non-commissioned officers, wives and children. Among the officers there was such a jubilee of mirth, mingled with grief for our lost comrades, as must be conceived, for never was there a Regiment in which harmony and unanimity were more perfect.

In the autumn the manufacturing districts, Glasgow, Manchester, Birmingham, etc., became much disturbed, and our soldiers, who invariably know everything first, insisted on it we should go to Glasgow. My Company was out at target practice with others, when we heard the assembly sound. "Hurrah for Glasgow!" said the men. We all marched home, and found we were to embark on board a man-of-war immediately. By four o'clock that afternoon [18 Sept.] we were

all on board the *Liffey*. Sir James Kempt had
succeeded Lord Howard of Effingham in the command at Portsmouth, and proud he was to see one of
his old Battalions in peace the same ready soldiers
they were in war. My wife remained behind to
go in the *Spartan* frigate, which had been recently
fitted up for the Duchess of Kent. The Captain
put her up superbly, and she reached Leith Roads
in time to join my Company on the march.*

---

* The 1st Battalion landed at Leith on 27th Sept. (Cope, p. 217.)

CHAPTER XXIX.

Glasgow (1819–1825)—radical disturbances—harry smith once more on the staff as major of brigade—george iv.'s visit to edinburgh—harry smith revisits paris—he rejoins his regiment in ireland.

Glasgow at this season of the year, October, is a most melancholy, dirty, smoky city, particularly the end in which the barracks are placed; and such was the state of the city, my wife had to live in barracks and we were again shut up in one room, as during the war. When matters approached the worst, I sent my wife to Edinburgh, where she received every kindness and hospitality. There was living there then Mrs. Beckwith, who had campaigned with her husband in Prince Ferdinand of Brunswick's time. She was then ninety-four, and lived afterwards to upwards of a hundred, the mother of Sir George Beckwith, my dear Sir Sydney, and several other sons. She was in full possession of her intellect, and was delighted to talk of war with my wife. The latter said one day, "I am afraid I do not speak English well enough to explain myself." "Not speak well enough! Why?" "Because I am a Spaniard, and have only recently learned to speak English." " A Spaniard ? Stand up, and let me look at your feet and ankles, for I have always heard your countrywomen celebrated for their neatness." My wife was still in heart a Spaniard, and as particular as ever in shoes and stockings, and the poor old lady was delighted. After talking for a certain time, she used to say, " Now go; I am tired."

Our duty in Glasgow was very laborious and irksome. We had neither enemy nor friends : a sort of *Bellum in Pace*, which we old campaigners did not understand. But, although constantly insulted by the mob in the streets, either individually or in a body, our deportment was so mild that we soon gained rather the respect than otherwise of the misguided and half-starved weavers. They had many old soldiers amongst them, and had organized themselves into sixteen Battalions. Many of these old soldiers I knew; one was a Rifleman— an old comrade who had lost his arm at New Orleans—and from him I ascertained their perfect organization. They had a General, or Central, Committee of Delegates ("a House of Lords"), and each district had a committee, who sent a delegate to the Central Committee. The regiments were formed by streets, so that in case of a turn-out they could parade—"Ah, just as we did in the towns of Spain and France," * my comrade said.

One day my Company was sent out with twenty

* See p. 166, bottom.

of the 7th Hussars, just before daylight, to arrest a party of delegates. We had magistrates, etc. with us, and succeeded in arresting every man. I saw a violent storm of mob assembling. I put the prisoners in the centre of my Company, under the command of my subaltern, Henry Havelock,* now a hero of Burma, Afghanistan, and Maharajpore celebrity, a clever, sharp fellow, and said, " Move you on collected to the barracks, and I will cover you with the Hussars." On my word, they were violent, and the Hussars, with the flat of their swords, as I particularly directed, did make the heads of some ache, while brickbats, stones, etc. were flying among us half as bad as grapeshot. The magistrates were horridly timid and frightened lest I should

---

* Henry Havelock, writing to his old Captain, then Major-General Smith, Oct. 3, 1840, refers perhaps to the events of this day. [Was it April 2, 1820 ? See Cope, p. 220.] " I feel that it is time I ought to be trying to ascend the ladder, if ever, for as the *Battle of Glasgow Green* was fought in 1820, I fear I must now be not very far from forty-six." It is perhaps not the least of Harry Smith's services to his country that he incited his subaltern, Henry Havelock, to make a serious study of the science of his profession. Havelock writes to him Sept. 5, 1840, as his " master," and writes of him on Oct. 2, 1847 (after his appointment to the Governorship of the Cape) : " When I was a boy, he was one of the few people that ever took the trouble to teach me anything ; and while all the rest around me would have persuaded me that English soldiering consisted in blackening and whitening belts with patent varnish and pipe-clay, and getting every kind of mercenary manœuvre, he pointed my mind to the nobler part of our glorious profession. As a public man I shall ever acknowledge his merits. He is an excellent soldier—one of the few now extant among us who have set themselves to comprehend the higher portions of the art. He has a natural talent for war, and it has been improved by the constant reflection of years, and much experience. There is no species of business which Harry Smith's mental tact will not enable him to grasp."—Marshman's *Memoirs of Sir H. Havelock* (1867), pp. 66, 165.

order the troops to fire. I said, " You command,"
which in those days they did, nor could the officer
fire, according to law, without their order.

The Commander-in-Chief in Scotland, Major-
General Sir T. Bradford, was then in Glasgow, and
also Sir W. Rae, the Lord-Advocate. Officers who
had been on duty were to report direct to the
Commander-in-Chief. This I did, and hardly was
my report received, when I was sent for to the
Inn where these authorities were. Sir Thomas,
ever a kind friend to me, met me at the door of
the room where they were, and said, " Smith, the
Lord-Advocate is most annoyed that you permitted
His Majesty's troops to be insulted this morning
with impunity, and desires to speak with you."
Sir W. Rae, although afterwards I found him a
capital fellow, was dictatorial in his manner, and
violent and pompous in his address. He sat when
I advanced towards him. I saw by his eye what
was coming, and my blood was as hot as his; and
the thought rushed into my mind, " What! to be
rowed by this man, who have ever been approved
of by *the Duke !*"

" Pray, sir, are you the officer who allowed His
Majesty's troops to be insulted in such a manner,
with arms in their hands? *I am surprised, sir.*
Why did you thus tamely act ?" So I replied,
quite as dictatorially as my lord, " Because, my
lord, I was acting under the officers of the law,
the magistrates, of whom you are the Commander-
in-Chief. They would not act, and I did not desire

to bring upon my head either the blood of my
foolish and misguided countrymen, or the odium
of the Manchester magistrates." (An affair of
Yeomanry * had lately occurred.) " I brought off
every prisoner ; but, my lord, since that is your
feeling, give me a written order to march through
Glasgow with the same party of soldiers and my
prisoners. A mob will soon attempt the rescue,
and d—— me, my lord, but I will shoot all
Glasgow to please you." I saw Sir Thomas Bradford biting his lips, and looking at me as much as
to say, " Gently, Smith." I turned on my heel,
and said, " Good morning, my lord."

From that day the Lord-Advocate took a great
fancy to me, and gave me some of the most laborious
night-marches I ever made, especially one to Galston
New Mills and Kilmarnock. It was so dark (and
an *ignis fatuus* dancing before us to make it
worse), I had a 6-pounder upset over a bridge.
Throughout my previous services I never had
more arduous duties than on this occasion.

A Battalion of Volunteer Riflemen were organized
here,† all young gentlemen, under the superin-

---

* " Peterloo," 16 August, 1819. It is amusing to contrast the
soldierly reference to an " affair of Yeomanry," with Shelley's *Masque
of Anarchy*, called forth by the same occurrence.

† " In 1819 and onwards for a few years, when the country was
supposed to be in danger from a rising of the " Radicals," and there was
certainly a good deal of disaffection, Glasgow was the centre of the agitation. In these circumstances it was resolved to re-embody the " Glasgow
Volunteer Sharpshooters," a Corps which in 1808 had made way for
the " Local Militia." This was accordingly done, the senior surviving
officer of the old corps, the well known Samuel Hunter, of the " Glasgow
Herald," being appointed Lieut.-Colonel Commandant, and Robert

tendence of my old Regiment, now called the Rifle Brigade.* This corps more nearly deserved the comprehensive appellation "soldiers" than any corps ever did, except those of the line. Their Colonel, Sam Hunter, walked twenty-two stone, an enormous man, with a capacity of mind fully proportioned to his corporeal stature. Many are the arduous duties I exacted of these Volunteers, and they were executed with cheerfulness and prompt obedience.

Sir Hussey Vivian came down to command, bringing with him as his Major-of-Brigade, my friend, (now Sir) De Lacy Evans. Evans did not wish to serve, but to study in London to prepare himself to be a senator, and he kindly went to the Horse Guards and said, " If my appointment is filled up by Harry Smith of the Rifles, I will resign." This arrangement was readily assented to, and I was again on the Staff, where I remained until 1825.

I had occasionally the most disagreeable duty, and always a difficulty to resist the importunity of the kindest hospitality that ever I and my wife received in this world. Immediately after I was

---

Douglas Alston, the Major. Colonel Hunter retired in 1822, and Major Alston became Colonel.

Colonel Alston was a capital officer, and the regiment, in appearance, discipline and drill, a very fine one. Some of the older citizens of Glasgow must still remember the grand reviews on the green, in which the Sharpshooters and Regulars took part under the command of Colonel Smith, afterwards Sir H. Smith, the hero of Aliwal."—*The Old Country Houses of the Old Glasgow Gentry*, 2nd edit., p. 6.

* " By an order dated ' Horse Guards, Feb. 16, 1816,' the 95th was removed from the regiments of the line, and styled *The Rifle Brigade.*"—Cope, p. 214.

appointed Major-of-Brigade, Major-General (now Sir T.) Reynell was appointed to command the district of Glasgow and the West of Scotland in place of Sir Hussey Vivian. In a year, as affairs in Glasgow assumed a more tranquil appearance, Queen Caroline's trial being finished and Her Majesty's death having occurred, Major-General Reynell was removed from the Staff of Glasgow, and went out in the *Glasgow* frigate to the East Indies to a command in Bengal, but I, the Major-of-Brigade, was kept on. My orders were to report direct to the Commander-in-Chief, Sir T. Bradford, in Edinburgh, and to receive no orders from any one but himself; and I could give any orders in his name which the exigencies of the moment required. Of course I was very cautious, fully aware of the delicacy of my position as regarded my senior officers, some of whom were very jealous of the authority vested in me, although personally I had never had a controversial word with them.

A great part of my duty in the summer was to inspect the various Corps of Yeomanry throughout the Western District, a most delightful duty. I was treated *en prince* by the Duke of Montrose, Lord Glasgow, Lord Douglas, Lord-Lieutenants of counties, Lord Blantyre, etc. The officers of the Corps of Yeomanry, too, all belonged to the aristocracy of the country, and their houses were open as their hospitable hearts.

In 1820 I had with me Sir John Hope's and Lord Elcho's Troops of the Edinburgh Light Horse,

consisting entirely of gentlemen of the highest class
in Scotland, and we were employed upon some
very arduous duty together. I have seen these
gentlemen after a long, heavy, and wet night's march,
every one dressing his own horse, feeding him, etc.,
like a German Hussar, ere they thought of anything
for themselves. One of the Troop, Corporal Menzies,
is now a Judge at the Cape, my most intimate
friend, and many is the laugh we have had at his
military experiences.

When we see the gentlemen of the country thus
devoted to it, we need have little fear of its continued prosperity. In my opinion there is no system
which can be adopted of such importance to our
country as the yearly calling-out of the Yeomanry
for a few days' exercise. It brings the educated
aristocracy in contact with the less favoured in life,
the cultivators of the soil,—landlords with tenants.
It shows the latter in their true character—honest,
manly, and liberal fellows, and teaches them to look
up to their superiors, while it also shows the former
what a noble set of men their tenants are, obedient,
but as proud as an English yeoman ought to be,
and that, thus engaged in the defence of our country
and in the maintenance of our rights as British
subjects, they are to be treated with the respect
due to every individual of the social compact.

When His Majesty George IV. paid a visit to
Edinburgh [15–27 Aug. 1822], I was ordered thither,
and sent to Dalkeith (where His Majesty was to
reside in the palace of the Duke of Buccleugh) to

superintend the guards and escorts, etc., for his Majesty's state (his *protection* was in the safe custody of the hearts of his loyal people); and when Sir Walter Scott and the Commander-in-Chief, Sir Thomas Bradford, had planned all the various processions, the organization and conduct of them was given to me, and His Majesty was kind enough to say they were conducted to his royal satisfaction. He never once was delayed in the streets by a check, thanks to the lesson I learnt in the Light Division how to regulate the march of a column.

Early every day I went, as I was ordered, to the palace to receive orders through the Gold Stick. The morning His Majesty was to leave Dalkeith, he sent for me to express his approbation of all I had done, and as I left the apartment Sir William Knighton followed me, and asked me, by the king's command, if there was anything I desired. I was so young a Lieutenant-Colonel, only of eight years' standing, with hundreds senior to me, that I neither desired to ask such an exorbitant thing as to be Aide-de-Camp to His Majesty, nor felt any inclination, on account of such pacific services, to be exalted above so many of my more meritorious comrades. Knighthood I would not accept, so I very quietly said, " I will ask a great favour of His Majesty—to give Sir Thomas Bradford's Aide-de-Camp the rank of Lieutenant-Colonel." Sir William said, " If the Commander-in-Chief will write me a note, it shall be done," and thus as good a fellow as ever lived got his rank. There is much honour attached to the charge of royalty, and as many of my old comrades were about the king, Barnard, Vivian, etc., I spent a most agreeable time, but the expense for myself and my wife was enormous. It cost me upwards of a year's income in new uniforms, court dresses, etc. His Majesty particularly admired my wife's riding.

Never was the old adage of " like master, like man" more exemplified than in the royal household. In the organization of the processions, etc. I was frequently engaged with the servants, coachmen, footmen, etc. I never saw such obedient, willing, and respectful fellows in my life ; and I never had to express more than a wish, to have any order implicitly, readily, and agreeably obeyed. Accustomed to the obedience of soldiers, I was particularly struck with equally obedient deportment on the part of those whom imagination had led me to believe to be a set of troublesome fellows. George IV. was a gentleman, and from His Noble Majesty was derived a "*ton*" which spread throughout his court and his household, an example and honour to the great nation he ruled.

In 1824 my gallant friend, Macdougall, requested me to accompany him to Paris to arrange a little matter of delicacy with a gentleman who had ill-used a lady, a great friend of Mac's family. We soon arranged that matter, the gentleman being one in fact, as well as in name, and acting as well as any could under the circumstances. Ten years had now elapsed since my first acquaintance with the

south of France, and six since I had quitted
Cambray. We landed at Boulogne, and had a long
journey to Paris by *diligence*, that renowned and
cumbrous and slow machine now replaced by the flying steam-coaches. Our *diligence* adventures were
numerous but not unusual. But my new visit to
France, and entry into Paris, forcibly brought
to mind the immense Armies assembled around
us in 1815,—the streets filled with uniforms of
every civilized nation, the public resorts ornamented
with the spoil of every nation in Europe except
Great Britain !

Paris was now a quiet city, much like any other,
and the only thing which attracted my attention
was the number of drunken soldiers in the streets.
In London such a thing is of rare occurrence indeed.
But it appeared to me that the French Army had
acquired some of those habits of the English which
we would willingly resign to them in perpetuity.
I visited my old quarters at Neuilly. My good old
landlady was no more. Imagination aroused a
variety of feelings closely cemented with the past,
while the present showed Paris aiming at English
habits, just as London was rapidly acquiring French
manners. In the streets of Paris we saw young
dandies driving tilburys in the last style, with
grooms in brown top-boots. To speak English
was becoming fashionable, whereas formerly any
Frenchman attempting to speak English was regarded as a Bourbonist, or an enemy to the blood-
acquired liberties of his country. We left France

now certainly flourishing, and speedily returned to our own land of fair and handsome faces, well-fed inhabitants, richly cultivated and enclosed fields. And oh, my countrymen, had you seen as many countries as I now have, and been banished so many years from your own, then would you bless that land of happiness and liberty which gave you birth, that land which was exempt from the horror of war through the ability of your statesmen, the blood of your sailors and soldiers, and the patriotism of the people!

During my residence in Glasgow, I twice went over to the Isle of Man, in expectation of succeeding to the Government of the House of Keys. The Governor was very ill, and desirous to retire. He got well, and forgot his former inclinations.

In 1825, such was the tranquillity in this immense manufacturing district, I was put off the Staff, and received from the Lord-Provost, Town Councillors, and Municipality every demonstration of their gratitude for the efficient aid I had afforded them to maintain tranquillity and subdue riots, mobs, and popular ebullitions.* My answer was, that the only merit I claimed was that in the service of my country and in the execution of this duty on very trying and most irritating occasions for five years, not a drop of my deluded countrymen's blood had been shed, though it was often indeed difficult in the extreme to avoid it.

The parting of myself and wife from our

* He was now admitted to the Freedom of the City of Glasgow.

numerous and most hospitable and kind friends in
Glasgow, and the whole of the West of Scotland, is
not to be described. My principal quarters I may
say were Elderslie House,* where the most amiable
and numerous family were ever to us a source of
happiness, Harhead, Lord Glasgow's, and Cumbernauld House, Admiral Fleming's, whose wife was
a county-woman of mine; but to name these houses
in particular is hardly fair, for throughout the country
we received equal hospitality. Certainly the happiest
five years of my life were spent in Scotland, amidst
the society of such people. Books were to be had
of every description, intellectual conversation was
ever enjoyed, and amidst the learned professors
of the colleges I have spent some of the most
agreeable evenings.

I was to join my Corps in Belfast, and as we
went down the Clyde in the steamer, the inmates
of every seat on its banks were assembled to wave
us, alas! a *last* farewell, for many of those dear and
valued friends are now in the silent grave. Glasgow,
with all your smoke, your riots, mobs, and dis-
affections, I look back to you with perfect happiness,
and I love the Scotch nation with a similar degree
of patriotism to that with which I have fought for
my native land, the words of my dear mother ever
ringing in my ears, " Remember, if ever you fight
for your country, you were born an Englishman."

Belfast, although then a flourishing city, showed

* Then the seat of Archibald Speirs, Esq. His family consisted
of five sons and nine daughters.—*The Old Country Houses of the
Old Glasgow Gentry*, 2nd edit. pp. 95, 96.

a great contrast to Glasgow in regard to the appearance of its population, although the gentlemen were as hospitable as possible, and most enthusiastic sportsmen, and, as I could ride a bit, I was soon at home among them. I was soon, however, ordered to Downpatrick, where my Company and two others were quartered. I was received by my dear old Regiment with every demonstration of affection, and spent a few months most happily at this little town of Downpatrick, among very amiable and kind people. The peasantry there were my delight, such light-hearted, kind creatures I never saw, and as liberal as primitive Christians. Not a day I had not sent me presents of eggs and butter, etc. It was painful occasionally to accept them, but as I saw that refusal created pain, I had no alternative. There were many of our old Light Division soldiers discharged and living in this neighbourhood, and every market day (Saturday) a re-enacting of old times was imposed on my patience. One, a noble soldier of the 43rd, celebrated every anniversary of a battle by getting gloriously drunk. On one occasion he was drunk without this exciting cause. I said, "Come, come, Murphy, this is too bad; to-day is no anniversary." "Maybe not, your honour, but, by Jasus, there are so many it is hard to remember them all, and the life's blood of me would dry up, if I missed the 'cilibration' of one of 'em—so it's safest to get drunk when you can."

CHAPTER XXX.

1825–1828 : HARRY SMITH ACCOMPANIES HIS REGIMENT
TO NOVA SCOTIA—SIR JAMES KEMPT—HARRY
SMITH PARTS WITH HIS OLD REGIMENT ON BEING
APPOINTED DEPUTY QUARTERMASTER-GENERAL IN
JAMAICA—HE HAS TO DEAL WITH AN EPIDEMIC
OF YELLOW FEVER AMONG THE TROOPS—AP-
POINTED DEPUTY QUARTERMASTER-GENERAL AT
THE CAPE OF GOOD HOPE.

SHORTLY after this, my Corps was ordered to embark at Belfast [30 July] for Nova Scotia on board
three transports, the *Arab*, the [*Speke**], and the
Joseph Green. I had the command of two Companies and a half in the last ship. When we arrived
on board, with the quantity of baggage, etc., the
ship was in a wild-looking state. The Captain and
the agent came to me and said, "We are ordered
to go to sea to-morrow, but this is impossible from
the state of the ship ; it is of no consequence, if you
would give us a certificate to this effect ; the day
after to-morrow will do quite as well." "The devil
it will," says I, "when you are ordered. Have
you everything belonging to the ship's stores on

* I supply this name from Cope, p. 226.

board?" "Everything." Johnny Kincaid was my subaltern, so I said, "Johnny, at daybreak in the morning turn out all hands, and prepare a certificate for my signature at eight o'clock if required." Eight o'clock arrived, and no man-of-war's decks were ever more ready for action—our baggage all stored below, our soldiers' arms and everything else arranged, and I told the Captain, "Now, you see, I need sign no certificate. We Riflemen obey orders and do not start difficulties." We were under way in no time. This Captain Lumsden was an excellent fellow; some years after he took Sir James Stirling out as Governor to Swan River and touched at the Cape, when I had an opportunity of returning some of his many acts of kindness.

Our voyage was much like other voyages across the Atlantic, but an odd circumstance occurred. Although each ship sailed from Belfast separately, and at an interval of two days, mine the last, we were all three sailing into Halifax Harbour the same day [1 Sept. ?], in the very order in which we left Belfast, and anchored within a few hours of each other. Our dear old friend, Sir James Kempt, the Governor there, was delighted with this odd re-union, and laughed and said, "I see my old comrades, whether separated by sea or land, get together in the old way, however distantly extended." In Halifax we were soon found by our other dear old friends, the 52nd Regiment. They had more old soldiers in their ranks than we had, having embarked for America two or three years before us; and oh, the greeting with us all, and the happiness of the old soldiers at meeting my wife again! They were inquiring after her horse Tiny, her dog, etc., and expecting all were alive as when we had parted at Bordeaux in 1814.

If ever happiness existed in this world, we may claim it for Halifax when the Government was administered by Sir James Kempt. Society, by the force of his example, was the most agreeable thing imaginable. Government House was princely in its style; we had private theatricals, races, sham-fights, regattas, and among all our varied amusements (to which were added in the winter four-in-hand and tandem driving-clubs, and picnics at the Half-way House), harmony the most perfect prevailed between civilians and officers, soldiers and sailors. (Our noble fellows of the Navy were commanded by Admiral Lake.)

We had a great re-union of Governors there one year; Lord Dalhousie, Governor-General of North America, Sir James Kempt, Governor of Nova Scotia, General Sir John Keane, Governor of Jamaica, Sir Howard Douglas, Governor of New Brunswick, and Colonel Reid, Governor of Prince Edward's Island—a regular court of magnates—and never were people more happy than all. For some time I had the command of the Regiment, Colonel Norcott that of the Garrison. I afterwards accepted an unattached half-pay majority, expecting to be brought in again, and I was appointed A.D.C. to my dear and valued friend, Sir James Kempt. I thus learned much of the administration of a Government, which was afterwards of the greatest possible use to me when administering a Government myself. I had often witnessed Sir J. Kempt's ability as a soldier ; but I cannot avoid saying he perfectly astonished me and all who knew him as a statesman and a ruler. Evincing such temper, such a clearness of judgment, such discretion and most uncompromising justice, he soon carried with him the Colony. The House of Assembly, and even the Whig opposition, admired his talent and never opposed any of his great acts, while, by his amiable manners and kind, though unostentatious, hospitality, society was cemented, and indeed, what the word implies, *social.*

The day I was gazetted out, my old Company came in a body to ask me to allow them to give me a dinner, " that is, we don't expect your honour to sit down with us, but we will have a dinner, and you will drink with us a parting glass." I readily consented, and sat down with them, too, for a few minutes. Old Johnny Kincaid, who succeeded me as Captain, and my subalterns, were present, and the parting glass was drunk with that mutual feeling of strong affection which exists between officers and soldiers. I was a most rigid disciplinarian, but good conduct was as much distinguished by me as bad was visited, and I carried all with me.

I was not long permitted to enjoy this comparative repose, but was appointed [23 Nov.]

Deputy Quartermaster-General in Jamaica. I speedily prepared to join, taking a passage on board a little brig for ourselves and our horses. I had a farewell dinner given me by the Governor and by the Admiral, and many of the kind inhabitants, and by every Regimental Mess, while the Regimental Order issued by Colonel Norcott speaks for itself.*

I had served twenty-five [twenty-one ?] years in this Corps during the most eventful periods. It had never been on service but I was fighting with some portion of it. No officer had ever posted it so often on outlying picquet, and I had fought where

---

* " Colonel Norcott feels himself bound by every principle of public and private duty to express to Lieutenant-Colonel Smith and the officers and battalion at large his most sincere and deep regret for the loss of an officer who has served for twenty-two years with such indefatigable zeal, distinguished bravery, and merit, and now retires from its active duties on promotion and an appointment on the staff in Jamaica, but to resume in that situation the same persevering devotion to his profession, his king, and country.

" The Colonel knows how truly every officer in the Brigade participates his feelings and sentiments, and is assured of the lively and warm wishes of every non-commissioned officer and soldier for the welfare of one who, with every attribute of as good and as gallant an officer as ever lived, invariably united the most kind and peculiar interest for the comfort and happiness of the soldier.

" At the particular request of this officer, it affords the Colonel much pleasure to release from confinement to barracks, and punishments of every description, all soldiers now under their sentences ; he only hopes, and is ready to believe, that they will prove sensible and grateful for Colonel Smith's kindness, shown up to the very last moment he remains amongst them, in addition to every noble and honourable feeling which all soldiers ought to show in the performance of their duty and conduct on every occasion, by a determination to relinquish every habit tending to injure the good of the service, their corps, and individual respectability, comfort, happiness, and future welfare.

" A. NORCOTT, *Colonel*.

" Halifax, Nova Scotia, June 4, [? Jan.] 1827."

it had not been; thus were severed no ordinary or transient ties.

The day we were to leave we can never forget. Sir James Kempt sent for me to his private room. I saw his warm heart was full. He said, "Harry, I am going to exact a promise of you. The climate you are going to is one where life and death so rapidly change places, it would be folly to rush into unnecessary danger, by exposing yourself to the effects of the sun or leading that life of violent exercise you have ever done. My desire, therefore, is your promise never to go out snipe-shooting or to ride any more races, in a tropical climate at least." Of course I promised. He then said, holding a letter in his hand, "Here are some notes for your guidance in Jamaica, and as you have paid three times more for your passage [than the allowance?], there is a note enclosed which makes up the difference." The tears rolled down his gallant cheeks, and I left the room in the deepest affliction.

On descending to the ball-room I found every gentleman of Halifax and every officer of the garrison awaiting to accompany us on board. Sir James, taking my wife under his arm, led the procession.

As I was with Sir James, three non-commissioned officers, one Rifles, one 52nd, and one 74th, came up and begged to speak to me. They said, "Your Honour, the whole garrison are turned out and in column in the street. There's the head of it to carry your Honour on board." By Jupiter, there they were, sure enough, in a column of sixes, one file Rifles, one 52nd, one 74th. They had a chair in which they seated me, and carried me after the procession of officers on board. These compliments *at the time* are impressive, but when we look back remind us of the pain of parting, and that many who were then most loud in their shouts of parting acclamation are long ago mingled with the mortal dust we shall all add to. The little brig was weighed immediately. All officers who had sailing boats accompanied us to the mouth of the harbour, and thus we parted from faithful friends, veteran comrades, and three of the most renowned Regiments of the Duke's old Army, and in a few hours found ourselves alone on the wide Atlantic, with a crew of one captain and seven sailors, and one quadrant the only nautical instrument on board. But as we were all in all to each other, so were we still in possession of the world. This quadrant the captain would leave about the deck in a careless manner when taking his observations. I almost worshipped it, and therefore watched over it accordingly. We had a very favourable passage, and dined every day on deck but one (for our cabin was not that of the *Royal Oak*), and ourselves and horses reached Jamaica in twenty-eight days all right. Soon after we landed, the crew, all but one man, an old German carpenter, died of yellow fever, and in the harbour commenced one of those awful visitations to the island which sweep off hundreds.

We landed at Kingston, where Sir J. Keane's

house was prepared for us. The Governor was at Spanish Town, but came in with his generous warmth of heart next day to entertain us. Our worthy friend, Admiral Fleming, of Cumbernauld House,* was in naval command. Mrs. Fleming was with him, so that, although in a new world, we were among faithful old friends.

As Quartermaster-General, my first attention was directed to the barrack accommodation, furniture, utensils, etc. The barracks at Upper Park was a Royal Establishment in every respect; the buildings were most beautifully provided, capacious, and built on arches with a current of air passing beneath; they had a bath-room, etc. The barracks in every other quarter of the island were Colonial Establishments, the buildings at many execrable, and the barrack furniture, bedding, etc., horrible. The soldier's bed was a blanket, though the very touch of a blanket in a tropical climate is disagreeable; and this, laid on the floor, was his all : a wooden floor certainly, but full of bugs, fleas, etc., to an incredible extent. So soon as I laid my report before Sir John Keane, he was most desirous to effect an improvement. We turned to and framed a statement to the Horse Guards (the Duke was then Commander-in-Chief), and in a few months every soldier had a bed, sheets, iron bedstead, etc., and every other requisite.

Still the troops did not escape the yellow fever, of which the seeds, as usual in its visitations, had

* See p. 336.

first germinated among the shipping (where the mortality was fearful). The disease spread to our troops—first to the Artillery at Port Royal, then to the 84th at Fort Augustus, next to the 22nd Regiment at Stony Hill (in both cases to an appalling extent), then partially to the 33rd Regiment at Upper Park Camp, the Royal Barracks. In about six weeks we buried 22 officers and 668 soldiers, out of the 22nd and 84th Regiments principally. Sir John (now Lord) Keane was up the country, and I had a *carte blanche* to do what I thought best. I therefore, in conjunction with the Acting Inspector-General of Hospitals, resolved to move the 84th from Fort Augustus to a bivouac at Stony Hill. Tents were sent up and huts were in progress. So soon as they were ready I marched the corps, and from that day the yellow fever ceased; there was only one admission afterwards. The day previously to the march of the poor 84th, I went down to Fort Augustus and paraded the Regiment. Only two subalterns were fit for duty, and although only sixty men were in hospital, seventeen died that day. The admissions into hospital were not so great in proportion as the mortality, one in four being the average of deaths. The Regiment was in a perfect state of despondency (it consisted like the 22nd Regiment, of young fresh soldiers recently arrived from England) ; but I cheered them up. I wheeled them into line a time or two, formed close column, and told them, whether a soldier died by yellow fever or on the battle-field, it was all in

the service of his country ; that I should move them
to a healthy spot the next day where they would
leave the yellow fever behind, and now three
cheers for his Majesty ! The poor fellows were all
alive again in no time. When we consider that
every officer but two was sick, that already upwards
of two hundred out of six hundred of their comrades had been buried, when death in this passive
shape lay hold of them, it is not to be wondered at
that a young (or any) Regiment should be appalled.

In Jamaica, while this yellow fever was raging,
I have ridden thirty-five miles in the sun and gone
sixteen miles in an open boat in one day, and been
for a long time in the wards of different hospitals,
where sickness and death in every stage was pro-
gressing around me. It is an awful sight to the
afflicted patients in the large wards of a hospital,
reduced by sickness to the excess of debility, to
see the men on either side probably dead or dying,
and there is no remedy and very little power of at
all alleviating such a calamity. Many a man who
would live if in a solitary room, dies from the power
of imagination on the debilitated frame. Then,
again, when a man has lost the fever, the surgeon
is obliged to discharge him, because he requires the
accommodation for recent admissions. He goes to
his Company, his appetite has somewhat recovered,
he eats heartily, a relapse ensues, he goes to
hospital and dies to a certainty. It is rarely indeed
that a case of relapse recovers. To obviate this,
I established convalescent hospitals. I had various

difficulties to contend with, but the success of the
institution was an ample reward for labour, and
established a precedent since equally advantageously
acted on.

Nothing can be more capricious than these
epidemics in tropical climates. On the very day
twelvemonth that I paraded the 84th and seventeen men died, Sir John Keane made his half-yearly
inspection of the corps at the same place, Fort
Augustus. There was not a man in hospital and only
one man out of the ranks ; he paraded in the rear of
his Company, being lame from a fractured leg.

The poor 22nd Regiment at Stony Hill suffered
equally with the 84th ; the Colonel, the Major, the
Paymaster, and five officers died in a few days. The
Adjutant's room, next the Orderly room, possessed
the mortal seeds of the yellow fever. Every one
who sat to write in the room was knocked down and
died in a few days ; in consequence I prohibited
the use of it. Major Stewart, a most excellent
officer, though not obedient in this instance, treated
the prohibition slightingly, wrote there *two* days,
on the fifth he was buried.

In a short time this fearful epidemic disappeared,
and the troops, five regiments in all on the island,
were healthy. Sir John Keane proposed a tour
of inspection throughout the island. He was to
sail in his yacht, landing every night. I, having
a terrestrial turn, drove my wife four-in-hand. The
daughter of the Receiver-General, Miss Stevenson,
accompanied us, the beauty of the island.

A very curious appearance presents itself nearly all round Jamaica. The coast is very bold, and ships to load sugar are navigated through sunken rocks within a few yards of the very shore. At a distance the ships look as if *on* shore, but they ride in perfect safety, the sunken rocks forming the protection of the harbour. To all these spots a road is made from the adjacent sugar estates, called a *barcadero*, from the Spanish *embarcaro*, "to embark."

The hospitality of the superb mansions we stopped at, the fortunate union with Sir John every night—for the sea-breeze blows so regularly he could calculate his arrival as by land—made this one of the most pleasant tours I ever made. Nothing can be more picturesque than the whole island, and its fertility exceeds anything I have ever seen ; while its population (slaves) were more happy, better fed, less worked, and better provided for in sickness than any peasants throughout the many parts of the world in which I have been. Slavery there was merely nominal ; the young were educated to a necessary extent, the able-bodied lightly worked, the sick comforted, the aged provided for. All had little huts, some very comfortable, according to the turn and industry of the occupants. All had a nice garden, and all were well fed.

After our tour we went to live in the Liguanea Mountains, in Admiral Fleming's Pen (as a country residence is there called) ; a most delightful spot, the climate luxurious, though enervating if you descend into the plains, which I did to my office regularly twice a week. In these hills you have constant thunder-showers; hence the gardens produce every European vegetable as good as in Covent Garden, and the fruits are unequalled.

While in this happy retreat, I received a note one evening from my worthy friend, Lord Fitzroy Somerset, to say *the Duke*, having been pleased with my exertions in Jamaica, had appointed me [24 July] to succeed my old friend John Bell (recently made Colonial Secretary) as Deputy-Quartermaster-General at the Cape of Good Hope. I never received any official communication of my appointment, and in forty-eight hours, bag and baggage, I was on board the *Slany* man-of-war, and under way for Nassau to Admiral Fleming, in the hope of some ship being ordered to proceed direct for the Cape, or to some intermediate port from whence I could take a fresh departure for my destination.

I was very fortunate in disposing of my furniture, carriage, buggy, horses, etc., particularly the latter, which I had brought from Halifax. They sold for three times what I had paid for them. They have an excellent breed of thoroughbred horses on the island, excessively dear, but for carriages the American horses are preferred.

Without egotism, our departure from Jamaica was as gratifying to us both as that from Halifax. Nothing could exceed the kindness of a vast number of friends, and I had a letter from every officer commanding a regiment.

CHAPTER XXXI.

AFTER STAYING THREE WEEKS AT NASSAU, HARRY
SMITH AND HIS WIFE SAIL FOR ENGLAND, AND
AFTER A MISERABLE VOYAGE LAND AT LIVERPOOL
—HE VISITS LONDON AND WHITTLESEY, AND
LEAVES ENGLAND (1829), NOT TO RETURN TILL
1847.

WE sailed in that, to appearance, heavenly
climate with a fresh sea-breeze, and as the magnificent Blue Mountains of Jamaica receded, the appearance of an island towering from the sea into
the very heavens became as it were a speck on the
mighty ocean. On our way to Nassau we passed
New Providence—the first land discovered by
Columbus, the joyful realization of his anticipations
and the fruit of his wonderful perseverance. The
transparency of the water in all the harbours of these
islands is very singular. At the depth of many
fathoms you see your anchor, cable, fish, etc., at the
bottom as distinctly as if no water intervened. A
sixpence may be discovered at a depth of twenty
fathoms.

On arrival at Nassau we found Admiral Fleming
away on a cruise. It was supposed he had gone to

Halifax. So, there being no chance of a man-of-war, we had to await the arrival of a brig called the *Euphemia*, which was daily expected, and which would sail again for Liverpool so soon as her cargo was landed and a fresh one shipped.

General Sir Lewis Grant was the Governor, and for three weeks he and his staff put Government House at our command in every way, and did all in their power to render our visit delightful, and to provide my wife with every little amusement the island afforded. The island of Nassau is a coral formation, but many parts of it are exceedingly fertile. The wells, which produce most excellent fresh water, rise and fall with the tide.

On the arrival of the *Euphemia* our passage was soon arranged, but I could have only half the stern (and only) cabin partitioned off with canvas during the night (the other half being already engaged for two officers of the West Indian Regiments), and a small mate's cabin for my wife's maid. The prospect before my poor wife was miserable enough, and we were afraid that in a three weeks' voyage we should not always have a fair wind, but her buoyant spirits laughed at the ideal distress.

We soon left the hospitable Governor and the happy island of Nassau. Luckily, I put on board ship goats and dry stock of every description, although the captain (a well-spoken, smart-looking young Scotchman, married to a Liverpool woman, on board with him) engaged to find us capitally. Our misery soon began. The ship sailed like a

witch, but we were constantly in a terrific storm,
with the little cabin battened down, no means of
cooking, and but little to cook if we had the means,
and we should have been literally starved but for
the things I fortunately shipped. We were upwards
of thirty days at sea. Our captain assured me he
had a timekeeper on board, and so he had, but he
knew no more how to use it than I did. We had
to lay to for forty-eight hours, during which we
shipped a sea which swept the boats, caboose, bin-
nacles, etc., clean off the deck. It was December,
and as we approached Liverpool the weather was
excessively cold, the sailors were frost-bitten in the
hands, and the captain had not a glass of grog on
board for them. I was, luckily, able to broach for
them a small cask of peculiarly good rum of great
antiquity, which I was taking as a present to an old
Glasgow friend. In the midst of all these miseries,
we fortunately fell in with a little Irish smack,
which put us into the Bristol Channel, for my
skipper knew no more where he was than the ship
did, the weather having been very cloudy, no
observations taken, and he and his mate execrable
navigators. We made the Tuskar Light most
accidentally, and then the previously cast-down
fellow was all elevation. We got hold soon after
of a Liverpool pilot. This was no small relief to
me, who, although I said nothing, saw what an
ignorant brute we were in the care of. He had
neither candles nor oil, and the very binnacle light
was supplied from my wax candles. He said he

was never before more than three weeks on the voyage, and his store (a pretty misnomer) was laid in only for that period. For the last two days the sailors had no biscuit, and three days more would have exhausted meat, flour, and water. The fellow was a capital seaman on deck, and managed the beautifully-sailing brig most skilfully, and whenever he did get a start of wind, as he termed it, he carried on like a man.

We reached our anchorage in the Mersey long after dark, so beautifully lighted is the approach, and lay at anchor all night in a strong north-east wind, cold enough to cut off our tropical noses. We left our dirty, miserable, exhausted, and stinking brig, and landed as soon as we could the next morning, about five o'clock, in a state of the most abject filth and misery.

We went to the Adelphi Hotel, where in a moment we were surrounded by every luxury and attendance our wealthy country so sumptuously affords. The sudden transition from a state of dire misery into such Elysian Fields is not to be described by me, or forgotten by myself and wife. It was like a miracle. No complaint ever escaped her while on board, but after baths and every imaginable want had been supplied in one of the best of English inns, she then exclaimed, " I hope we may never again experience such a month of wretchedness, misery, and tempest ; and if we must, that we may bear it equally well (for it was a heavy task), be equally protected by Divine Providence, and as happily situated after it as at this moment."

The next day I made every inquiry about ships, and found a very fine brig, the *Ontario*, bound for Calcutta without a passenger. She was to sail in a fortnight. The captain offered to take me, provided the underwriters would allow him to go into Table Bay without an additional premium; and this they assented to, the season of the year being favourable.

My wife stayed at Liverpool, and I started for London, to make a few arrangements for our voyage and to thank Lord Fitzroy Somerset and the Duke. While I was with Lord Fitzroy Somerset, who was delighted to see me, he said, "Hardinge, the Secretary at War, wants to see you." I offered to go, but he said, "No, he will come, he told me, if I would let him know when you are here." That able soldier and Secretary at War and statesman (now Governor-General of India) was soon with us, and made as useful and practical inquiries about barracks, etc., in Jamaica as if he had been there. I then parted with these two of the Duke's staff with a full heart, and went to Downing Street.

The Duke was just appointed First Lord of the Treasury. I found my old friend and brother staff-officer with Sir John Lambert, Greville * (as good a

* Algernon Frederick Greville (1798–1864), younger brother of the author of the *Greville Memoirs* (see p. 216), after being present as an ensign at Quatre Bras and Waterloo, served as aide-de-camp during the occupation of France, first to Sir John Lambert and afterwards to the Duke of Wellington. When the Duke became Commander-in-Chief, January, 1827, Greville became his private secretary, and continued so during the Duke's premiership.

fellow as ever breathed), the Duke's private secretary. Greville was delighted to see me, and expected his Grace every moment. He said the Duke as Prime Minister was as light-hearted and as lively as when comparatively idle at Cambray, that no great question seemed to stagger him, and the facility with which all business progressed under his conduct was truly wonderful. Greville added, " I will give you an anecdote. The Duke is very fond of walking from Apsley House to Downing Street, and we go through the Park, from which a small door opens into the Prime Minister's office. We arrive regularly at ten, and the porter is ready to open and close the door. One day we were rather late, and the porter looked like a weary sentry and was moving very slow. The Duke observed this, and in his usual emphatic manner said, 'Greville, look at that careless fellow; I will turn his flank, by G——.' The Duke watched his opportunity, slipped in unperceived, and says to the porter, 'Hallo, you sir, a pretty *look-out* this!' and laughed, and enjoyed the feat, as much as he did when he played the same flank-turning game in war." This little anecdote depicts the character of the man of mind, free, unshackled from thought until the question is brought before him, and then his powerful mind is absorbed in it, and in it solely.

I waited until three, when I was obliged to go, as I was to dine with Sir John Lambert, and leave town for my father's in Cambridgeshire by seven o'clock. I was a few hours with my dear sister,

Mrs. Sargant, and then dined in my travelling costume. Dear, warm-hearted Sir John Lambert had all his family to bid me farewell. O what a happy and united family of brothers and sisters! and his own children were perfectly beautiful.

At daylight the next day I was in my native place, Whittlesea. O home, our happy home! how altered! I stayed in the house of my third Waterloo brother, now settled as Captain of the Troop of Cavalry, magistrate, etc.; but I could not remain more than forty-eight hours, when I was again on my road back to London. Here I stayed a few hours with my sister, and then off to Liverpool to join my lonely wife, a total stranger and a foreigner in a great, commercial city!

My baggage, by the kind and civil attention of the Custom-house officers, was transferred from one brig to the other without the usual and laborious ordeal of landing. My new things arrived from London, and in a few days we were summoned to embark. It was daybreak, and the brig was floating in dock ready for the gates to be opened. We were soon on board; I had taken a little shore-boat to row me the few yards across. After paying my outfit, my bill at the inn, passage, insurance of baggage, etc., the last remains of my money was half a crown. "There," says I, "my friend!" "Lord, sir, my fare is only threepence." "Keep it," says I, "and drink the health of a man banished from his native land." The fellow stared at me at first as if looking at a convict. At last, in that manner so peculiarly English, he made up his mind, "He must be a gentleman." "I'll drink to your Honour's health, depend on it, and success attend you wherever you go." My friend and his boat were the farewell to my native land. It was then January, 1829 ; this is 1844, and I have never been home since.

APPENDIX I.

" E'er since reflection beam'd her light upon me
You, sir, have been my study ; I have plac'd
Before mine eyes, in every light of life,
The father and the king.   What weight of duty
Lay on a son from such a parent sprung,
What virtuous toil to shine with his renown,
Has been my thought by day, my dream by night :
But first and ever nearest to my heart
Was this prime duty, so to frame my conduct
Tow'rd such a father, as, were I a father,
My soul would wish to meet with from a son.
And may reproach transmit my name abhorr'd
To latest time, if ever thought was mine
Unjust to filial reverence, filial love."

                                        MALLET.

1806. *Nov.* [*Oct.*?] 9*th*.—Sailed from Falmouth under convoy
of His Majesty's ship *Ardent* (Capt. Donnelly), *Unicorn* frigate,
Daphne, 20-guns ship, *Pheasant* and *Charwell*, Sloops-of-war,
with a fleet of about 25 transports, a store-ship for the Cape of
Good Hope, and a merchant ship for the East Indies.   The force
consists of a Company of Artillery, under Capt. Dixon; three
Companies of the 2nd Battalion Rifle Regiment, under Major
T. C. Gardner; 17th Light Dragoons, Col. Loyd; 40th Regiment
of Foot, Col. Browne ; and 87th, Col. Sir Edward Butler ; the
whole under Brigadier-General Sir Samuel Auchmuty.   Brigadier-
General the Hon. William Lumley, Brigadier of the Horse ;
Lieut.-Col. Bradford, Deputy Adjutant-General; Lieut.-Col. Bourke,
Deputy Quartermaster-General; Captain Blake, Assistant Adju-
tant-General ; Lt. Tylden, Brigade-Major to Sir Samuel ; Captain
Roach, Brigade-Major to General Lumley ; Mr. Baddock,

Deputy Paymaster-General; Mr. Bissett, Deputy Commissary of Accompts; Mr. Redman, Deputy Inspector of Hospitals. A fine breeze until the 12th, when we were becalmed in the Bay of Biscay. Lovely weather.

13th.—A breeze sprung up which increased into a gale. Blew dreadfully hard. Sea ran mountains high. Continued until the 16th, when it gradually died away; a heavy sea still running, with the heavy rolling of the ship, sprang the main piece of our rudder. We made a signal of distress, which was instantly answered by the Commodore, who made a signal to the *Charwell* to come along-side us, which she did, and hailed us. She immediately sent a boat on board with her carpenter. Soon after the *Unicorn* came up with us. She also sent a boat on board, with a lieutenant, mid-shipman, and carpenter, with everything requisite to repair our rudder, which was soon done. A steady breeze until the 18th, when it again blew hard. The *Daphne* and a Transport with 150 men of the 40th Regiment parted convoy in the night. Still con-tinued to blow until the 23rd, when we were becalmed. Lovely weather. Captain of the ship took an observation for the first time since at sea. Latitude 47° 35' North.

24th.—Breeze sprung up. Lat. 39° 37'. Breeze freshened. Continued until the 30th. Commodore lost a man overboard. Lovely weather. In the evening observed two large whales close to the ship. They followed us some time and greatly amused us. Lat. 32° 9'.

Nov. 1st.—At daybreak discovered land, to our great delight. It proved to be the Canary Isles. In sight of them the whole of the day. The ground appeared mountainous and barren, with an aspect bleak to a degree. Beautiful weather, with a fine breeze which soon carried us into the Trade winds. The flying-fish begin to be innumerable.

Nov. 4th.—Lat. 23°. A shark passed close under our stern.

Nov. 5th.—Lat. 21° 40'. Fine fresh breeze. The *Harriet* Transport, with the Artillery on board, made a signal of distress, which proved to be from the death of her captain. Flying-fish so numerous, they resemble large flocks of larks. Some of them were by accurate observation seen to fly from 100 to 200 yards and upwards.

Nov. 6th.—Lat. 18° 31'. Fine fresh breeze. In the evening an unfortunate flying-fish flew on board us, being close pursued by an enemy, which measured 8 inches from head to tail, and 9½ from the extreme of each wing. Tail forked like a mackerel. Cooked him for breakfast the next morning. Every one tasted him.

Nov. 7*th.*—Lat. 16° 53'. Thermometer 80 in the shade. Weather very warm. Signal from Commodore for Commanding Officers of Corps. A fine turtle close to the ship. We wished for him on board. To our astonishment, although a considerable distance from land, we were in shoal water the whole of the day, supposed to be a sand-bank, the water by times being quite discoloured. Commodore, not meaning to put into any port, made a signal for the troops and seamen to be put on short allowance of water, two quarts per man, all ranks.

Nov. 8*th.*—Lat. 15° 19'. Therm. 84°. Scorching hot. Speared some fish at the bow of the ship.

Nov. 9*th.*—Lat. 15° 12'. Therm. 82°. Fine weather, but no breeze. Caught two venata with bait. They resemble a mackerel as much as possible, except that they are about twice as large. Cooked them. Coarse, hard and bad eating. A flying-fish flew on board and fell into a tub of water.

Nov. 10*th.*—Lat. 14° 34'; long. 23°. Therm. 83°. *Pheasant*, Sloop-of-war, made sail in search of land, which must be the Cape de Verd Isles. Suppose she made it, as she joined convoy in the evening.

Nov. 11*th.*—Lat. 12° 57'. Therm. 82°. Venata are innumerable. It is very amusing to see them leap out of the water in pursuit of the poor flying-fish.

Nov. 12*th.*—Lat. 10° 49'. Therm. 82°.

Nov. 13*th.*—At 10 a.m. every appearance of a storm. The clouds put on a terrible aspect. Fortunately it was not violent, going off with torrents of rain. Five minutes before 5 p.m. a waterspout was observed to the westward, which emptied itself in torrents over the bow of the *Pheasant* without intermission, until 5 minutes past 5.

Nov. 14*th.*—Dark cloudy weather. No observations.

Nov. 15*th.*—Lat. 7° 53'. Therm. 83°. A boat of the *Charwell's* swamped as they were about to hoist it up. All hands overboard, but saved. Went on board the Commodore with returns to the General.

Nov. 16*th.*—Lat. 6° 38'. Therm. 86°. Sultry close weather, with storms of thunder and lightning. Stark calm, with tremendous showers, the rain coming down in torrents, not drops.

Nov. 17th.—Lat. 6° 17'. Therm. 82°. Weather less sultry, with heavy showers. A large flight of birds resembling ducks ahead, so close together in the water they resemble a floating island. Loaded rifles and fired at them, but to no purpose.

Nov. 18th.—Lat. 6° 1'. Therm. 84°. No breeze. Tremendous thunderstorm, with torrents of rain.

Nov. 19th.—No observation, being cloudy dirty weather. A signal for masters of transports to go on board Commodore. A brig sent home for inattention and not obeying signals. The troops on board her were distributed on board different ships. Wrote letters home in hopes of being able to send them by her, but a breeze springing up prevented our lowering a boat, to my great disappointment.

Nov. 20th.—Lat. 4° 44'. Therm. 82°. Nice breeze but rather ahead. At 6 p.m. the *Pheasant* passed us under all sail. On coming alongside the Commodore she hoisted his ensign, which was immediately returned by him. It is always done when a ship parts convoy. Suppose she is sent forward to Buenos Ayres.

Nov. 21st.—Lat. 3° 45'; long. 26° 38' West. Therm. 82°. Fine breeze.

Nov. 22nd.—Lat. 3° 14'. Therm. 81°. Squally. Wind changing often and suddenly.

Nov. 23rd.—Lat. 2° 30'. Therm. 80°. Weather cool, considering how near we are to the sun.

Nov. 24th.—Lat. 1° 49'. Therm. 82°. Fine breeze but rather ahead. Evening squally. A strange sail to windward. Proved to be an American.

Nov. 25th.—Dark and cloudy. No observation. Plenty of wind.

Nov. 26th.—Lat. 15' South; long. 32° West. One of the sailors caught an immense large albacore with a spear. Took three men to haul him in. He had a curious prickly fin upon his back, which he could completely hide in a crevice so as not to be perceived, and when hurt would set it up. Sea completely covered with flying-fish. A signal made for our ship to take in tow the *Three Sisters*, a small brig, she being to leeward. Ran down to her and obeyed the signal.

Nov. 27th.—Lat. 1° 29'; long. 32°. Speared another large

albacore, which measured 4 feet long and 2 feet 9 inches in circumference.

Nov. 28*th.*—Lat. 3°. Therm. 82°. Signal made by Commodore signifying land in sight, bearing south-south-west, upon which he altered his course one point more to the westward. Supposed to be the island Ferando Noronha.

Nov. 29*th.*—Lat. 4° 12'. Therm. 84°.

Nov. 30*th.*—Lat. 5° 27'; long. 34° 15'. Therm. 81°. Took in tow the *Osborne*, a large ship with Dragoons on board.

Dec. 1st.—Lat. 6° 39'. Therm. 82°. At 6 o'clock a.m. a signal made by Commodore signifying land in sight, supposed to be Cape Augustin.

Dec. 2nd.—Lat. 8° 20'. Therm. 82°. Have observed for these two or three days the flying-fish have almost entirely disappeared.

Dec. 3rd.—Lat. 10° 3'. Therm. 81°. The two merchant ships, the *Lincoln* and *Loyalist*, the former bound to the East Indies, the latter store-ship for the Cape of Good Hope, parted convoy. On altering their course every ship hoisted her ensign, which was returned by them by way of farewell. Had a pretty effect.

Dec. 4th.—Lat. 12° 42'. Therm. 81°. Lovely breeze. A signal for masters of transports to caulk and prepare their boats for landing.

Dec. 5th.—Lat. 15° 24'. Therm. 80°. A schooner in sight to the westward bearing down for us. Overhauled by the *Charwell*, and proved to be a Portuguese bound for San Salvador.

Dec. 6th.—Fresh breeze. No observation.

Dec. 7th.—Lat. 19° 26'. Therm. 82°. Observed a shark which followed the ship a long time, accompanied with three pilot fish. Threw a bait to him, upon which one of his pilot fish swam to it and tasted, and reported accordingly to its master. Observed the breeze to die away by day and blow by night.

Dec. 8th.—Lat. 20° 8'. Therm. 86°. Dreadfully hot.

Dec. 9th.—Lat. 20° 48'; long. 39° 34'.

Dec. 10th.—Lat. 22° 5'; long. 40° 29'.—A signal from Commodore signifying land in sight, supposed at first to be Rio Janeiro, afterwards proved to be Cape Trio, about 40 miles distant from it. Therm. 85°. A tremendous thunderstorm, louder than anything I ever heard.

"Loud thunder from the distant poles ensue,
  Then flashing fires the transient light renew."

Dec. 12*th.*—Beating all day off Cape Trio, endeavouring to get into port. Wind ahead. At 9 p.m. wind came round. Weathered Cape Trio.

Dec. 13*th.*—Made the bay. On the first appearance of the land it put me in mind of the following lines in Thomson's *Hymn on the Seasons :*—

"Should fate command me to the farthest verge
  Of the green earth, to distant barbarous climes,
  Rivers unknown to song ; where first the sun
  Gilds Indian mountains, or his setting beams
  Flame on th' Atlantic Isles, tis nought to me,
  Since God is ever present, ever felt,
  In the void waste as in the city full,
  And where *He* vital spreads, *there* must be joy."

Appearance of the land before the entrance of the harbour, mountainous and woody. At 7 p.m. came to an anchor at the mouth of the harbour. The darkness of the night prevented our going in. The hills surrounding illuminated with the most vivid lightning I ever saw, equally beautiful as awful.

Dec. 14*th.*—At 12 weighed anchor. The entrance of the harbour is very grand. On the left hand is an immense rock called the Sugar-loaf, which it correctly resembles. At the foot of it is a strong battery. On the right hand is a pretty little fort, apparently very strong, having three tiers of heavy guns. At a small distance from the mouth of the harbour is a little island with a fort upon it, which gives the bay a pretty and rather romantic appearance. As soon as the Commodore came to an anchor, he fired a salute of 19 guns, which was immediately returned by the different batteries, the echo of which in the surrounding hills was beyond description grand.

General, Staff, and Commodore went on shore to call upon the Viceroy. When in the boat the *Ardent* fired a salute of 15 guns to them. The General obtained permission for the officers and a proportion of men to go on shore.

Dec. 15*th.*—Went on shore, and was highly delighted with the town of Rio Janeiro. It is very large but irregularly built, situated on a spacious and commodious bay. You land nearly opposite the Viceroy's palace, which stands on the south side of a large and regular square. You see nothing scarcely but poor slaves carrying immense loads, and friars in their cocked hats going to and from the monasteries. Their carriages resemble in some manner our single-horse chaises, but badly made and drawn by two mules. On the near one rides the charioteer, in a huge cocked hat; the off one is in the shafts. They go astonishingly quick. Saw but few horses, those small and bad. The mules are most beautiful animals, and the inhabitants tell you are much more serviceable then the horses. They are as clean about the legs as our race-horses, and full of spirit. Fowls and ducks plentiful, but rather dear. The oxen and sheep are small and bad. Pigs in abundance. Fruits of all sorts. Pines are larger than ours, but not so fine flavoured; you get them for 6*d.* apiece. Oranges, lemons, limes, sweet and sour, bananas, yams, etc., etc. They make no butter or cheese. They get it from England or America. The grandees, when they appear abroad, are carried in a kind of palanquin, which is borne on two negroes' shoulders. Most of these are blue, and adorned with fringes in general of the same colour. They have a velvet pillow, and above the head a kind of tester with curtains. He may either lie down or sit up. (See Guthrie.)

I must think, from what we have seen of the inhabitants, Guthrie speaks too harshly of them. They paid us every attention—nay, so much so that they were troublesome; and were honest in their dealings. The canoes afforded us great amusement. They are rowed by two or three negroes, according to the size of them—not with oars, but a thing resembling a spade. They appear, as they go along, to be digging the water.

I went into one of their monasteries, the chapel of which was very grand. There was also a capital library. The monks were extremely polite, and showed us everything particular. Their service is in Latin. There are four monasteries, and two nunneries filled with poor wretches of girls, who are not allowed to speak to their own fathers. I dined in what they call a cooking-house. The host showed us into a miserable back room looking into the kitchen, where was a black fellow cooking. My stomach was not yet turned. No glass in the window (but that is the case with all the houses, except those of the grandees), and the light shining through the pantiles over our heads. We had for dinner first some macaroni soup, half oil, and scraped cheese to eat with it; afterwards some mutton chops swimming in grease, pork chops in a similar way, a pair of fowls we could scarcely pull to pieces, not an atom of flesh on their bones. There was also a piece of thin beef rolled up with the stuffing in it and roast —a famous dish for a hungry mastiff dog. These being removed, we then had a cold plum-pudding, which was very good. We drank at dinner bad American bottled ale, afterwards some decent port wine. When we called for our bill, we were all amazingly astonished. It came to 4880—*whats*, we could not tell. We afterwards found it was about six dollars. They give you always their bills in that way in some imaginary coin about half a farthing value.

Dec. 16*th.*—Did not go on shore. At 6 p.m. a Portuguese brig came into harbour, laden with poor wretches of slaves just taken from the Guinea coast—the most horrid sight imaginable.

Dec. 17*th.*—Went to see a grand review of the Portuguese troops. They performed pretty well. There was a regular regiment of militia, and a volunteer, with some dragoons and artillery, amounting in all to about 2000 men. After it was over, all the English officers were presented to the Viceroy. Nothing more worth setting down. All of us quite tired of the place, and anxious to get away.

Dec. 23*rd.*—Sailed for Buenos Ayres. Nice breeze.

Dec. 24*th.*—Lat. 24° 47'. Out of sight of land. Therm. 80°.

Dec. 25*th.*—Lat. 25° 32'. Therm. 76.° Blows hard, with a heavy sea.

Dec. 26*th.*—Lat. 26° 51'.—Heavy swell and no breeze. An immense shoal of porpoises swimming towards the north. In hopes of a fair wind, as they always swim against the wind.

Dec. 27*th.*—Lat. 27° 48'. Stark calm. At 4 a.m. a strong breeze sprung up, but quite ahead.

Dec. 28*th.*—Lat. 27° 52'.

Dec. 29*th.*—Lat. 27° 29'; long. 47° 9'. Went on board the Commodore. A large shoal of porpoises by their swimming portending a fair wind, which soon sprung up.

Dec. 30*th.*—Lat. 30° 21'.

Dec. 31*st.*—Lat. 32° 11'. Anxious to get along, but the wind against us.

1807. *Jan.* 1*st.*—Lat. 32° 20'; long. 51° 15.'

Jan. 2*nd.*—Lat. 32° 30'. Wind against us.

[Remainder apparently written afterwards.]

Landed four miles north of Monte Video 16th Jan., had a sharp skirmish with the enemy.

19*th.*—A regular battle. Licked them confoundedly.

20*th.*—A very severe action. The enemy's loss very great.

3*rd Feb.*—Stormed the fortress of Monte Video. A severe conflict. Indeed, our loss, as well as that of the enemy, was very great.

16*th Jan.*, 1807.*—Sharp skirmishing with enemy.

17*th.*—Ditto.

18*th.*—Ditto.

19*th.*—A regular and victorious battle in the open field.

20*th.*—They made a sortie ; were repulsed with great loss.

From the 20th Jan. to 3rd Feb. constant skirmishes. On the morning of the 3rd Feb. stormed the fortress of Monte Video with severe loss on both sides ; but carried it.

7*th April*, 1807 [7 *June* ?].—Colonel Pack made a sortie from Colonia with 1000 men to meet Colonel Elio, whose force consisted of 1500. Entirely routed him, and took six pieces of cannon.

3*rd June* [5 *July* ?].—Attacked Buenos Ayres by assault. Was made prisoner, and confined three days and three nights.

Embarked for England, and arrived at Falmouth 5th Nov.

1808.—Embarked at Harwich for Sweden latter end of May [April ?]. Sailed soon afterwards. Was two months in Gottenburg harbour, when we sailed for England, and refitted at Portsmouth for Portugal. Landed about 30 miles north of Lisbon latter end of July [August ?]. Marched through the south of Portugal into Spain. Had a very hot action with the French between Villa Franca and Calcavellos 3rd Jan., 1809. The loss was nearly equal on both sides. Take it all together, the most severe conflict I ever saw.

Embarked at Corunna in January, and reached England soon after.

Ready to embark again.

* In this and the following items, the story given above is repeated.

APPENDIX II.

Letter I. Endorsed—"*7th May*, 1813. *From Eleanor on Stona's
marriage.—H. G. S.*"

Whittlesea, May 7th, 1813.

My Dear Henry,

From the ardent desire which you have long expressed
concerning Stona's marriage, it will, I am convinced, give you
pleasure to hear that the nuptials are at last solemnized. The
ceremony took place on Tuesday, which was the fourth of May.
Mr. Coleman was father, and of course led the bride to church.
Stona, Kate, Charles, and Anna Maria followed, and my Uncle
Ground's John in a handsome livery, and Stona's own servant
(who is a particular smart-looking young man) dressed in a drab
coat, and a gold band on his hat—all new for the occasion—
attended to receive the bridesmaids' parasols at the church door,
and remained there in waiting during the ceremony. When
concluded, the party returned to breakfast at my Uncle Ground's,
where were assembled to meet them a group of relations consisting
of about two and twenty. Each of us was presented with a white
favour, the ringers and servants also. There were forty favours
given away. The bride and bridegroom, accompanied by Catherine,
set off at twelve for Cambridge, and from thence they proceeded
to London. I assure you they cut a dash. The postboy of
course had a favour on his hat, and James, Stona's man, attended
them on horseback as far as Ramsey. Unfortunately it was a
Newmarket meeting, and Cambridge was so full that they could
not get beds, were therefore obliged to proceed another stage
that evening. About five the next day they arrived in the

Metropolis, and when they had dined, they dressed for Covent
Garden Theatre. Stona repeatedly expressed a great wish that
it was possible to meet you in town. Neither the bride nor brides
maid would, I can venture to say, have had any objection to that.
Never poor fellow I think was in a greater agitation than Stona
during the ceremony and two days before. When he was
being married he trembled in such a manner that Anna Maria
expected no other than he would drop the ring—and he was
himself much afraid lest he should have fainted at the altar. . . .

I must not omit to tell you what a very pretty place Stona's
house is, and so handsomely furnished that I declare it is enough
to make me long to be married. . . .

We are now always changing our Curates; next week Mr. Cook
is going to leave us, and that handsome gentlemanlike man, whom
I mentioned to you in my last, Mr. Powis, is to take his place.
The young ladies, they say, will become very religious, and many
of them attend prayers.

I have, since writing the above, received a letter from you
for which I thank you a thousand times. Believe me, I am not
offended at the remark you made respecting my age, and the
next time I hear from you, I expect the letter addressed to
" Mrs. Eleanor Smith." You will, my dear Henry, be six and
twenty in June.

My Mother, I am happy to say, is better than when I last
wrote, though still rather delicate. My Father goes into quarters
on Sunday. Wisbeach, as usual, is to be head-quarters.

Mrs. W——, I fear, has not added much to her happiness by
marrying W——, for he is excessively idle, an *epicure*, a free *drinker*,
and a *notorious debauchee*. With such a man, can any woman be
truly happy ? . . .

I hope you will lose no opportunity of writing, for, as I have
frequently observed, it is the greatest pleasure I can have in your
absence. Would to God we could have you among us. I never
wished for you more than I do now. My Mother is quite delighted
that you wish to see us.

As you do not say anything about Tom, I conclude he is
well. Pray give my love to him, and tell him that Mary Smith *
is a pretty little black girl, and generally allowed to be more
interesting than ever her sister was.

* Afterwards married to Charles Smith.

All your friends, my dear Henry, join in affectionate remembrance to you and Tom; and sincerely wishing you health and happiness, believe me to remain, dearest Henry, your truly affectionate sister,

ELEANOR.

Addressed—

Brigade-Major Smith,

2nd Light Brigade,

Light Division,

Portugal.

Pd. 3/

Letter II.　　Endorsed—" 19th *August*, 1813.　*The last letter my dear Mother ever wrote to me.　She died on the 12th December, 1813, Sunday.—H. G. Smith."*

Whitt^a, Augst 19, 1813.

MY BELOVED CHILD^N,

What words shall I find sufficiently expressive to congratulate you upon y^r great escape from the great perils and dangers you have been exposed to, where so many of y^r brave countrymen have fallen? But to God alone must the praise be given, who has preserved you both, I hope to be an ornament to y^r country and a blessing to y^r friends, and may God Almighty of his infinite mercy still hold his protecting Arm over you both, and may we never lose sight of him, and have always his goodness in our sight as never to neglect our duty for his great mercies towards us at this time and all others.

This, my dear Harry, is an anxious time, and, tho' we have not a Lett^r from you, by the *Gazette* we know that you are safe.

As for Tom, I think he never intends to write to eith^r of us again, but I am proud to hear of him from you as being so brave a fell^w, and hope to have Lett^{rs} by the next dispatches. We can make every allowance for not hearing from you at this time, as indeed you must be so much ingaged, but pray write whenever you can, and indeed it is one of my greatest comforts.

I have been very ill, so much so that I never expected seeing eith^r of you again, but with the blessing of God I am a very great deal bett^r, and with the kindness of y^r Fath^r and the attention of y^r Sis^{rs} I look forw^d with the hopes of seeing my beloved boys once more under their parental roof. . . .

We have been extremely healthy for a length of time that y Fath^r and Bro^r make great complaints some time for want of something to do.

Poor R^d Binfield is no more. He payd the great debt of nature about three weeks ago, after being a very great sufferer. When he was taken to be buried, his Corpse was preceeded by six Girls dressed in white with white turbans, and baskets of flowers in their hands, wh^h they throwed into the grave as soon as the Corpse was let down. The Pall was supported by six of the scho^{rs} in white Hat-bands, and the whole Sch^l follw^d in the same way. It altogether was a pretty sight, but rath^r too romantic, but you know the woman. . . .

Y^r Sis^r Sargant is not in very good health, and is gone to Cromer. It is upon the Norfolk coast, and is a very fashionable Bathing-place. The rest of the Family, I am happy to say, are well. As for y^r dear Fath^r, I think if you could see him you wou^d think he had grown fat. We all Unite in Love to you and Tom, with best wishes for y^r healths and prosperity. Pray write soon, and may God Almighty preserve you both is the fervent prayer of y^r affec^e Moth^r,

E. SMITH.

Eleanor desires me to say she is much oblidged to you for y^r Lett^r and will write soon, and Betsy also says that unless Tom will write to her she never will write again.

Addressed—
Brigade-Major Smith, Light Brigade,
2nd Light Division, Portugal.

Post paid to Falmouth.

Letter III. Endorsed—"15th Oct. 1813. *From my Father, saying my Mother was pleased with my Letter after a fight in Spain.—H. G. S.*"

Whittlesea, Octr 15th, 1813.

MY DR HARRY,
Your Mother receiv'd your letter the other day and myself one about a fortnight back, both of which gave us great satisfaction, particularly as you were both in good health and safe. We were in hopes as the French were so much beaten by our

brave fellows, and Soult having had so good a specimen of the superior Abilities of Marshal Wellington (superior they are indeed, for he is certainly the first General in the world), that he wou'd have been glad to have got hived, and not have exposed himself again to the second part of the same tune.

I was very sorry to hear of your Horse's accident, as it must be a great loss, but it was an accident and cou'd not have been prevented. My Horse I bought for you to send into Portugal has turned out very unfortunate. He has had a bad Cough on him for near a year, which continued getting worse, and I was fearful of its terminating in Glanders. Had he been quite well he was worth two hundred. However, I was under the necessity of sending Long Will to Bridge Fair, and selling him for what he wou'd fetch, which was fifteen pounds, leaving me a loser of at least £100, for I was at great expence with him.

I was happy to find Cap^n Stewart's horse turn'd out so well, but you clapt your seal over the amount and we cou'd not read it. Send me the amount when you write again. As to news I have none, for Eleanor gives you that in all her letters.

I must say I feel hurt at Thos not writing at all. . . . I am very proud to hear so high a character of him as an adjutant. Major Percival came from Portsmouth with Bob Hotchkin to London, and seeing an offic^r in the coach in 95th uniform, he asked him if he knew Capt. Smith, and he asked him which, Henry or Tom. They had a great deal of conversation, and he said he believ'd Tom to be one of the best adjutants in the service. A poor unfortunate Cripple he was. Bob was with Gen. Murray at that noble business. He came Home extremely ill indeed of Dysentery.

I am sorry to tell you poor Mr. Moore * I think is wearing up fast. He has been severely afflicted with Rheumatism. He is better of Pain, but left so weak and low that he can scarcely ride on horseback. . . .

If any one is coming home that you can trust, I wish you wou'd send me some flower seeds, but I am in great hopes you will bring them yourself.

The Allies seem to be licking the French in Germany well, and I hope will drive them into Peace.

* Vicar of St. Mary and St. Andrew, Whittlesey, and cousin to Harry Smith's mother.

We one and all unite in Love and affection to self and Tom, praying God to protect you both is the prayer of your affect. Father,

JN^O SMITH.

Addressed—

Brigade-Major Smith, 95th Reg^t, Rifle Corps,
Light Division, Light Brigade.
Serving under
Marshal Wellington,
Spain.

Letter IV. Endorsed—"14th *Dec^r*, 1813. *My dear Father's Letter announcing my poor Mother's Death.—H. G. S."*

Whittlesea, Decr 14th, 1813.

We have received, my Dr Harry, your letter dated Sante Pe, Novr 14th, and it was read by myself, your *Dr Mother*, Brothers, and Sisters with infinite pleasure in finding you were both unhurt, and with gratitude to the Almighty for the preservation of you both in this and in every other danger you have so often been expos'd to.

But, my *Dr Boys*, what pain, what affliction is it to me to tell you it is the last letter your poor dear Mother will ever hear or read more from you.

You have been apprised of her ill health by your Sister Elean^r, and we did not wish to distress your feelings by repeatedly telling you the ill state of her health, for we were in hopes she might have got well again. But alas! her D^r soul quited this earthly abode on Sunday morning, Decr 12th, in hopes of a joyful resurrection, which her pious, virtuous, good life entitled her to hope for in her blessed Lord and Redeemer. Oh Harry! she prayed constantly for the return and welfare of you both; she suffer'd much in anxiety; she dearly, very dearly lov'd you and adored you, and in her last prayers never lost sight of her dear Boys abroad. She died in her perfect senses even to the last moment. I hope she did not suffer very much in the separation of soul and body. . . . Your poor distrest father, Brothers and sisters all unite in the strongest love and affection for you both. God Bless you.

JN^O SMITH.

Send a proper direction. Pray write to me on the Receipt of this.

Remember, my Dr Boys, that this letter is equally addrest to you both by your very much afflicted Parent.

Addressed—

> Brig^d-Major Smith,
>> Light Brigade,
>>> Light Division,
>> Commanded by Col. Colborne,
>>> Serving under Marq. Wellington,
>>>> France.

Letter V. Endorsed—"*19th Feb^{ry}, 1814, after my poor mother's death, from my sister Eleanor.—H. G. S.*"

Whittlesea, Feb^{ry} 19th, 1814.

My Dearest Henry,

I received your melancholy and affectionate letter on the seventeenth, and only waited to answer it until we could purchase a pair of Wild Ducks to send with it to Mr. Angelo, who has very politely offered at any time to forward our letters abroad. Heaven has indeed, my dear Brother, thought proper to lay upon us a most heavy affliction; every day proves to us the severity of our loss and the inestimable value of her who is gone. You have indeed, my poor Henry, lost your best friend. Never parent more truly loved a child than she did you. Never shall I forget her the last time she read a letter from you. When I went in, she raised her languid face from the pillow, and holding up the letter to me, said with a heavenly smile, " I am quite purely [i.e. *well*] to-day, my love, for I have had such a delightful cordial "—meaning your letter. I have witnessed two deaths and heard of many, but never such a one as our angel mother's. For two months before her death, she was not able to walk upstairs, but was carried up and down every day, and laid upon a sopha in the dining-room. On the 10th of December,* she was so much worse, that we requested her not to leave her bed, but she earnestly begged to be brought downstairs, and as soon as she had recovered a little from the fatigue of being dressed and removed, she told us that

* Query, 11th ?   See preceding letter.

she felt her end approaching, and summoning my grandmama, my aunts, and all her children around her, she took a long and affectionate farewell of every one separately with as much calmness and composure as if she was only going a short journey. With my father she requested to be left alone, and continued talking with him for a considerable time. She lamented greatly that she could not see her other three boys, and wept when she left you her blessing. All the day she spent in dozing, praying, and speaking peace and comfort to her afflicted husband and children. Frequently she held up her hands to look at her poor black nails, and would often request my father and brother to feel her pulse, and begged they would tell her if it did not get lower every time. She mentioned every particular respecting the disposal of her clothes, and gave orders about being laid out and for her funeral, and turning to my father, meekly said, " If not too much expense, I should like a vault." Oh, Henry, what a day was that! To describe our feelings is impossible, but from your own on receiving the intelligence of her death, you may form some idea of ours who witnessed it. It was some consolation to us that she did not die below. She loved to be carried upstairs. My father lay by her side all night, and from her calm and comfortable slumbers was in hopes she would awaken rather better. But when she awoke, she complained of being in a little pain, which did not continue long. In about an hour after, with her hands clasped in prayer, she breathed her last. Who, who beheld such a scene as this could refrain from exclaiming, ' May I die the death of the righteous, and may my last end be like hers !' The highest respect we can pay to her ever-lamented memory is to aim, my dear Henry, at her perfection, that by a virtuous life here, we may be re-united to her in Heaven. My poor Father is better than he was, but still continues to feel his loss greatly, as do we all. But the conviction of the eternal happiness of her for whom our tears flow blunts the edge of our affliction. Our loss is most assuredly her gain. It is for ourselves that we lament, and selfish indeed should we be to wish for her return. Elizabeth is my father's housekeeper, and Anna Maria and her, by their attention to him, endeavour to assuage the bitterness of his regret. Charles, by his own wish and the request of his dear departed mother, is under the tuition of my Uncle Davie, who performs to the uttermost—nay, I must say, exceeds the extent of his promise, a convincing proof of his regard for her to whom he made it. Charles neither boards nor sleeps in our house. At least, he does not breakfast or dine with us, but he always comes in at eleven for some refreshment, drinks tea, and sups with us constantly every evening, and on Sunday we have his company all day. He is a very amiable, promising youth, and I cannot speak too highly of my aunt and uncle's kindness to him, nor of his gratitude to them. Sam, by his own choice, is to be a surgeon and apothecary, and by his good talents and attention has gained the approbation of his father and brother. He is a very respectable English scholar, and might have been a good Latin one if Mr. Binfield had taught him properly, but by experience it is proved that, though Mr. B. may understand that language himself, he is incapable of teaching it to others. An opportunity has, however, presented itself for Sam learning Latin in perfection, if he will be but diligent. Mr. Pratt, our new curate, is allowed to be a classical scholar of considerable eminence, and he has promised to instruct Sam. . . . Since my father was in practice, he never had so little business as he has had for these last two years. It is the general remark, that such a healthy time for so long a continuance was never remembered. I was concerned to see your friend Captain Eeles' name in the list of wounded at the late Engagement in Holland. I sincerely hope that the war is nearly at an end, and that we may again meet, though the late melancholy change in our family will render it both a happy and painful meeting. But you must be confident that you have still many friends left, who dearly love you, and believe me, no one better than myself. . . . All your friends, my dear Henry, join in affectionate remembrance to yourself and Tom, and believe me to remain if possible more than ever

Your truly affectionate Sister,
ELEANOR MOORE SMITH.

Letter VI. Endorsed—" 13*th* *July*, 1815. *From my Father after Waterloo, thanking God he had three sons unhurt.—H. G. S.*"

Whittlesea, July 13, 1815.

MY D*R* HARRY,

Never did I receive two Letters with such pleasure as your two last since the fight at Waterloo. For three of you to have been engag'd and to come off unhurt, must have been not the fate of chance, but Providence seem'd to have watch'd over you all and protected you.   How grateful we all ought to be to the Almighty.   I assure you my Prayers have ever been offered up to the Throne of Grace, praying for the Protection of you all, and a safe return to England.   This has been one of the most glorious, and most decisive, Battles that has been fought this War.   What a shocking sight to see the *Gazette*, it contain'd full four Columns and a half of kill'd and wounded, and amongst them so many Names I had so often heard spoke of.   Poor Major Bringhurst is among the kill'd, an only Son, and his poor father almost broken-hearted.

Poor Mr. Moore is at my house, broken-hearted, and a most distrest object in Health. . . .

Poor Sudbury is dead, he has been a poor creature for many Weeks. . . .

Your Mare was put to Cervantes, a Horse of Ld Fitzwilliam's; she is very well, and lying in my Wash ground with my Mare and foal, I think the handsomest I ever saw.   I am sorry to hear Charles' Mare is like to have bad feet; if so, the sooner she is disposed of, the better.   Tell Tom and Charles I expected to have heard from them long ago.

Give my Love to your Wife and tell her how much I felt for her, before I heard of your fate, well knowing that she must have been dreadfully alarm'd.

Your blood Mare is worth, Buckle tells me, a great deal of Money.   Her Dam is dead, and they have sent to him for her to Newmarket to breed from.

Your sisters have told all the News, therefore I conclude with my Love to your Wife and Brothers join'd with all at home.

I am your affect. father,

J. SMITH.

Write soon.

Addressed—

Major Smith,
95th Reg^t of Rifles,
Serving under the
Duke of Wellington,
France.

Letter VII. Endorsed—" 31ˢᵗ *Decʳ*, 1816. *My Father's Letter announcing the death of my good Grandmother, 83 years old.—H. G. Smith, Col.*"

Whittlesea, Decʳ 31ˢᵗ, 1816.

My Dᴿ Harry,

After a very short tho' not painful illness, your poor old Grandmother paid the last debt of nature in the 83ʳᵈ yʳ of her Age. During the whole of the time she lay on her death-bed she retained her senses, and died calm and reposed, a Blessing which God grant we may all do in the same manner as she did, a Pattern of true Piety and Benevolence. The changes in our family have within these last seven yʳˢ been great, and *one of them* painful and very distressing to me, having lost that Companion whose Conduct endeared her to every one who at all knew her, and, that being the case, how much more so must I have felt her Loss! But these are trials we must all expect to meet with, and let none of us in our *gay moments* forget how soon the case may be our own. . . .

I find the House is to be sold, but times are so bad here now that no one has got any money to purchase, however desirable they may be. I hope if Charles and his Lady shou'd marry, they may become the Purchasers. . . .

Since the Death of poor old Jack, I have lost my Uria Mare, which I was obliged to have shot. I afterwards bought a fine big Horse five yʳˢ old, one I expected wou'd have proved valuable. After keeping him about ten Weeks he made his exit as rotten as a Hare, so you see I am one of those unfortunate Beings in the Horse way. I must now be satisfied with my little Mare and my good old Gig Horse; when you are tired of your bay Mare, forget not she is a particular favourite of mine. . . .

Remember me most kindly to all my friends, particularly Col. Achmuty, Bell, and my old friend St. John.

Tell Charles we have not written to him as you wou'd be able to tell him every particular. I hope his Mare turns out well and that he is able to hunt her. How are all your Horses? I ope you have had good hunting ; it has been very wet here, and very heavy riding. I suppose the same with you.

Give my Love to Juana, and tell her the whole of her Brothers and Sisters do also.

I remain,

My Dr Harry,

Your affect. father,

J_N^O SMITH.

Addressed—

Lieut.-Col. Smith,

Rifle Brigade,

Town Major,

Cambray,

France.

Post p^d.

Letter VIII. Endorsed—" 18th *March,* 1822. *Eleanor as to the Genealogy of my Mother's family.—H. G. S."*

Whittlesey, March 18th, 1822.

MY DEAR HARRY,

. . . You have desired me to collect for you all the information I can of the Moore family, but that is very little. My good grandfather Moore always used to say that he was descended from that great though unfortunate man Sir Thomas Moore, who was beheaded in the reign of Henry the eighth. Alice always says that she is sure we are descendants, the arms are undoubtedly the same. When my poor Mother was very young, my aunt Stona told her that she was descended from no mean family, and to prove it unfurled a genealogical table which reached half over the room, but my Mother was then so young that she never could recollect much about it. She used to say that she remembered seeing a number of Gabriel Moores. This table I am sorry to say was destroyed during the riots in London. At that time my aunt Stona lived in London and lost a great many valuable things. Our great great grandfather was the first of the Moores who lived in Whittlesey, and he was an Attorney and came out of Buckinghamshire.

. . . I must now say farewell, and with kindest love to yourself and Juana, believe me, dear Harry, to remain your truly affectionate sister,

ELEANOR MOORE SMITH.

Addressed—

Lieut.-Colonel Smith,
Rifle Brigade,
Glasgow,
Scotland.

Letter IX. Endorsed—" 2*nd* Sep*r*, *reporting the death of my poor and venerable Father,* 2*nd* Sep. 1843, ¼ *before five o'clock in the Morning;* rec*d* *at Cawnpore* 31*st* Oct*br*, 1843.—H. G. S."

Whittlesea, Sep*r* 2, 1843.

MY DEAREST HARRY,

. . . Our beloved father breathed his last this morning at ¼ before 5 o'clock. . . .

About three weeks ago Charles perceived an evident alteration in his appearance. He became ill in health that week, and on Wednesday, Aug*st* 16*th*, he took to his bed. His poor mind was in a most distressed state and his terrors extreme. Unable to bear the suspense, Anna Maria and myself set off for Whittlesea, Saturday, Aug*st* 19*th*. Eleanor had come to Charles's from Northampton a few days before, and on the Monday morning as we got to W. on the Sunday Tom arrived. We found our poor father very ill, but certainly not like immediate dissolution, tho' his state was very precarious. We tried to rouse him to recollection and to soothe him, and oh, blessed be the Almighty for the mercy, we so far succeeded as to be convinced that we restored him to happiness and peace. Tho' not able to retain recollection of us for many minutes together, he was ever conscious that his children were about him; he blessed us, recognized us, asked us to pray for him, to repeat the Lord's Prayer, and one day he told us he had *hope*, that God was a God of mercy. He never uttered indeed two connected sentences, and he rambled incessantly, but the character of his ramblings was altered—bits of hymns, parts of the Psalms, exclamations to the Deity took the place of cries of terror, etc. He was *happy*—our voices reached him and soothed him, and he would reward us with a word or a look of love. He would lie in bed and amuse himself with fancied dressings of himself, talk of driving, etc., entreat to get out of bed, and would sit a few minutes in his chair. On this day week we got him out of bed, when his happiness was beautiful, but oh, the heartrending appearance he made ! He was *literally* a skeleton ; he had not an ounce of flesh on his whole body, he was a breathing death. He knew us all, smiled on each (the four daughters and Charles), dressed himself in imagination for a walk and a drive, tied his handkerchief on his neck, and when he had fidgetted away the blanket in which he was wrapt, and I put a light chair cushion in his lap, saying, " It is cold, we must pull up the apron of the gig," he smiled and said, " What fun it is ! " After a little while he asked to go home ; we laid him in bed and thought he was dying. It was, however, but exhaustion, and he rallied again, but he was never more so rational as this.

Oh, Harry, all my desire now was to gain something for you. I tried him, asked him if he recollected you, spoke the name " Harry " in a marked manner, and oh, Harry, you will thank me for this—at length he said, " Harry, yes, God bless him." I had touched the string. Some time after he addressed a set speech (made of broken sentences) to Col. Smith, in which he said he " thanked "—" noble deeds "—" to be praised "—and much more that could not be gathered ; but this was enough, his darling son was not forgotten. He spoke much of William, always saying, " William, I am coming," and once he said, " Stop, Stona—I'll go with you." He took decided notice of Anna Maria, but he held all our hands as we sat by him, and would stroke them and take them to his cheek, and even to his lips and kiss them. When he awoke in tears and we spoke to him, it vanished and he became calm ; and even when we prayed by his side, if we told him not to interrupt us, he would become quiet, seem to catch some sentences, become soothed and fall asleep. The last three days he became very ill and the pains of death racked him greatly, and it was *very* sad to see his sufferings. He was dying all yesterday and all the night, and oh, what an awful night we passed by his bedside ! He

appeared to suffer a good deal from convulsive affection of th
muscles, but the strength of his constitution was really wonderful
It was a hard struggle indeed for the victory.   After many hours
most laboured breathing, he became gradually lower and lower
and at length with one sigh, one struggle, one effort, he breathed
his last at ¼ before 5 o'clock this morning, Sept. 2nd, having reached
the great age of 87.   We mean to lay him beside our beloved
mother on Wednesday afternoon. . . .

I must close my letter, praying God to bless and comfort
you, and grant that hereafter we may all meet in Heaven and
there form one happy family again. . . . Kind love to you both
from all.

Believe me your fond sister and friend,

J. A. SARGANT.

END OF VOL. I.

PRINTED BY WILLIAM CLOWES AND SONS, LIMITED, LONDON AND BECCLES.